RELIGIOUS LIBERTY IN AMERICA

RELIGIOUS LIBERTY IN AMERICA

Political Safeguards

Louis Fisher

University Press of Kansas

Published by the University Press of Kansas (Lawrence, Kansas 66045), which was
organized by the Kansas Board of Regents and is operated and funded by Emporia
State University, Fort Hays State University, Kansas State University, Pittsburg State
University, the University of Kansas, and Wichita State University

Library of Congress Cataloging-in-Publication Data

Fisher, Louis.
  Religious liberty in America : political safeguards / Louis Fisher.
    p. cm.
  Includes bibliographical references and index.
  ISBN 978–0–7006–1201–7 (cloth : alk. paper)
  ISBN 978–0–7006–1202–4 (pbk. : alk. paper)
    1. Freedom of religion—United States. 2. Church and state—United
States. 3. Legislative power—United States. I. Title.
  KF4783 .F57 2002
  342.73'0852-dc21   2002004616

British Library Cataloguing in Publication Data is available.

EU Authorised Representative Details: Easy Access System Europe

Mustamäe tee 50, 10621 Tallinn, Estonia I gpsr.requests@easproject.com

To my brother Lee,
for a long and sustaining friendship

Contents

Acknowledgments

Friends, colleagues, and my brother helped with this project. In particular, I want to express my appreciation for comments and suggestions from David Ackerman, Elizabeth Bazan, Lackland Bloom, Neal Devins, Garrett Epps, Lee Fisher, James Hutson, Gregg Ivers, Douglas Laycock, Leonard W. Levy, Carolyn Long, Louis Talley, and Roger Walke. The University Press of Kansas asked two outside scholars to review the book manuscript: Allen Hertzke and Mark Rozell. I am indebted to both for preparing incisive evaluations. I also appreciate the continued support and friendship of Mike Briggs of Kansas Press.

Some of the themes in this book first appeared in the *University of Cincinnati Law Review* in "Nonjudicial Safeguards for Religious Liberty," published in the fall 2001 issue, in "Indian Religious Liberty: To Litigate or Legislate?" published in Volume 26 (2002) of the *American Indian Law Review,* and in "Statutory Exemptions for Religious Liberty," published in the spring 2002 issue of the *Journal of Church and State.*

I am very pleased to dedicate this book to a special person who has read my materials for a long time, offering both interest and support: my brother.

Note on Citations

Several standard reference works are abbreviated in my footnotes by using the following system:

Elliot
Jonathan Elliot, ed., The Debates in the Several State Conventions, on the Adoption of the Federal Constitution, 5 vols. (Washington, D.C., 1836–1845)

Farrand
Max Farrand, ed., The Records of the Federal Convention of 1787, 4 vols. (New Haven, Conn.: Yale University Press, 1937)

The Founders' Constitution
Philip B. Kurland and Ralph Lerner, eds., The Founders' Constitution, 5 vols. (Chicago: University of Chicago Press, 1987)

Landmark Briefs
Gerald Gunther and Gerhard Casper, eds., Landmark Briefs and Arguments of the Supreme Court of the United States: Constitutional Law (Bethesda, Md.: University Publications of America)

Richardson
James D. Richardson, ed., A Compilation of the Messages and Papers of the Presidents, 20 vols. (New York: Bureau of National Literature, 1897–1925)

Stokes
Anson Phelps Stokes, Church and State in the United States, 3 vols. (New York: Harper & Bros., 1950)

Swindler
William F. Swindler, ed., Sources and Documents of United States Constitutions, 10 vols. (Dobbs Ferry, N.Y.: Oceana Publications, 1973–1979)

Thorpe
Francis Newton Thorpe, ed., The Federal and State Constitutions, Colonial Charters, and Other Organic Laws,

                    7 vols. (Washington, D.C.: Government Printing Office,
                    1909)

Wkly. Comp.   Weekly Compilation of Presidential Documents, pub-
Pres. Doc.   lished each week by the Government Printing Office since
                    1965.

Introduction

This book runs against the grain. We are taught that courts, not the political process, protect individual rights. Legislative bodies, operating by majority vote, are supposedly insensitive to minority interests. This proposition seems axiomatic, almost self-evident, but it is not true. For most of U.S. history and certainly up to World War I, one finds it difficult to locate court decisions that uphold individual rights in any area. In seeking legal remedies, blacks, women, and other minorities turned not to the judiciary but to the legislative and executive branches. While it may seem logical that a majoritarian institution like Congress cannot be trusted to protect isolated and politically weak minorities, history has not followed logic. We should take to heart John Dickinson's advice at the Philadelphia Convention: "Experience must be our only guide. Reason may mislead us."[1] For two centuries American legislatures have performed quite well in protecting minority rights, while courts during that period were often insensitive and unreliable.

This general lesson of constitutional law applies equally well to the protection of religious liberty. The origin and growth of an individual's right to believe or not believe, and the securing of that right, have occurred almost entirely outside the courtroom. Though it may seem counterintuitive, the regular political process has safeguarded the religious freedom of minorities as well as—and often better than—the courts. Citizens, legislators, and executive officials often act jointly to support minority rights left unsecured by the courts. Sometimes the checks to misguided federal court decisions are rulings by state courts that are more generous to religious freedom. Individual rights are best protected by society as a whole, operating through the regular political process and with vigorous exchanges between federal and state courts.

1. 2 The Records of the Federal Convention of 1787, at 278 (Max Farrand ed. 1937).

Courts nudge society at times, but the impact is usually marginal rather than central. Twelve years after the desegregation case of 1954, a federal appellate court remarked: "A national effort, bringing together Congress, the executive and the judiciary may be able to make meaningful the right of Negro children to equal educational opportunities. *The courts alone have failed.*"[2] The political process, responsible for such statutes as the Civil Rights Act of 1964, advanced individual and minority rights far more than courts could do on their own.

Religious lobbies press their agenda on all three branches at the national level and on state governments. On the whole, when they operate in concert for broad national goals, they have exercised a positive and constructive influence. When they pursue narrow, sectarian objectives, they are checked by other interest groups. Over the past decade, religious groups have been more inclined to rely on Congress than on the courts to advance their interests. To that extent, there is a fundamental shift from the "minoritarian politics" of the courts to the majoritarian and consensus-seeking politics of the legislative process.

The case studies in this book explain how Supreme Court rulings on religious liberty have been challenged and countermanded by public pressure, legislation, and independent state action. The chapter on conscientious objectors describes how society as a whole, with little involvement of the courts, recognized and protected the rights of religious minorities not to participate in war. The next chapter is devoted to what happened after the Court in 1940 sustained a compulsory flag salute. The ruling so inflamed the public and professional organizations that the Court, under attack, reversed itself within three years. The same chapter covers a Court decision in 1986 that upheld an Air Force regulation that prohibited an observant Jew in the military from wearing a skullcap. The Court's opinion unleashed a political storm, prompting Congress to intervene within a year to pass legislation to repair the damage. Other chapters treat such controversies as the school prayer decision of 1962, Indian religious freedom, the religious use of peyote, and various statutory exemptions for religious organizations.

I have not attempted to cover every religious dispute. At times I give only glancing recognition to public funding of religious schools, displays

---

2. United States v. Jefferson County Board of Education, 372 F.2d 836, 847 (5th Cir. 1966) (emphasis in original), responding to Brown v. Board of Education, 347 U.S. 483 (1954).

of crèches and menorahs, Sunday closings, and other important controversies. However, the issues I select are sufficient to support my central
thesis that we must understand the political—and not just the judicial—
context for the safeguards that protect religious minorities. By and large
this is an American success story, but one we comprehend poorly.
Understanding this history shows why it is inaccurate to claim that it
"advances the cause of realism in American constitutional law to say that
the Constitution is what the judges say it is."[3] Even a cursory review of
the past two centuries reveals the inadequacy of that position. Instead of
promoting realism, such statements advance the cause of illusion and
misunderstanding.

3. Frank J. Sorauf, The Wall of Separation: The Constitutional Politics of Church
and State 3 (1976).

1

WHO PROTECTS MINORITY RIGHTS?

From James Madison to the present, it is widely argued that courts stand as sturdy sentinels to shield individuals and minorities from majoritarian assaults. Madison believed that by adding the Bill of Rights to the Constitution, "independent tribunals of justice will consider themselves in a peculiar manner the guardians of those rights."[1] It didn't work out that way, unless we want to speculate on what Madison meant by "peculiar manner." For the first century and a half, individual rights were decided almost exclusively by the majoritarian process. On the rare occasions when such issues were brought before the federal courts, judges were more likely to side with government and corporations rather than with individuals and minorities.[2]

Conventional Views

While the record of state and federal courts in the past half century has improved, contemporary scholars continue to exaggerate the extent to which judges can be trusted to protect individual and minority rights. Insulated somewhat from political forces, the judiciary is said to have the independence and technical expertise to defend constitutional rights, especially those of minorities.[3] The political branches and the

1. 1 Annals of Cong. 439 (1789).
2. Henry W. Edgerton, "The Incidence of Judicial Control over Congress," 22 Corn. L. Q. 299 (1937).
3. Laurence H. Tribe, God Save This Honorable Court 20 (1985) ("Even when the Congress and the President can be counted upon to defend most of us from the infringement of fundamental liberties, because the political majorities to which those departments of government answer demand such protection, the Supreme Court often stands alone as the guardian of minority groups. The democratic political process, by its very nature, leaves political minorities vulnerable to the will of the majority. True, the Supreme Court's record in championing the cause of oppressed minorities is hardly unstained.").

general public—operating through legislatures that vote on majoritarian grounds—are supposedly less sensitive to personal rights and liberties.[4] Scholars claim that political power must be invested in an unelected Court to protect minorities "from democratic excess."[5] In his famous footnote in *Carolene Products,* Justice Stone said that a "more searching judicial inquiry" may be required to protect "discrete and insular minorities."[6]

The Supreme Court's record in safeguarding minority and religious rights has never been that attractive or reliable. The Court barely began to sketch out a jurisprudence of religious freedom until 1940.[7] Thus, for a century and a half, the duty of protecting religious liberties was left essentially to the regular political process. The record did not change greatly even after courts became more active. Individuals and private organizations, in their efforts to protect the rights of conscience, often turn to elected officials for relief. Instead of the Court serving as the exclusive or even dominant guardian of individual rights, a powerful dialogue operates between judicial and nonjudicial bodies, with the courts often playing a secondary role. Caught in this crossfire, the Court can be overridden by a majoritarian process that advances religious liberties beyond what is available from the judiciary.

There should be nothing astonishing about the proposition that the Supreme Court has a limited role to play in protecting individual liberties, including religious freedom. Congress, the President, and state governments have major institutional strengths and responsibilities and are frequently driven by private groups that are well organized and effective in articulating and advancing their values, preferences, and agendas. Despite the belief that nonjudicial institutions cannot protect minority rights, Congress and the President often champion the cause of individuals after they have been rebuffed by the courts. As one study noted: "The Court has not been behaving as the counter-majoritarian force of its textbook description. It has instead been heeding quite carefully the

4. Jesse H. Choper, Judicial Review and the National Political Process 2 (1980) ("although judicial review is incompatible with a fundamental precept of American democracy—majority rule—the Court must exercise this power in order to protect individual rights, which are not adequately represented in the political processes.").

5. William Mishler & Reginald S. Sheehan, "The Supreme Court as a Countermajoritarian Institution? The Impact of Public Opinion on Supreme Court Decisions," 87 Am. Pol. Sci. Rev. 87, 87 (1993).

6. United States v. Carolene Products Co., 304 U.S. 144, 153 n. 4 (1938).

7. Cantwell v. Connecticut, 310 U.S. 296 (1940).

policies endorsed by the majoritarian branches of government."[8] Throughout American history, the elected branches and the general public have played a major role in guarding individual and minority rights.[9]

Early Lessons (1789–1861)

Judicial supremacy would have been alien to the members of the First Congress. Long before there were any court decisions to provide guidance on constitutional questions and individual rights, legislators and the President had to tackle such complex issues as judicial review, the Bank of the United States, Congress's investigative power, slavery, internal improvements, federalism, the war-making power, treaties and foreign relations, interstate commerce, and the President's power to remove executive officers.[10] They turned not to case law but to first principles of constitutional democracy.

NEUTRALITY PROCLAMATION

An early dilemma faced by President George Washington illustrates how the political process can keep elected officials sensitive to constitutional principles. In 1793, he issued his neutrality proclamation to prevent Americans from siding militarily in the war between France and England. In English law, proclamations had been used to give public notice of anything the king thought fit to advertise to his subjects. Washington instructed law officers to prosecute all persons who violated his proclamations, but enforcement proved difficult. The check on executive

8. Leslie Friedman Goldstein, "The ERA and the U.S. Supreme Court," 1 Law & Policy Stud. 145, 154–55 (1987).

9. John J. Dinan, Keeping the People's Liberties: Legislators, Citizens, and Judges as Guardians of Rights (1998).

10. William G. Andrews, Coordinate Magistrates: Constitutional Law by Congress and the President 1–20 (judicial review), 21–43 (Bank), 44–64 (slavery), 65–95 (interstate commerce), 109–30 (removal power), 131–44 (war powers) (1969); William Letwin, ed., A Documentary History of American Economic Policy Since 1789, at 53–84 (1961) (early debate on internal improvements); James Hart, The American Presidency in Action 78–111 (treaties and foreign relations), 152–248 (removal power) (1948); Charles Miller, The Supreme Court and the Uses of History 52–70, 205–10 (removal power), 101–18 (investigative power), 140–59 (interstate commerce) (1966); Abraham D. Sofaer, War, Foreign Affairs and Constitutional Power (1976) (discussing deliberations by Congress from 1789 to 1829); David P. Currie, The Constitution in Congress: The Federalist Period, 1789–1801 (1997).

overreaching came not from the courts but from ordinary jurors, whether bakers or blacksmiths. It was their judgment that criminal law in the United States must be made by Congress—through the regular legislative process—and not by presidential proclamations. They did not want the President to decide criminality by decree.[11]

Federal courts continued to try persons for violations of neutrality, with indictments based on common law and the law of nations,[12] but the lack of statutory authority convinced the government to drop other prosecutions. President Washington was now compelled to ask Congress to pass legislation to give him the legal footing he needed to make prosecution effective. He told legislators that it rested with "the wisdom of Congress to correct, improve, or enforce" the policy his proclamation had established. It would be expedient, he said, "to extend the legal code" and the jurisdiction of federal courts in order to have effective enforcement.[13] In short, he needed authority from the only branch that could provide it: Congress. Lawmakers responded by passing the Neutrality Act of 1794.

SEDITION ACT

With the Sedition Act of 1798, the political process first failed but later corrected itself in protecting minority rights. The United States veered toward war because of French aggression against American commerce. In April 1798, Congress learned of the "XYZ dispatches," disclosing French efforts to extract bribes and gifts from U.S. diplomats. As partisanship mounted, Federalists and Republicans (present-day Democrats) accused each other of having disloyal and treasonous motives. Republican newspapers unleashed attacked on President John Adams, calling him a "libeller" whose hands reeked with blood from the attempt to embroil the nation in war with France. Federalist journals called Republicans "frog-eating, man-eating, blood-drinking cannibals."[14] John Allen, Federalist from Connecticut, defended the legislation as necessary to deal with publications of "the most shameless falsehoods" against

11. Francis Wharton, State Trials of the United States during the Administrations of Washington and Adams 84–85, 88 (1849); 2 John Marshall, The Life of George Washington 273 (1832).

12. 1 Charles Warren, The Supreme Court in United States History 115 n. 2 (1937).

13. Annals of Cong., 3d Cong., 1–2 Sess. 11 (1793).

14. Walter Berns, "Freedom of the Press and the Alien and Sedition Laws: A Reappraisal," 1970 Sup. Ct. Rev. 109, 112.

lawmakers.[15] The Sedition Act provided penalties for writing, printing, uttering, or publishing "false, scandalous and malicious" statements against the federal government, either House of Congress, or the President.[16]

Some lawmakers regarded the statute as a blatant violation of press freedoms protected by the First Amendment. Nathaniel Macon, Republican from North Carolina, warned that the bill would force opponents of the government to form corresponding societies and communicate in secret, rather than in public.[17] Supporters of the bill, he said, had not "gone into the Constitutional question; no one has shown what part of the Constitution will authorize the passage of a law like this." He believed that "none such could be adduced."[18] Albert Gallatin, Republican from Pennsylvania, estimated that out of ten presses in the country, nine supported the administration. The Federalists, he said, wanted to use force "to suppress the limited circulation of the opinions of those who did not approve all their measures."[19] He added that the bill was designed "as a weapon used by a party now in power, in order to perpetuate their authority and preserve their present places."[20] Within a short time the bill would have the opposite effect: driving the Federalists from power and into oblivion.

Gallatin said that appeal "must be made to another tribunal, to the Judiciary in the first instance," to challenge the unconstitutionality of the law.[21] Macon, insisting that Congress lacked authority to pass the bill, "could only hope that the Judges would exercise the power placed in them of determining the law an unconstitutional law, if, upon scrutiny, they find it to be so."[22] However, there was little likelihood that Federalist judges, linked by ideology and patronage to the administration, would declare the law invalid or restrain its use against Republican newspapers.

Justice Samuel Chase, who handled a number of the sedition cases, earned a reputation for delivering intemperate and partisan statements during a trial. In one of his charges to the jury, he said he could not "suppress my feelings at this gross attack upon the President."[23] He described

15. 8 Annals of Cong. 2093 (1798).
16. 1 Stat. 596, § 2 (1789).
17. 8 Annals of Cong. 2105.
18. Id. at 2106.
19. Id. at 2109.
20. Id. at 2110.
21. Id. at 2111.
22. Id. at 2152.
23. Francis Wharton, State Trials of the United States during the Administrations of Washington and Adams 672 (1849).

one publication as "the boldest attempt I have known to poison the minds of the people."[24] The publication, he said, was "evidently intended to mislead the ignorant, and inflame their minds against the President, and to influence their votes on the next election."[25] He stated his determination not "to oppress, but I will restrain, as far as I can, all such licentious attacks on the government of the country."[26] Chase's partisan conduct on the bench led to his impeachment by the House on March 12, 1804.[27] A year later, the Senate voted not to remove him from office.

The constitutionality of the Sedition Act, which expired by its own terms in 1801, was never determined by the courts. Instead, it was decided by the people in the national elections of 1800, which drove the Federalist party out of government. The newly elected President, Thomas Jefferson, called the Sedition Act a "nullity" and pardoned every person prosecuted under it.[28] He denied that only the judiciary could decide the validity of the Sedition Act. Nothing in the Constitution "has given them a right to decide for the Executive, more than to the Executive to decide for them. Both magistracies are equally independent in the sphere of action assigned to them."[29] If judges believed the Sedition Act constitutional, they had the power to pass a sentence of fine and imprisonment. But the President was equally free to denounce the Act as unconstitutional and "remit the execution of it."[30] To give judges the right to decide what laws are constitutional not only in their own "sphere of action" but in the legislative and executive spheres as well "would make the judiciary a despotic branch."[31]

Congress also felt at liberty to make independent determinations about the constitutionality of the Sedition Act. It passed private bills to reimburse those who had been fined under the law. For example, in 1840 it provided $1,060.96, with interest from February 9, 1799, to the heirs of Matthew Lyon.[32] The accompanying report from the House Committee on the Judiciary stated that the Sedition Act was "unconstitutional, null, and void, passed under a mistaken exercise of undelegated power, and the mistake ought to be corrected by returning the fine so obtained, with

24. Id. at 675.
25. Id. at 676.
26. Id. at 678.
27. 1 Warren, The Supreme Court in United States History, at 273–82.
28. 11 Writings of Thomas Jefferson 43–44 (Bergh ed. 1904).
29. Id. at 50 (letter to Mrs. John Adams, September 11, 1804).
30. Id. at 51.
31. Id.
32. 6 Stat. 802, c. 45 (1840).

interest thereon, to the legal representatives of Matthew Lyon."[33] The Supreme Court later acknowledged that the Sedition Act was struck down not by a court of law, but by "the court of history."[34]

PROTECTION OF BLACKS

A similar record of nonjudicial activity applies to American blacks kept in slavery. Opposition to slavery arose from the general public, not from the judiciary. The creative and prevailing force in constitutional law lay outside the courts. Individual Americans, untutored in the fine points of constitutional law, viewed slavery as repugnant to fundamental political and legal principles, especially those embedded in the Declaration of Independence. The essential antislavery documents were private writings and speeches, not court decisions or legislative statutes.[35] Citizens felt a strong duty to express their opinions on constitutional rights. They deferred neither to courts nor legislatures. Americans of the mid–nineteenth century "were not inclined to leave to private lawyers any more than to public men the conception, execution, and interpretation of public law. The conviction was general that no aristocracy existed with respect to the Constitution. Like politics, with which it was inextricably joined, the Constitution was everybody's business."[36]

England abolished slavery in 1833.[37] In that same year, the American Anti-Slavery Society was founded and concerted efforts were made to keep slavery out of the territories. The Compromise Act of 1820 prohibited slavery north of the 36° 30' line, but its repeal by the Kansas-Nebraska Act of 1854 propelled the nation toward civil war. Leadership was desperately needed at the national level to moderate the passions and the call for war.

James Buchanan, elected President in 1856, wanted to discuss the slavery issue in his inaugural address on March 4, 1857. He solicited the advice of several Justices on the Supreme Court, asking whether the pending *Dred Scott* case was about to be decided. Justice Catron wrote to him on

33. H. Rept. No. 86, 26th Cong., 1st Sess. 2 (1840), reprinted in part in Louis Fisher, American Constitutional Law 25–26 (4th ed. 2001).

34. New York Times Co. v. Sullivan, 376 U.S. 254, 276 (1964).

35. William M. Wiecek, The Sources of Antislavery Constitutionalism in America 1760–1846 (1977).

36. Harold M. Hyman, A More Perfect Union: The Impact of the Civil War and Reconstruction of the Constitution 6 (1975).

37. Abolition Act, 1833, 3 & 4 Will. 4, ch. 73.

February 19, 1857, suggesting that at the Inaugural, Buchanan could "safely" say: "That the question involving the constitutionality of the Missouri Compromise line is presented to the appropriate tribunal to decide; to wit, to the Supreme Court of the United States. It is due to its high and independent character to suppose that it will decide & settle a controversy which has so long and seriously agitated the country, and which *must* ultimately be decided by the Supreme Court."[38]

On February 23, 1857, Buchanan received from Justice Grier further details on the case, even indicating how the Court would split and along what lines.[39] Fortified by these confidential communications, Buchanan included within his inaugural address the naive expectation that the explosive issue of slavery could be decided solely by the Supreme Court. The dispute over slavery in the territories, he said, "is a judicial question, which legitimately belongs to the Supreme Court of the United States, before whom it is now pending, and will, it is understood, be speedily and finally settled. To their decision, in common with all citizens, I shall cheerfully submit, whatever this may be."[40]

When the Court handed down *Dred Scott* two days later, the citizens of the United States did not "cheerfully submit" to the Court's decision. Citizens in the North fought it tooth and nail. The Court held that Scott (and all other black slaves and their descendants) was not a citizen of the United States or of Missouri. The Court also ruled that Congress was without power to prevent the spread of slavery to the territories in the West.[41] Unlike Buchanan's willingness to accept any decision, regardless of its merits, citizens took sides. The *New York Tribune* remarked: "The decision, we need hardly say, is entitled to just as much moral weight as would be the judgment of a majority of those congregated in any Washington bar-room."[42] Newspapers in the South, of course, accepted the Court's decision as the last word. According to the *Louisville Democrat*, the decision "is right, and the argument unanswerable, we presume, but whether or not, what this tribunal decides the Constitution to be, that it is; and all patriotic men will acquiesce."[43]

38. 10 Works of James Buchanan 106 (John Bassett Moore ed. 1910) (emphasis in original).

39. Id. at 106–08.

40. 7 Richardson 2962.

41. Dred Scott v. Sandford, 60 U.S. (19 How.) 393 (1857).

42. Stanley I. Kutner, The Dred Scott Decision: Law or Politics? 47 (1967).

43. Don E. Fehrenbacher, The Dred Scott Case: Its Significance in American Law and Politics 418 (1978).

A historic challenge came in Illinois in 1858, when Senator Stephen A. Douglas debated a largely unknown challenger, Abraham Lincoln. Douglas supported *Dred Scott* without reservation. Lincoln accepted the decision only as it affected the particular litigants: "In so far as it decided in favor of Dred Scott's master and against Dred Scott and his family, I do not propose to disturb or resist the decision."[44] However, he renounced the larger policy questions decided by the Court, denying blacks the right to be citizens and prohibiting Congress from excluding slavery in the territories. Lincoln considered those parts of the decision a nullity, to be left to political resolution outside the courts.[45]

Lincoln rejected the implication in *Dred Scott* that the nation should remain divided between freemen and slaves. Drawing principles from the Declaration of Independence, he concluded that Congress had the right to exclude slavery from the territories. He asked Douglas and his supporters if they wanted to amend the Declaration of Independence so that it would read "all men are created equal except negroes."[46] Lincoln continued:

> I have said that I do not understand the Declaration to mean that all men were created equal in all respects. They are not our equal in color; but I suppose that it does mean to declare that all men are equal in some respects; they are equal in their right to "life, liberty, and the pursuit of happiness." Certainly the negro is not our equal in color—perhaps not in many other respects; still, in the right to put into his mouth the bread that his own hands have earned, he is the equal of every other man, white or black.[47]

Lincoln refused to accept the moral and political teachings of *Dred Scott.* He regarded the Court as a coequal, not a superior, branch of government. In his inaugural address in 1861, he denied that constitutional questions could be settled solely by the Court. If government policy on "vital questions affecting the whole people is to be irrevocably fixed" by the Supreme Court, "the people will have ceased to be their own rulers, having to that extent practically resigned their Government into the hands of that eminent tribunal."[48]

---

44. 2 Collected Works of Abraham Lincoln 516 (Roy P. Basler ed. 1953).
45. Id.
46. Id. at 520.
47. Id.
48. 7 Richardson 3210.

We have been accustomed to look to the U.S. Supreme Court for the protection of essential liberties, but over its first century the Court played at most a marginal role on issues ranging from free speech to criminal procedures. Throughout the nineteenth century, citizens were more likely to find protection from state courts and state legislatures. In 1854, the Supreme Court of Indiana held that a "civilized community" could not put a citizen in jeopardy and withhold counsel from the poor.[49] In 1859, the Wisconsin Supreme Court called it a "mockery" to promise a pauper a fair trial and then tell him he must employ his own counsel.[50] The U.S. Supreme Court would not awake to these elementary facts until 1963.[51]

After the Civil War

Dred Scott was overturned by the Thirteenth, Fourteenth, and Fifteenth Amendments, which were ratified from 1865 to 1870. However, before those amendments nullified the Court's ruling, Congress and the President had already taken action to repudiate the main tenets of the decision. The two political branches formed their own constitutional views on the rights of blacks, independent of what the Court had announced.

ELECTED BRANCH RESPONSE TO *DRED SCOTT*

Congress passed legislation in 1862 to prohibit slavery in the territories. The statute provided: "From and after passage of this act there shall be neither slavery nor involuntary servitude in any of the Territories of the United States now existing, or which may at any time hereafter be formed or acquired by the United States, otherwise than in punishment of crimes whereof the party shall have been duly convicted."[52]

If Supreme Court decisions can be overturned only by constitutional amendment, it would seem that someone during the congressional debate would have objected to reversing *Dred Scott* by statute. However, lawmakers did not even mention the Court's decision.[53] Congress never doubted

---

49. Webb v. Baird, 6 Ind. 13 (1854).
50. Carpenter v. Dane, 9 Wis. 249 (1859).
51. Gideon v. Wainwright, 372 U.S. 335 (1963).
52. 12 Stat. 432, c. 111 (1862).
53. Cong. Globe, 37th Cong., 2d Sess. 2030, 2041–54, 2061–64, 2066–69, 2618, 2624, 2769 (1862).

its constitutional power to prohibit slavery in the territories and proceeded to announce its independent interpretation, with or without the Court.

Also in 1862, Attorney General Bates released a detailed opinion in which he held that neither color nor race could deny American blacks the right of citizenship. He pointed out that "freemen of all colors" had voted in some of the states.[54] The idea of denying citizenship on the ground of color was received by other nations "with incredulity, if not disgust."[55] The Constitution was "silent about *race* as it is about color."[56] With regard to *Dred Scott,* he held that the case, "as it stands of record, does not determine, not purport to determine," the question of blacks to be citizens.[57] What Chief Justice Taney said about citizenship was pure dicta and "of no authority as a judicial decision."[58] Bates concluded: "*The free man of color,* . . . if born in the United States, is a citizen of the United States."[59]

The Court's record in guarding the rights of blacks after the Civil War was no better than before the conflict. Two years before ratification of the Fourteenth Amendment, Congress passed the Civil Rights Act of 1866 to extend to blacks the same legal rights enjoyed by whites. The statute made all persons born in the United States, excluding Indians not taxed, citizens of the United States. Such citizens, "of every race and color," had the same right in every state and territory, "to make and enforce contracts, to sue, be parties, and give evidence, to inherit, purchase, lease, sell, hold, and convey real and personal property, and to full and equal benefit of all laws and proceedings for the security of person and property, as is enjoyed by white citizens."[60]

President Andrew Johnson vetoed the bill, claiming that the power to confer the right of state citizenship "is just as exclusively with the several States as the power to confer the right of Federal citizenship is with Congress." He objected to forcing this policy on the southern states and questioned whether blacks, newly emerged from slavery, had the "requisite qualifications to entitle them to all the privileges and immunities of citizens of the United States."[61] Congress promptly overrode the veto,

---

54. 10 Att'y Gen. 382, 387 (1862).
55. Id. at 397.
56. Id. at 398 (emphasis in original).
57. Id. at 409.
58. Id. at 412.
59. Id. at 413 (emphasis in original).
60. 14 Stat. 27, § 1 (1866).
61. 8 Richardson 3604.

the Senate by a vote of 33 to 15 and the House by a margin of 122 to 41. The Court proceeded to eviscerate the statute with narrow, technical decisions.[62]

One of the great losses in rights for blacks came with the Court's decision in the *Civil Rights Cases* of 1883, which struck down legislation passed by Congress in 1875 giving blacks equal access to public accommodations.[63] The statute attempted to close the gap between the Declaration of Independence and the Constitution by stating, in the preamble, "Whereas, it is essential to just government we recognize the equality of all men before the law."[64] The statute provided for equality of all races in using public accommodations in inns, "conveyances" (transportation), theaters, and other places of public amusement. One of the sponsors, Representative Benjamin Butler, forcefully rejected the argument of opponents who claimed that the bill attempted to impose a national standard of "social equality" among blacks and whites:

> Social equality is not effected or affected by law. It can only come from the voluntary will of each person. Each man can in spite of the law, and does in spite of the law, choose his own associates.
>
> But it is said we put them into the cars. The men that are put into the cars and the women that are put into the cars I trust are not my associates. There are many white men and white women whom I should prefer not to associate with who have a right to ride in the cars. That is not a question of society at all; it is a question of a common right in a public conveyance.
>
> There is not a white man [in] the South that would not associate with the negro—all that is required by this bill—if that negro were his servant. He would eat with him, suckle from her, play with her or him as children, be together with them in every way, provided they were slaves.[65]

Congress did not attempt to make blacks and whites equal on a social plane. That remained a private matter. What the statute did intend, and what Congress had a right to require, was granting blacks equal access to accommodations available to the general public. Yet the Court in 1883 invalidated the statute as a federal encroachment on the states and an

62. E.g., Blyew v. United States, 80 U.S. (13 Wall.) 581 (1872).
63. The Civil Rights Cases, 109 U.S. 3 (1883).
64. 18 Stat. 335 (1875).
65. 3 Cong. Rec. 940 (1875).

interference with private relationships. In his dissent in the *Civil Rights Cases,* Justice Harlan pointed out that for centuries the common law had prohibited private parties from acting in a discriminatory fashion toward travelers who needed access to inns and restaurants. Because of the Court's action, what could have been accomplished in 1875 had to await the Civil Rights Act of 1964, finally giving blacks equal access to public accommodations.

WOMEN'S RIGHTS

At the same time the Court denied blacks their rights, it accorded women similar treatment. The struggle over slavery had helped stimulate the cause of women's rights. One of the leaders of women's rights, Elizabeth Cady Stanton, became involved in the antislavery movement. In 1840 she married Henry Brewster Stanton, an abolitionist, and they set sail immediately for London to attend the World's Anti-Slavery Convention. At the convention, Mrs. Stanton found the exclusion of women delegates highly offensive and thereafter determined to alter the traditional restrictions placed on women.[66]

In 1848, Elizabeth Cady Stanton worked with Ernestine Rose and other women to change the New York property law to give married women, for the first time, a legal basis for holding and retaining property. The real and personal property of married women would no longer become the sole property of the husband.[67] At a women's rights convention in Seneca Falls, New York, Elizabeth Cady Stanton helped write a Declaration of Sentiments, using the Declaration of Independence as a model to hold "these truths to be self-evident: that all men and women are created equal."[68]

Whatever victories women gained during this period came from legislative action, not from the courts. In 1869, the Supreme Court of Illinois held that Myra Bradwell could not be admitted to practice law in the state. Of her qualifications the Court had "no doubt."[69] However, the decision advised her, or any other interested person, to present the issue to the state legislature for relief. If changes needed to be made in the legal

---

66. 3 Notable American Women 342–43 (E. James ed. 1971).
67. Miriam Schneir, ed., Feminism: The Essential Historical Writings 72–74 (1972).
68. Id. at 79.
69. In re Bradwell, 55 Ill. 535, 536 (1869).

position of women, "let it be made by that department of the government to which the constitution has entrusted the power of changing the laws."[70] The Illinois legislature passed a law in 1872, stating "that no person shall be precluded or debarred from any occupation, profession or employment (except military) on account of sex: *Provided,* that this act shall not be construed to affect the eligibility of any person to an elective office."[71]

After this legislative victory, Myra Bradwell's case continued to the U.S. Supreme Court, which held that denying women the right to practice law did not violate the Fourteenth Amendment guarantee of privileges and immunities.[72] Concurring in the judgment, Justice Bradley insisted that the "natural and proper timidity and delicacy which belongs to the female sex evidently unfits it for many of the occupations of civil life."[73] The "divine ordinance" assigned to women specific duties in the domestic sphere: "The paramount destiny and mission of woman are to fulfil the noble and benign offices of wife and mother. This is the law of the Creator."[74]

Similar rhetoric appears in other court decisions. In Wisconsin, R. Lavinia Goodell requested permission to practice before the Wisconsin Supreme Court. The court ruled that the "law of nature" destines women to bear and nurture children, take care of the custody of homes, and love and honor their husbands. Although females might be fit for many employments, the "profession of the law is surely not one of these."[75] The court explained why:

> The peculiar qualities of womanhood, its gentle graces, its quick sensibility, its tender susceptibility, its purity, its delicacy, its emotional impulses, its subordination of hard reason to sympathetic feeling, are surely not qualifications for forensic strife. Nature has tempered woman as little for the juridical conflicts of the court room, as for the physical conflicts of the battle field. Womanhood is moulded for gentler and better things.[76]

70. Id. at 540.
71. 1872 Illinois Laws 578 (March 22, 1872) (emphasis in original).
72. Bradwell v. State, 83 U.S. (16 Wall.) 130 (1873).
73. Id. at 141.
74. Id.
75. In re Goodell, 39 Wis. 232, 245 (1875).
76. Id.

The Wisconsin Supreme Court felt a special obligation to protect
women from the hazards of the law profession, which has "essentially and
habitually to do with all that is selfish and malicious, knavish and criminal, coarse and brutal, repulsive and obscene, in human life."[77] Women
should not be permitted to mix professionally in "all the nastiness of the
world which finds its way into courts of justice."[78] Here the court set forth
a terrifying list of sordid subjects, almost all of them quite familiar to
women. Into the courtroom came

> all the unclean issues, all the collateral questions of sodomy, incest,
> rape, seduction, fornication, adultery, pregnancy, bastardy, legitimacy,
> prostitution, lascivious cohabitation, abortion, infanticide, obscene
> publications, libel and slander of sex, impotence, divorce: all the
> nameless catalogue of indecencies, *la chronique scandaleuse* of all the
> vices and all the infirmities of all society, with which the profession has
> to deal, and which go toward filling judicial reports which must be
> read for accurate knowledge of the law. This is bad enough for men.[79]

It was left to Congress to remove the legal disabilities that prevented
women from practicing law. The House of Representatives, voting 169 to
87, passed legislation in 1878 to provide that any woman who was a
member of the bar of the highest court of any state or territory or of the
Supreme Court of the District of Columbia for at least three years, maintained a good standing before such court, and was a person of good moral
character, should be admitted to practice before the U.S. Supreme
Court.[80] Congressman Alexander White asked whether that question
had ever been brought before the Court. Congressman Roderick Butler
answered: "It has; and they have decided that as the law now stands
women cannot be admitted."[81]

The Senate Judiciary Committee reported the bill adversely, concluding that such matters should be left to courts to handle through their own
internal rules.[82] During floor debate, Senator Aaron Sargent pointed out
that the legislatures of many states recently admitted women to the bar.
He concluded that there was "no reason in principle why women should

77. Id.
78. Id.
79. Id. (emphasis in original).
80. 7 Cong. Rec. 1235 (1878).
81. Id.
82. Id. at 1821.

not be admitted to this profession or the profession of medicine. . . . I think the Supreme Court should not have required further legislation, but they seem to have done so, and that makes the necessity for this legislation which I have now offered."[83]

The Senate delayed action on the bill until February 7, 1879. Senator Joseph McDonald supported the bill because it was improper to permit a woman to handle a case in a state court, or in the District of Columbia, and then be forced to transfer the case to a man if it came before the U.S. Supreme Court.[84] He conceded that the Court might change its rules to permit practice before it, "but as it does not seem inclined to do so, I do not think it is wrong for us to prescribe in this case a rule for the Supreme Court."[85] Senator Sargent reviewed the progress of women in the professions, showing a sensitivity to women's rights that could not have come from the courts:

> It is generally recognized that women are taking to themselves a wider sphere of action and filling it well. . . . The medical universities of the world are receiving women and instructing them in medicine and surgery. . . . There are in various States of the Union women lawyers; and women in literature have won a very high place. No man has a right to put a limit on the exertions of the sphere of woman. That is a right which only can be possessed by that sex itself.
>
> I say again, men have not the right, in contradiction to the intentions, the wishes, the ambition, of women, to say that their sphere shall be circumscribed, that bounds shall be set which they cannot pass. The enjoyment of liberty, the pursuit of happiness in her own way, is as much the birthright of woman as of man. In this land man has ceased to dominate over his fellow—let him cease to dominate over his sister; for he has no higher right to do the latter than the former. It is mere oppression to say to the bread-seeking woman, you shall labor only in certain narrow ways for your living, we will hedge you out by law from profitable employments, and monopolize them for ourselves.[86]

Senator George Hoar rejected the argument that the Supreme Court should be left alone to decide by its own rules who may practice before it:

83. Id. at 2704.
84. 8 Cong. Rec. 1083 (1879).
85. Id.
86. Id. at 1084.

"Now, with the greatest respect for that tribunal, I conceive that the law-making and not the law-expounding power in this Government ought to determine the question what class of citizens shall be clothed with the office of the advocate."[87] Echoing the reasoning of Senator McDonald, Hoar said: "Is it tolerable that the counsel who has attended the case from its commencement to its successful termination in the highest court of the State should not be permitted to attend upon and defend the rights of that client when the case is transferred to the Supreme Court of the United States?"[88]

The bill passed the Senate, 39 to 20. Thus, an all-male legislative body provided impressive support to women's rights—rights that were unavailable from the Supreme Court. As enacted, the bill provided that any woman "who shall have been a member of the bar of the highest court of any State or Territory or of the Supreme Court of the District of Columbia for the space of three years, and shall have maintained a good standing before such court, and who shall be a person of good moral character, shall, on motion, and the production of such record, be admitted to practice before the Supreme Court of the United States."[89]

Within a few weeks, Belva Lockwood, who had lobbied vigorously for this legislation, became the first woman admitted to practice before the U.S. Supreme Court.[90] When Mrs. Lockwood was denied the right to practice in Virginia and appealed to the U.S. Supreme Court, the Court deferred to the state court's ruling that state law restricted legal practice to men.[91]

Prohibiting Polygamy

While members of Congress were upholding the rights of blacks and women after the Civil War, did they infringe upon the religious rights of Mormons by abolishing polygamy? Legislation in 1862 prohibited polygamy by the Church of Jesus Christ of Latter-day Saints (the Mormon Church). When the Church refused to comply with the statute, Congress resorted to other sanctions in 1882: making polygamists ineligible to serve on juries, to vote, or to hold territorial or federal office. Finally, in

87. Id.
88. Id.
89. 20 Stat. 292, ch. 81 (1879).
90. 2 Notable American Women 414 (James ed. 1971).
91. In re Lockwood, 154 U.S. 116 (1894).

1887, Congress passed legislation to confiscate Church property. Each time Congress made it clear that it was placing restrictions on *practice,* not religious beliefs. All of the statutes were later upheld by the Supreme Court on that same ground.

Joseph Smith, the founder of the Mormon Church, was born in 1805 and brought up in Vermont and New York. In 1827 he claimed that the angel Moroni appeared to him in a vision, directed him to a cache of golden plates inscribed with hieroglyphics, and enabled him with a set of seer stones to read the plates.[92] In March 1830, Smith published the Book of Mormon. Facing hostility and persecution from local people, the Mormons fled westward to Ohio, Missouri, and Illinois. Smith founded the town of Nauvoo in Illinois, served as its Mayor, created a military force under Illinois militia law, and announced his candidacy for President of the United States in 1844. It was during this period that he introduced several new doctrines, including polygamy. He was arrested for suppressing the opposition newspaper in Nauvoo by destroying its press and scattering its type. On June 27, 1844, a mob broke into the jail at Carthage, Illinois, and shot Smith and his brother.[93]

Brigham Young succeeded Smith and led the Mormons to the Great Salt Lake Basin, where they founded the state of Deseret. In 1848, following the Mexican War, the territory of Utah came under U.S. control. The Mormons wanted to create a constitution for the State of Deseret and asked Congress to admit it into the Union on that basis.[94] However, congressional legislation in 1850 established a "Territorial Government for Utah" and stipulated that all the laws passed by the Utah legislature and governor "shall be submitted to the Congress of the United States, and, if disapproved, shall be null and of no effect."[95] Brigham Young became the first territorial governor.

Although some of the Mormons had practiced polygamy, it was not

92. Sydney E. Ahlstrom, A Religious History of the American People 501–2 (1972); Leonard J. Arrington and David Bitton, The Mormon Experience: A History of the Latter-day Saints 8–9 (2d ed. 1992).

93. Ahlstrom, A Religious History of the American People, at 505–6; Dallin H. Oaks, "The Suppression of the *Nauvoo Expositor,*" 9 Utah L. Rev. 862, 868, 876 (1965); Edwin Brown Firmage and Richard Collin Mangrum, Zion in the Courts: A Legal History of the Church of Jesus Christ of Latter-day Saints, 1830–1900, at 106–17 (1988).

94. Eric Michael Mazur, The Americanization of Religious Minorities 72 (1999).

95. 9 Stat. 455, § 6 (1850).

until 1852 that the practice was openly acknowledged at a general church conference.[96] In 1856, President Franklin Pierce decided not to reappoint Brigham Young as territorial governor. Tension mounted in 1857–1858 when President James Buchanan sent federal troops into Utah, and the Mormons responded with military force to destroy supply trains and forts belonging to U.S. troops.[97]

In 1860, Congress began debate on a bill to prevent the practice of polygamy in the territories and to annul certain acts of the Legislature of Utah that had sanctioned polygamy.[98] In reporting the bill, the House Judiciary Committee argued that "the whole civilized world regard the marriage of one man to one woman as being alone authorized by the law of God," and that marriage "is the foundation of civil society."[99] It noted that every state treated polygamy as a crime, generally punished as a felony.[100] The bill passed the House, 149 to 60.[101]

Two issues dominated the debate. One was whether Congress could prohibit not only polygamy in the territories but slavery as well.[102] The Supreme Court's decision in *Dred Scott* was referred to repeatedly.[103] Lawmakers pointed to the Republican platform of 1856, which stated that the Constitution conferred on Congress "sovereign power" over the territories and that it was "both the right and duty of Congress to prohibit in the Territories those twin relics of barbarism—polygamy and slavery."[104]

The second issue related to enforcement. Congressman John McClernand predicted that the Mormons would not comply with a statute passed by Congress: "Does not every one know that the Mormons will not enforce such a law against themselves? that a grand jury of polygamists will not indict a polygamist? and that a petty jury of polygamists will not convict a brother polygamist? Does not every sane man know

96. Arrington & Bitton, The Mormon Experience, at 199.
97. Elbert B. Smith, The Presidency of James Buchanan 66–67 (1975).
98. Cong. Globe, 36th Cong., 1st Sess. 1150–51, 1409–12, 1492–1501, 1512–23, 1540–46, 1557–60 (1860).
99. H. Rept. No. 83, 36th Cong., 1st Sess. 1, 2 (1860).
100. Id. at 1.
101. Cong. Globe, 36th Cong., 1st Sess. 1559 (1860).
102. Id. at. 1499 (statement by Cong. Lamar), 1516 (Cong. Noell), 1517 (Cong. Noell), and 1543 (Cong. Barksdale and Gooch).
103. Id. at 1497 (Cong. Etheridge), 1498 (Cong. Etheridge), 1517 (Cong. Reagan), and 1518 (Cong. Olin).
104. Id. at 1542 (Cong. Branch).

that?"[105] Congressman Eli Thayer, noting that the bill was written as a penal statute, asked: "Will it be enforced? I say no . . . there is nobody here who claims that it is the purpose of any party to vote money or instruction to enforce this penal statute."[106] The question of enforcement would preoccupy Congress over the coming years.

The Senate did not act on the legislation until 1862. Senator Justin Morrill explained that the Senate bill was almost identical to the earlier passed House measure. The only difference, he said, was that the House bill "excepted from its provisions the District of Columbia, and that exception is stricken out of this bill."[107] With little debate the bill passed the Senate by voice vote.[108] After further action by the two chambers, the bill punished not only polygamy but also cohabitation without marriage. The Senate, after deleting the latter provision, passed the bill 37 to 2.[109] As enacted, the bill was limited to polygamy.

The statute remained a "dead letter" because indictments and convictions could not be expected as long as Mormons controlled the jury process.[110] Prospects for enforcement improved when Congress passed legislation in 1874 to give federal judges and federal officials greater authority over the Utah courts.[111]

In passing legislation in 1862, Congress respected constitutional principles by taking aim at religious practices, not religious beliefs. The prohibition on polygamy did not interfere with the right "to worship God according to the dictates of conscience."[112] The sole purpose was to annul laws that countenanced "the practice of polygamy, evasively called spiritual marriage."[113] In 1879, the Supreme Court upheld the statutory prohibition by drawing the same distinction between belief and practice: "Laws are made for the government of actions, and while they cannot interfere with mere religious belief and opinions, they may with practices."[114] The Court noted that if human sacrifices were part of

105. Id. at 1514.
106. Id. at 1520.
107. Cong. Globe, 37th Cong., 2d Sess. 1847 (1862).
108. Id. at 1848.
109. Id. at 2506–7.
110. Orma Linford, "The Mormons and the Law: The Polygamy Cases" (Part I), 9 Utah L. Rev. 308, 316 (1964).
111. 18 Stat. 253 (1874).
112. 12 Stat. 501, § 2 (1862).
113. Id.
114. Reynolds v. United States, 98 U.S. 145, 166 (1879).

religious worship, government could nonetheless pass legislation to prohibit it.[115]

In 1882, Congress passed legislation to extend the polygamy statute to cohabitation with more than one woman, making it a misdemeanor.[116] Moreover, sections 5 and 8 of the statute added teeth to the 1862 law by denying several rights to any polygamist, bigamist, or person cohabitating with more than one woman. They lost the right to sit on juries, to vote, and to hold either a territorial or a federal office. Section 9 explained that voting rights were being denied to those who *practiced* polygamy, bigamy, or cohabitation, not to those who entertained an "opinion" on the subject. In reporting the bill, the House Judiciary Committee said that anyone who violated the 1862 statute "that is justified and demanded by the positive sentiment of civilization" is not "excused or defended under the guise of religion."[117] The bill passed the Senate by voice vote and the House by a margin of 199 to 42.[118]

The Supreme Court upheld the 1882 statute, remarking that the "people of the United States, as sovereign owners of the National Territories, have supreme power over them and their inhabitants."[119] The Court endorsed the reasoning behind the statutory ban on polygamy:

> For certainly no legislation can be supposed more wholesome and necessary in the founding of a free, self-governing commonwealth, fit to take rank as one of the co-ordinate States of the Union, than that which seeks to establish it on the basis of the idea of the family, as consisting in and springing from the union for life of one man and one woman in the holy state of matrimony; the sure foundation of all that is stable and noble in our civilization; the best guaranty of that reverent morality which is the source of all beneficent progress in social and political improvement.[120]

In 1890, the Court upheld an Idaho law that withheld the privilege of voting or holding public office from bigamists or polygamists. The Court stated that bigamy and polygamy "tend to destroy the purity of the marriage relation, to disturb the peace of families, to degrade woman and to

115. Id.
116. 22 Stat. 31, § 3 (1882).
117. H. Rept. No. 386, 47th Cong., 1st Sess. 1 (1882).
118. 13 Cong. Rec. 1217, 1877 (1882).
119. Murphy v. Ramsey, 114 U.S. 15, 44 (1885).
120. Id. at 45.

debase man. . . . To call their advocacy a tenet of religion is to offend the common sense of mankind."[121] Further, the Court said it was never intended that the First Amendment "could be invoked as a protection against legislation for the punishment of acts inimical to the peace, good order and morals of society."[122]

Continued noncompliance by Mormons provoked Congress to add further legislative sanctions in 1887. To get the Church's attention, Congress confiscated its property and repealed the act that incorporated the Church. The statute exempted buildings occupied exclusively for the worship of God, parsonages related to those buildings, and burial grounds.[123] The 1862 statute (never enforced) had already placed a limit of $50,000 on real estate held by the Mormon Church. With the 1887 legislation, any real estate held by the Church in excess of that amount "shall be forfeited" to the United States.[124]

In reporting the bill to confiscate Church property, the House Judiciary Committee referred to "the Biblical origin of our race . . . one man and one woman—the dual unity—constituted the Divine appointment of the family."[125] During floor debate, Senator George Edmunds emphasized that the bill "deals with conduct and states of fact, not opinions, faiths, or beliefs."[126] The Supreme Court upheld the 1887 statute on several grounds, including the general and plenary constitutional grant of authority to Congress over the territories, and the organic statute of the Territory of Utah that reserved to Congress the power to disapprove and annul the acts of its legislature.[127] The Court dismissed the argument that the practice of polygamy constituted "a religious belief" to be protected by the Constitution: "No doubt the Thugs of India imagined that their belief in the right of assassination was a religious belief."[128]

Following the Court's opinion, the head of the Mormon Church, President Wilford Woodruff, issued an announcement against polygamy, stating that he would submit to federal law and advising all Mormons "to refrain from contracting any marriage forbidden by the law of the land."

121. Davis v. Beason, 133 U.S. 333, 341–42 (1890).
122. Id. at 342.
123. 24 Stat. 637 [§ 13], 638 [§ 17] (1887).
124. 12 Stat. 501, § 3 (1862).
125. H. Rept. No. 2735, 49th Cong., 1st Sess. 3 (1886).
126. 17 Cong. Rec. 407 (1886).
127. Mormon Church v. United States, 136 U.S. 1, 42, 44 (1890).
128. Id. at 49.

His statement was approved by a general conference of Mormon representatives, who accepted his declaration concerning polygamy as "authoritative and binding."[129]

Congressional legislation in 1894 enabled the people of Utah to form a constitution and be admitted as a state. Congress set forth these distinctions between religious beliefs and religious practices: "That perfect toleration of religious sentiment shall be secured, and that no inhabitant of said State shall ever be molested in person or property on account of his or her mode of religious worship: *Provided,* That polygamous or plural marriages are forever prohibited."[130] Those principles were repeated two years later when President Grover Cleveland proclaimed that Utah had been admitted to the Union.[131]

Although these steps largely resolved the issue of polygamy, other disputes continued. In 1946, the Supreme Court upheld the convictions of six Mormons who transported women across state lines to make them a plural wife or to cohabit with them. The fact that the men were motivated by religious belief was no defense. The case involved enforcement of the Mann Act, which prohibits the transportation in interstate commerce of any woman or girl for the purpose of prostitution, debauchery, "or for any other immoral purpose," to cover polygamy.[132] In 1953, in Short Creek, Arizona, law enforcement officers arrested more than a hundred Mormons for practicing polygamy.[133] Other incidents with fundamentalist Mormons, having multiple wives, occurred in the 1970s and 1980s.[134]

In 2000, Utah prosecuted Tom Green, a Mormon, for bigamy. With ten wives since 1970 and five at the time of the legal action, Green had for years publicly defended his multiple marriages. The state charged that the five wives were between thirteen and sixteen years old when he married them. From these marriages Green had twenty-nine children; several of his wives were expecting to give birth in 2001. On May 19, 2001, the Utah court found him guilty of four counts of bigamy and one count of

129. 2 Stokes 280; Orma Linford, "The Mormons and the Law: The Polygamy Cases" (Part II), 9 Utah L. Rev. 543, 582–83 (1965).

130. 28 Stat. 108, § 3 (1894) (emphasis in original).

131. 29 Stat. 876 (1896).

132. Cleveland v. United States, 329 U.S. 14 (1946).

133. Ken Driggs, "After the Manifesto: Modern Polygamy and Fundamentalist Mormons," 32 J. Church & State 367 (1990).

134. Id. at 386–87.

nonsupport of his offspring. On August 24, the court sentenced him to five years in prison and ordered him to pay $78,868 to support his wives and children.[135]

Twentieth-Century Disputes

Congressional efforts to regulate child labor, either by the Commerce Clause or the Taxing Power, were invalidated by the Court in 1918 and again in 1922.[136] When the constitutionality of using the taxing power was before the Court, Solicitor General Beck's brief advised the Court that congressional statutes should be struck down only when "an *invincible, irreconcilable,* and *indubitable repugnancy* develops between a statute and the Constitution."[137] Beck further stated: "The impression is general—and I believe that it is a mischievous one—that the judiciary has an unlimited power to nullify a law if its incidental effect is in excess of the governmental sphere of the enacting body."[138] It was an "erroneous idea," he continued, that the Court is the "sole guardian and protector of our constitutional form of government," for that belief leads to an impairment within Congress and the people of "what may be called the constitutional conscience."[139]

Despite its failures in protecting minorities, the Court somehow managed to retain its reputation as guardian of individual rights. In 1937, when the Senate Judiciary Committee repudiated President Franklin D. Roosevelt's court-packing plan, the committee report claimed that minority political groups "no less than religious and racial groups, have never failed, when forced to appeal to the Supreme Court of the United States, to find in its opinions the reassurance and protection of their constitutional rights."[140] The committee said that the framers "never wavered in their belief that an independent judiciary and a Constitution defining with clarity the rights of the people, were the only safeguards of the

135. "Putting Polygamy on Trial in Utah," Washington Post, December 8, 2000, at A49; "Polygamist Is Found Guilty of Bigamy," Washington Post, May 20, 2001, at A2; "Utahan Is Sentenced to 5 Years in Prison in Polygamy Case," New York Times, August 25, 2001, at A9.

136. Hammer v. Dagenhart, 247 U.S. 251 (1918); Bailey v. Drexel Furniture Co., 259 U.S. 20 (1922).

137. 21 Landmark Briefs 51 (emphases in original).

138. Id. at 52.

139. Id. at 59.

140. S. Rept. No. 711, 75th Cong., 1st Sess. 20 (1937).

citizen."[141] That may have been the framers' hope, but the judicial record fell far short of that standard.

At the time of the Senate's consideration of the court-packing bill, Henry W. Edgerton, who would later become a federal judge, had completed an analysis of the extent to which judicial review had protected individual liberties, especially those of a "relatively poor and unprivileged majority on the one hand, or of a relatively well-to-do minority on the other."[142] In the whole series of cases from 1789 to 1937, Edgerton could not find a single one that protected the civil liberties of speech, press, or assembly. Instead, the Court regularly protected the interests of government and corporations. A few years after Edgerton's study, Henry Steele Commager concluded that the Court had "intervened again and again to defeat congressional efforts to free slaves, guarantee civil rights to Negroes, to protect workingmen, outlaw child labor, assist hard-pressed farmers, and to democratize the tax system."[143] In the memorable words of Justice Holmes: "It must be remembered that legislatures are ultimate guardians of the liberties and welfare of the people in quite as great a degree as the courts."[144]

The desegregation decision of 1954 probably represents, in the minds of many people, the clearest example of the Court protecting minority rights. In important ways, *Brown v. Board of Education* aroused the public conscience and articulated constitutional values.[145] That decision by itself, however, did little to integrate public schools. Part of the ineffectiveness of the desegregation decision resulted from the Court's ruling a year later, announcing guidelines for implementing the integration of schools. The Court deferred largely to local school authorities and gave a green light to obstruction and procrastination by using such phrases as "practical flexibility," "as soon as practicable," "a prompt and reasonable start," and "all deliberate speed."[146] In fact, the unanimity happily achieved in 1954 relied on obfuscatory language for the implementation phase.[147]

---

141. Id. at 19.
142. Henry W. Edgerton, "The Incidence of Judicial Control over Congress," 22 Corn. L. Q. 299, 301 (1937).
143. Henry Steele Commager, Majority Rule and Minority Rights 55 (1943).
144. Missouri, Kansas & Texas Ry. Co. v. May, 194 U.S. 267, 270 (1904).
145. 347 U.S. 483 (1954).
146. Brown v. Board of Education, 349 U.S. 294 (1955).
147. See the boxed material in Louis Fisher, American Constitutional Law 853 (4th ed. 2001).

The Court's insistence on desegregation in 1954, followed by its announcement of judicial supremacy in the Little Rock case in 1958,[148] had little impact on integrating schools. As late as 1964, the Court complained that there "has been entirely too much deliberation and not enough speed" in enforcing *Brown*.[149] A federal appellate court noted in 1966: "A national effort, bringing together Congress, the executive and the judiciary may be able to make meaningful the right of Negro children to equal educational opportunities. *The courts acting alone have failed*."[150]

What finally turned the tide were a series of legislative enactments: the Civil Rights Act of 1964, the Voting Rights Act of 1965, and the Fair Housing Act of 1968. Congressional action in 1964 attracted top-heavy majorities of 289–126 in the House and 73–27 in the Senate. Bipartisan support was solid. The House voted 153–91 Democrat and 136–35 Republican. The party split in the Senate was 46–21 for Democrats and 27–6 for Republicans. It was this broad consensus, acting through the regular political process, that allowed progress toward racial equality. Many private groups lobbied for the legislation, creating a political base that was essential to educate citizens. The rights of blacks were secured far better through this majoritarian process than through a Court decision, even when unanimous.

The movement for women's rights in the twentieth century came largely from legislatures, not from courts. Federal judges held fast to anachronous legal doctrines. It was not until 1971 that the Supreme Court decided a case that struck down sex discrimination.[151] The judicial record was so bleak that one study concluded that "by and large the performance of American judges in the area of sex discrimination can be succinctly described as ranging from poor to abominable."[152]

Action by the U.S. House of Representatives in 1970 and 1971 on the Equal Rights Amendment was driven in large part by the sorry record of the Supreme Court. Congresswoman Martha Griffiths, the leading force behind the ERA, told her colleagues that what the ERA sought to do,

---

148. Cooper v. Aaron, 358 U.S. 1, 18 (1958).

149. Griffin v. School Bd., 377 U.S. 218, 229 (1964).

150. United States v. Jefferson County Board of Education, 372 F.2d 836, 847 (5th Cir. 1966) (emphasis in original).

151. Reed v. Reed, 404 U.S. 71 (1971) (voiding an Idaho law that preferred men over women in administering estates).

152. John D. Johnston, Jr. & Charles L. Knapp, "Sex Discrimination by Law: A Study in Judicial Perspective," 46 N.Y.U. L. Rev. 675, 676 (1971).

"and all it seeks to do, is to say to the Supreme Court of the United States, 'Wake up! This is the 20th century. Before it is over, judge women as individual human beings.'"[153]

The last three decades record other efforts by Congress and the President to protect individual and minority rights, often in response to judicial rulings. A 1976 decision by the Supreme Court, *United States* v. *Miller*, held that bank depositors were not protected by the Fourth Amendment when the government wanted to gain access to microfilms of checks, deposit slips, or other bank records.[154] Congress, concerned about the privacy rights of depositors, passed legislation to provide procedural rights and protections that had not been protected by the Court.[155]

Also in 1976, the Court supported a company's disability plan that gave benefits for nonoccupational sickness and accidents but not for disabilities arising from pregnancy. The Court decided that the plan did not violate Title VII of the Civil Rights Act of 1964.[156] Congress passed the Pregnancy Discrimination Act of 1978 to reverse the Court. The statute amended Title VII to prohibit employment discrimination on the basis of pregnancy and to require fringe benefit and insurance plans to cover pregnant workers.[157] In 1993, Congress passed the Family and Medical Leave Act, requiring employers with fifty or more employees to provide workers with up to twelve weeks of unpaid leave for the birth or adoption of a child or the illness of a close family member. The option is available to both fathers and mothers.[158]

In 1978, the Court upheld the right of law enforcement officers to use a search warrant on the premises of a newspaper.[159] The newspaper was not a suspected party to a crime. Instead, it was a "third party," and previous cases had placed substantial restraints on third-party searches. After the press appealed to lawmakers for help, Congress passed legislation in 1980 to offer greater protection to newspapers and to First Amendment interests. The statute directs law enforcement officers to use subpoenas as a less intrusive method of obtaining documents.[160] Once again, lawmak-

---

153. 117 Cong. Rec. 35323 (1971).
154. 425 U.S. 535 (1976).
155. 92 Stat. 3697 (1978).
156. General Electric Co. v. Gilbert, 429 U.S. 125 (1976).
157. 92 Stat. 2076 (1978).
158. 107 Stat. 7 (1993).
159. Zurcher v. Stanford Daily, 436 U.S. 547 (1978).
160. 94 Stat. 1879 (1980).

ers gave greater protection to individual rights than could be obtained from the judiciary.

In a decision handed down in 1980, the Court held that states are prohibited only from *purposefully* discriminating against the voting rights of blacks. Abridgement of voting rights had to be intentional, not incidental. To be held invalid, a voting plan had to be conceived for the purpose of furthering racial discrimination.[161] Finding the Court's test unacceptable, Congress amended the Voting Rights Act to allow plaintiffs to show discrimination solely on the *effects* of a voting plan. The statute borrowed language from an earlier Court opinion.[162] In 1986, the Court accepted the constitutionality of the "results test."[163]

These Court-Congress dialogues form a vital part of the development of constitutional law and individual freedoms. The dialogue embraces not just structural issues—separation of powers and federalism—but basic rights and liberties. Religious liberty is no exception. The regular political process is called upon to protect religious liberty, and not merely for powerful religious groups but small ones as well. This process underscores Alexander Bickel's observation that courts find themselves engaged in a "continuing colloquy" with political institutions and society at large, a process in which constitutional principles are "evolved conversationally not perfected unilaterally."[164] As explained in the next chapter, the principles of religious liberty were articulated by individuals, not political institutions.

161. Mobile v. Bolden, 446 U.S. 55 (1980).
162. 96 Stat. 134, § 3 (1982); White v. Regester, 412 U.S. 755 (1973).
163. Thornburgh v. Gingles, 478 U.S. 30 (1986).
164. Alexander Bickel, The Least Dangerous Branch 240, 244 (1962).

2

THE STRUGGLE FOR RELIGIOUS LIBERTY

Religious freedom did not reach America on the wings of court decisions. The active, driving force for creating and preserving religious liberty has been the political—not the judicial—process. No rulings guided
the early settlers, who drew inspiration from their hearts and minds.
Calling on tradition, experience, and personal values, Americans of the
seventeenth and eighteenth centuries forged the principles that preceded
by centuries whatever guidance courts would later offer. Independent
and headstrong pioneers were willing to confront authority, suffer punishment, and face exile. Their hard-fought and painful battles eventually
found expression in the religion clauses of the First Amendment: "Congress shall make no law respecting an establishment of religion or prohibiting the free exercise thereof." In the context of this struggle over
four centuries, the role assigned to courts has been necessarily reactive
and marginal. Moreover, an assertive judiciary has not always had a benign impact on religious liberty.

Colonial Precedents

Bitter religious wars erupted in Europe in the sixteenth century. After
one bloody inquisition, Dutch revolutionaries drafted the Union of
Utrecht of 1579 to proclaim that "each person must enjoy freedom of religion, and no one may be persecuted or questioned about his religion."[1]
The Netherlands would be both a haven for religious dissenters and a
point of departure for passage to America. The Puritans, who dissented
from the Church of England, founded colonies at Plymouth in 1620 and
in Massachusetts Bay in 1629.

The Puritans brought with them the principles of theocracy developed

---

1. John Witte, Jr., Religion and the American Constitutional Experiment 18 (2000).

by John Calvin in Geneva. In Massachusetts Bay, suffrage and property were restricted to members of the Congregationalist Church. The government levied taxes to support the clergy and the church, compelled all persons to attend church services regardless of their beliefs, and subjected non-Congregationalists to trial and punishment for heresy, blasphemy, and idolatry.[2] Church authorities in Massachusetts believed that "in any society only one orthodox regime should be allowed and that the civil magistrate should suppress and, if necessary, extirpate every form of ecclesiastical or doctrinal dissent."[3]

Into this tightly disciplined community sailed an independent spirit, Roger Williams. Landing at Boston in February 1631, he began to challenge the doctrines and policies of the Puritans. He objected to the restriction of the franchise and public office to Congregationalists, the compulsory attendance at religious services, and taxes supporting the ministry.[4] He moved to the Pilgrim colony of New Plymouth, just south of Boston, and joined ranks with William Bradford and others who considered themselves "Separatists" from Anglicanism (the Church of England).[5] Driven from Massachusetts Bay in 1635, Williams and his followers reached the head of Narragansett Bay and founded the settlement of Providence.

The first articles of incorporation, drafted by Williams in 1637, extended political authority "only in civil things."[6] Civil society and religious society were to be kept separate: "As it would be confusion for the *Church* to censure such *matters* and acts of such persons as belong not to the *Church;* so it is *confusion* for the *State* to punish *spiritual* offenses, for they are not within the *sphear* of a *civil jurisdiction.*"[7] The inhabitants of Providence drew up an agreement in 1640, providing "as formerly hath bin the liberties of the town, so still, to hould forth liberty of Conscience."[8] A charter in 1663 guaranteed religious liberty to all persons, while a 1716 statute stipulated that salaries for ministers be "raised by a free contribution and no other way."[9]

2. R. Freeman Butts, The American Tradition in Religion and Education 19 (1950).

3. Perry Miller, Roger Williams: His Contribution to the American Tradition 23 (1953).

4. Sanford H. Cobb, The Rise of Religious Liberty in America 181–85 (1902).

5. William G. McLoughlin, Rhode Island: A History, 6–7 (1986).

6. Gerald V. Bradley, Church-State Relationships in America 27 (1987).

7. Cobb, The Rise of Religious Liberty in America, at 426 (emphases in original).

8. Henry Steele Commager, ed., Documents of American History 25 (1973).

9. Bradley, Church-State Relationships in America, at 27.

A publication by Williams, *The Bloudy Tenent* (1644), marks an inquiry into religious persecution and the cause of conscience. He begins by saying that "the blood of so many hundred thousand soules of *Protestants and Papists*, spilt in the *Wars* of *present* and *former Ages*, for their respective *Consciences*, is not *required* nor *accepted* by *Jesus Christ* the *Prince* of *Peace*."[10] The "most lamentably true *experience* of all Ages" is that "*persecution* for cause of Conscience hath ever proved pernicious" and that the result of such persecution against both saints and sinners "fill'd the *Streams* and *Rivers* with their *blood*."[11] Taking up the sword against so-called non-believers produced "a whole *Nation* of *Hypocrites*."[12]

Part of Williams's separation of church and state depended on his notion of the "Two Tables" of the law. The first four commandments—honor to God, no graven images, no blasphemy, and Sabbath worship—defined man's duty to God. In this realm the state had no role. Government's jurisdiction was limited to the remaining commandments (including murder and theft) that defined one's duties to the community.[13]

Williams thought about religious freedom within a Christian context: "I have offerd and doe . . . discusse by Disputation . . . these 3 positions: First that forc'd Worshpp stincks in Gods Nostrills, 2 That it denies Christ Jesus yet to come . . . 3 That in these flames about Religion . . . there is no other prudent Christian Way of preserving peace in the World but by permission of differing Consciences."[14] However, he articulated two principles of great power: separation of church and state, and religion as a matter of personal conscience. Rhode Island was "the first commonwealth in modern history to make religious liberty (not simply a degree of toleration) a cardinal principle of its corporate existence and to maintain the separation of church and state on these grounds."[15]

Maryland, founded by the Catholic leader Lord Baltimore in 1633, offered another experiment in religious liberty. An act of 1649 provided that "noe person . . . professing to believe in Jesus Christ, shall from

10. 3 The Complete Writings of Roger Williams 3 (1963) (emphases in original).

11. Id. at 182 (emphases in original).

12. Id. at 136 (emphases in original).

13. Stephen Phillips, "Roger Williams and the Two Tables of the Law," 38 J. Church & State 547 (1996).

14. 2 The Correspondence of Roger Williams 617 (1988) (letter to Major John Mason and Governor Thomas Prence, June 22, 1670).

15. Sydney E. Ahlstrom, A Religious History of the American People 182 (1972). See Timothy L. Hall, "Roger Williams and the Foundations of Religious Liberty," 71 Boston U. L. Rev. 455 (1991).

henceforth bee any waies troubled . . . for his or her religion nor in the free exercise thereof . . . nor any way compelled to the beliefe or exercise of any other Religion against his or her consent."[16] Notwithstanding these declared sentiments, religious discord prevailed in Maryland among Catholics, Protestants, and other sects.[17] During this same period, religious liberty flourished in several towns in Maine. A law in 1649 provided that "all gode people . . . shall have full liberty to gather themselves in to a Church estate." The proviso, however, required them to "doe it in a Christian way: with the due observation of the rules of Christ revealed in his worde."[18] While these precedents in Maryland and Maine would not count as "religious liberty" today, they were liberal compared to the Congregationalist control that held sway in Massachusetts.

The first two Quakers (Society of Friends) reached Boston in 1656. They were promptly shipped back to their point of origin, as were others who arrived. With their belief in an "inner light" that allowed each person to experience religious faith, Quakers were a natural antagonist to organized churches and religious authorities. They engaged in provocative activities by "interrupting church services to testify against false worship or going naked to symbolize the condition of their opponents' spiritual state."[19] Massachusetts passed laws to inflict penalties on Quakers: imprisonment, fines, whipping, branding, ear-cropping, tongue-boring, and death by hanging. In 1659, two Quakers were hanged on Boston Commons for returning a third time to preach their views. Several other hangings followed.[20] Not until 1672 were Quakers allowed to preach in Boston without being arrested.[21]

Pennsylvania made important contributions to religious liberty. From its founding in 1682, Pennsylvania "stood for noncoercion of conscience, divorce of the institutional church from the state, and the cooperation of the church and state in fostering the morality necessary for prosperity and good government."[22] William Penn supplied the leadership. While a student at Oxford, he had been imprisoned because of his association with

16. Witte, Religion and the American Constitutional Experiment, at 21.
17. Thomas J. Curry, The First Freedoms: Church and State in America to the Passage of the First Amendment 31–53 (1986).
18. 1 Charles Edward Banks, History of York Maine 175 (1931).
19. Curry, The First Freedoms, at 21.
20. William C. Braithwaite, The Beginnings of Quakerism 404 (1955).
21. McLoughlin, Rhode Island, at 35–37.
22. J. William Frost, A Perfect Freedom: Religious Liberty in Pennsylvania 2 (1990).

Quakers. After he reached America, he urged liberty of conscience and refused to force individuals to pay taxes or tithes to support a form of worship they did not profess.[23]

Penn exacted some conditions before one could enjoy full religious freedom. His charter of 1701 begins by noting that "no People can be truly happy, though under the greatest Enjoyment of Civil Liberties, if abridged of the Freedom of their Consciences, as to their Religious Profession and Worship." However, one had to first "confess and acknowledge *One* almighty God, the Creator, Upholder and Ruler of the World" before receiving the following benefits: not to be "molested or prejudiced" because of conscientious persuasion or practice, not to be compelled to frequent or maintain any religious worship, or to suffer any other act contrary to their religious persuasion.[24] Only persons who professed to believe in "*Jesus Christ,* the Saviour of the World," were entitled to serve in governmental positions.[25] Penn also set aside a day of rest and religious study "to the end, that looseness, irreligion, and Atheism may not creep in under any pretense of Conscience in this Province."[26]

Locke's Influence

The framers read John Locke with great care, borrowing ideas that could be applied to American society while rejecting or modifying those that did not. In fashioning principles of religious liberty, they studied closely his 1689 publication, *A Letter Concerning Toleration.* Jefferson made detailed notes of this work.[27] Samuel Adams, writing in 1772, relied extensively on Locke's study of religious liberty.[28]

Locke regarded toleration as "the chief characteristical mark of the true church."[29] The qualities of being a true Christian—charity, meekness, and "goodwill in general towards all mankind, even to those that are not true christians"—were incompatible with religious persecution, "torments," destruction, and killing "upon pretense of religion."[30] He

23. Id. at 15.
24. Commager, Documents of American History, at 40 (emphasis in original).
25. Id. at 40–41 (emphasis in original).
26. Cobb, The Rise of Religious Liberty in America, at 443.
27. 1 The Papers of Thomas Jefferson 544–48 (Boyd ed. 1950).
28. 5 The Founders' Constitution 60.
29. 5 The Works of John Locke 5 (1824).
30. Id. at 6.

condemned those who were "cruel and implacable towards those that differ from him in opinion."[31]

Church and state needed to be kept separate by distinguishing "the business of civil government from that of religion, and to settle the just bounds that lie between the one and the other."[32] The civil interest was directed toward life, liberty, health, and the possession of such things as money, land, houses, and furniture. It had nothing to do with "the care of souls." Nor could such power be vested in the civil magistrate, even with the consent of the people. No one "can so far abandon the care of his own salvation, as blindly to leave it to the choice of any other, whether prince or subject, to prescribe to him what faith or worship he shall embrace. . . . [F]aith is not faith, without believing."[33] Here Locke enters the domain of conscience, a realm so inherent and personal that no outside force is authorized to violate it.

Although members of the community are entitled to their own religious beliefs, Locke encourages an open dialogue in society. Individuals may argue, admonish, and try to convince another of religious error. However, it is unacceptable to resort to penalties, beatings, or compulsion. Only "light and evidence . . . can work a change in men's opinions."[34] Persuasion, yes; persecution, no.

To Locke, religious belief is individual and personal. He denied that religion is passed automatically from parent to child, because everyone "joins himself voluntarily" to a religious society.[35] "No way whatsoever that I shall walk in against the dictates of my conscience, will ever bring me to the mansions of the blessed." One cannot be saved by a religion he distrusts or a worship he abhors. "Faith only, and inward sincerity, are the things that procure acceptance with God."[36]

On these points, Jefferson, Madison, and other advocates of religious liberty would agree. It was Locke's concept of *toleration* that they found unacceptable. When members of a community gathered together to worship God, Locke said that the magistrate "ought to tolerate" their meetings.[37] To the framers, toleration was an act of grace, something an

31. Id. at 8.
32. Id. at 9.
33. Id. at 11.
34. Id. at 12.
35. Id. at 13.
36. Id. at 28.
37. Id. at 29.

official could initially bestow but later withdraw. On matters of religious belief and conscience, many of the framers thought the magistrate lacked authority to be either tolerant or intolerant. It was not his business to intervene at all. No one was required to ask permission from a magistrate to do what was a natural right: to believe in accordance with one's conscience.

At times Locke seemed to understand this. The magistrate "has no power to enforce by law either in his own church, or much less in another, the use of any rites or ceremonies whatsoever in the worship of God."[38] He later acknowledges, as would the framers, that the magistrate may forbid some ceremonies, such as the sacrifice of infants.[39] But Locke would go further. If a religious group is subject to a foreign prince and is prepared to seize the government, they "have no right to be tolerated by the magistrate."[40]

Through this reasoning Locke justified British constraints on Catholics because of their allegiance to Rome, and on Muslims, who might look to Constantinople.[41] Moreover, the magistrate did not have to tolerate those who denied the existence of God. "Promises, covenants, and oaths, which are the bonds of human society, can have no hold upon an atheist."[42] Elsewhere Locke seems more accepting of non-Christians: "If we may openly speak the truth, and as becomes one man to another, neither pagan, nor mahometan, nor jew, ought to be excluded from the civil rights of the commonwealth, because of his religion."[43]

Jefferson credited Locke with advanced views on religious freedoms, but cautioned: "Where he stopped short, we may go on."[44] Tench Coxe, writing in 1790, explained the deficiencies of religious toleration: "Mere toleration is a doctrine exploded by our general condition; instead of which have been substituted an unqualified admission, and assertion, that their own modes of worship and of faith equally belong to all the worshippers of God, of whatever church, sect. or denomination."[45] The following year, Thomas Paine offered his views about religious toleration:

38. Id.
39. Id. at 33.
40. Id. at 46.
41. Id. at 47.
42. Id.
43. Id. at 52.
44. 1 The Papers of Thomas Jefferson 548 (Boyd ed. 1950).
45. 5 The Founders' Constitution 94.

"Toleration is not the opposite of intoleration, but is the counterfeit of it. Both are despotisms. The one assumes to itself the right of withholding liberty of conscience, and the other of granting it."[46] President George Washington, in his famous address to the synagogue at Newport, Rhode Island, remarked: "It is now no more that toleration is spoken of, as if it was by the indulgence of one class of people, that another enjoyed the exercise of their inherent natural rights. For happily the government of the United States, which gives to bigotry no sanction, to persecution no assistance, requires only that they who live under its protection should demean themselves as good citizens."[47]

Thomas Jefferson wrote about the "poor Quakers" who fled from persecution in England, hoping to find the American colonies to be asylums of civil and religious freedom, but discovering them "free only for the reigning sect."[48] Benjamin Franklin's assessment was similar: "If we look back into history for the character of present sects in Christianity, we shall find few that have not in their turns been persecutors, and complainers of persecution. The primitive Christians thought persecution extremely wrong in the Pagans, but practiced it on one another."[49] Jefferson looked in part to the leadership of William Penn and the Quakers for guidance on what should be done in Virginia. Pennsylvania and New York, he noted, "have long subsisted without any establishment at all," yielding an "unparalleled" harmony that "can be ascribed to nothing but their unbounded tolerance."[50]

The Virginia Statute of 1786

On several occasions the Supreme Court has recognized that the religion clauses "had the same objective and were intended to provide the same protection against governmental intrusion on religious liberty as the Virginia statute."[51] The Virginia Statute for Establishing Religious Freedom—the handiwork of Jefferson and James Madison—helps explain

46. Id. at 95.
47. 31 The Writings of George Washington 93 n.95 (Fitzpatrick ed. 1939).
48. Notes on Virginia, 2 The Writings of Thomas Jefferson 218 (Bergh ed. 1903).
49. 5 The Founders' Constitution 58.
50. Id. at 224. The record of establishment and disestablishment in America is detailed in Leonard W. Levy, The Establishment Clause: Religion and the First Amendment (1994).
51. Everson v. Board of Education, 330 U.S. 1, 13 (1947). See also Reynolds v. United States, 98 U.S. 145, 162–64 (1879).

the motivations behind the religion clauses. Both men deplored the sectarian battles, intolerance, narrow creeds, and doctrinal wrangling that
split their state. For them, religion was a moral code to be practiced, not
preached. "On the dogmas of religion," wrote Jefferson, "as distinguished
from moral principles, all mankind, from the beginning of the world to
this day, have been quarreling, fighting, burning and torturing one another, for abstractions unintelligible to themselves and to all others, and
absolutely beyond the comprehension of the human mind."[52] He believed
that religion and its free exercise represented a fundamental human right
over which the state could not intrude: "Our rulers can have authority
over such natural rights, only as we have submitted to them. The rights of
conscience we never submitted, we could not submit."[53]

As with other colonies, Virginians suffered from religious cruelty and
intolerance among the competing sects. Madison lamented the "diaboli-
cal, hell-conceived principle of persecution" that raged about him in
1774.[54] Baptists, Presbyterians, Catholics, Quakers, and other minority
groups were whipped, fined, imprisoned, and forced to support the established Anglican (Episcopal) Church. Madison's Baptist neighbors kept
him sensitive to the injustice of religious persecution. From one-half to
two-thirds of Virginia's population were non-Episcopalians.[55]

In 1776, Virginia's Declaration of Rights proclaimed that religion "can
be directed only by reason and conviction, not by force or violence; and
therefore all men are equally entitled to the free exercise of religion, according to the dictates of conscience."[56] As originally drafted, the clause
on religion provided that "all men should enjoy the fullest toleration in
the exercise of religion according to the dictates of conscience." Madison
objected to the word *toleration* because it belonged to a system where an
established church granted a certain liberty of worship, "not of right, but
of grace; while the interposition of the magistrate might annul the
grant."[57] By removing this concept of toleration, the language now expressed a fundamental human right.

---

52. 10 Writings of Thomas Jefferson 67–68 (Ford ed.) (letter to Mathew Carey, November 11, 1816).
53. 3 Writings of Thomas Jefferson 263 (Ford ed.)
54. 1 Writings of James Madison 21 (Hunt ed.).
55. Edward Frank Humphrey, Nationalism and Religion in America, 1774–1789, at
366 (1924).
56. 7 Thorpe 3814.
57. Cobb, The Rise of Religious Liberty in America, at 491–92.

Virginia's Declaration triggered a large number of petitions urging that the laws favoring the Anglican Church be repealed.[58] Responding to these petitions, Jefferson drafted language to disestablish the Church and exempt dissenters from contributing to it.[59] In December 1776, Virginia repealed its laws directed against heretics and nonattendance and exempted dissenters from giving financial support to the Anglican Church.[60]

The next step toward disestablishment took place in 1779 when Virginia repealed all laws requiring even members of the Anglican Church from supporting their own ministry. Joining in this campaign for disestablishment were Baptists, Quakers, Presbyterians, Lutherans, and other religious groups.[61] Denied preferential treatment, the Anglican Church lobbied for a general tax to benefit all Christian religions and supported legislation to fund teachers of Christianity. The bill that emerged from the legislature allowed taxpayers to designate a church to receive their share of the tax. Nonreligious taxpayers could direct their taxes to general educational purposes.

Those who supported the general assessment bill claimed that Christianity and public morals would suffer without state financial aid. However, the Baptists and some Presbyterians, although they would have received funds under this arrangement, opposed the legislation. So did the Quakers, Roman Catholics, and some of the Methodists.[62] Madison, in his famous "Memorial and Remonstrance Against Religious Assessments," argued that religion should be left to the conviction and conscience of the individual. To Madison, religion consisted of voluntary acts "wholly exempt" from governmental control. He objected to religious assessments partly because "experience witnesseth that ecclesiastical establishments, instead of maintaining the purity and efficacy of Religion, have had a contrary operation. . . . What have been its fruits? More or less in all places, pride and indolence in the Clergy; ignorance and servility in the laity; in both, superstition, bigotry and persecution."[63]

Madison's slashing attack, underscoring the incompatibility between private religious beliefs and public financial support, helped defeat the

58. 1 Papers of Thomas Jefferson 526 (Boyd ed. 1950).

59. Id. at 530–35.

60. H. J. Eckenrode, Separation of Church and State in Virginia 50–52 (1910).

61. Michael W. McConnell, "The Origins and Historical Understanding of Free Exercise of Religion," 103 Harv. L. Rev. 1410, 1439 (1990).

62. 5 The Framers' Constitution 103.

63. 2 Writings of James Madison 187 (Hunt ed.).

general assessment bill. Virginia now prohibited financial aid to religion both on a preferential and nonpreferential basis. Flush from this victory, Madison introduced Jefferson's Statute for Establishing Religious Freedom, which passed in January 1786. The statute provided that "Almighty God hath created the mind free; that all attempts to influence it by temporal punishments or burthens, or by civil incapacitations, tend only to beget habits of hypocrisy and meanness." Compelling individuals to contribute money to propagate religious opinions that they disbelieve "is sinful and tyrannical." Even legislation that allows someone to direct funds to their church deprives that person of the liberty of giving contributions to a particular pastor, "whose morals he would make his pattern, and whose powers he feels most persuasive to righteousness." Financial contributions of any kind tend "to corrupt the principles of that religion it is meant to encourage, by bribing with a monopoly of worldly honours and emoluments." The statute assumed that "truth is great and will prevail if left to herself, that she is the proper and sufficient antagonist to error, and has nothing to fear from the conflict." The bill further stated that

> no man shall be compelled to frequent or support any religious worship, place, or ministry whatsoever, nor shall be enforced, restrained, molested, or burthened in his body or goods, nor shall otherwise suffer on account of his religious opinions or belief; but that all men shall be free to profess, and by argument to maintain, their opinion in matters of religion, and that the same shall in no wise diminish, enlarge, or affect their civil capacities.[64]

The statute acknowledged that the Virginia assembly had no control over what succeeding assemblies decided to do on the same question, "yet we are free to declare, and do declare, that the rights hereby asserted are of the natural rights of mankind, and that if any act shall be hereafter passed to repeal the present, or to narrow its operation, such act will be an infringement of natural right."[65] Years later, in evaluating religious institutions in Virginia after they had been denied public funding, Madison remarked that "it is impossible to deny that Religion prevails with more zeal, and a more exemplary priesthood than it ever did when established

64. 12 William Waller Hening, The Statutes at Large: Being a Collection of All the Laws of Virginia 86 (1823).
65. Id.

and patronised by Public authority."[66] A resolution passed by Congress in 1988 contains this Madisonian sentiment: "Religion is most free when it is observed voluntarily at private initiative, uncontaminated by Government interference and unconstrained by majority preference."[67]

Virginia offers an unusually strong example of religious toleration. Attitudes and practices in other colonies and states were quite different. A number of states continued to provide assistance to established churches after 1786. The Congregational ministry in Connecticut controlled government, public policy, and the schools until church and state were finally separated in the period from 1802 to 1818.[68] The Congregationalist Church ruled Massachusetts until 1833.[69] Other states with an established church included New Hampshire (Protestant), South Carolina (Protestant), Maryland (Christianity), and Delaware (Trinitarian Christianity).[70]

Meeting at Philadelphia

On May 29, 1787, at the Philadelphia convention, Charles Pinckney's draft constitution included a provision that the national legislature "shall pass no law on the subject of Religion."[71] However, his plan was never acted upon.[72] The subject of religion was not addressed at the convention, except for debate on a national university and language in Article VI. Three days before adjournment, Madison and Pinckney moved to give Congress the power "to establish an University, in which no preferences or distinctions should be allowed on account of religion." With little discussion the motion was defeated, 6 to 4, with one state divided.[73] Article VI provides that Members of Congress, members of state legislatures, and all executive and judicial officers—both federal and state—"shall be bound by Oath or Affirmation, to support this Constitution; but no religious Test shall ever be required as a Qualification to any Office or public Trust under the United States."

66. 9 Writings of James Madison 102 (Hunt ed.).

67. 102 Stat. 1772 (1988).

68. Anton Phelps Stokes & Leo Pfeffer, Church and State in the United States 74 (1964).

69. Id. at 76–78.

70. Id. at 78–81.

71. 3 Farrand 599.

72. Levy, The Establishment Clause, at 80, n. 1.

73. 2 Farrand 616.

OATH OR AFFIRMATION

The provision on oaths and affirmations took several forms. Although political societies had long required oaths to ensure honest testimony, several colonies provided religious exemptions to the oath requirement. Carolina, New York, and Massachusetts from the late 1600s to the 1740s allowed Quakers to substitute affirmation for an oath.[74] Quakers, Mennonites, and other religions objected to oaths "on the ground that they were unnecessary—a Christian man was under obligation to speak the truth on all occasions."[75] They took literally the biblical injunction "Swear not at all" (Matthew 5:34). The Bible also instructed: "But above all things, my brethren, swear not, neither by heaven, neither by the earth, neither by any oath: but let your yea be yea, and your nay, nay; lest ye fall into condemnation" (James 5:12). Objections were raised to oaths because they were associated with the "test oaths" that insisted on allegiance to a particular denomination, such as the Church of England.[76]

As originally proposed in the Virginia Plan in 1787, the legislative, executive, and judicial powers "within the several States ought to be bound by oath to support the articles of Union."[77] Delegates later extended the pledge to cover both federal and state officials and added the option "or Affirmation."[78] Unlike an affirmation, an oath is generally understood to be directed to a deity or divine authority.[79]

In his *Commentaries,* Joseph Story explains why officeholders have a choice between taking an oath and making an affirmation: "Oaths have a solemn obligation upon the minds of all reflecting men, and especially upon those, who feel a deep sense of accountability to a Supreme being." In the administration of justice, oaths are an important procedure to remind witnesses who give testimony that they must "guard against malice, falsehood, and evasion." However, Story noted that the taking of any oath is offensive to some religions: "There are known denominations of men, who are conscientiously scrupulous of taking oaths (among which is that pure and distinguished sect of Christians, commonly called Friends, or Quakers) and therefore, to prevent any unjustifiable exclusion from

74. McConnell, "The Origins and Historical Understanding of Free Exercise of Religion," 103 Harv. L. Rev. at 1467–68.

75. Stokes & Pfeffer, Church and State in the United States, at 482.

76. Id. at 483.

77. 1 Farrand 22.

78. 2 Farrand 461, 468.

79. 1 Stokes 524.

office, the constitution has permitted a solemn affirmation to be made instead of an oath, and as its equivalent."[80]

RELIGIOUS TESTS

Article VI provides that "no religious Test shall ever be required as a Qualification to any Office or public Trust under the United States." Whereas the oath/affirmation requirement applies to all public officers—state and federal—the test ban covers only federal officials.

On August 20, Charles Pinckney offered a number of propositions to be referred to the Committee of Detail. Among the entries was this language: "No religious test or qualification shall ever be annexed to any oath of office under the authority of the U.S."[81] There was no discussion of this provision on that day. Apparently the Committee of Detail chose to exclude the reference to a religious test, because on August 30 Pinckney had to offer the language again, prompting Roger Sherman to say he "thought it unnecessary, the prevailing liberality being a sufficient security agst. such tests."[82] Yet when Pinckney's motion was put to a vote, it passed without further debate.

At the Massachusetts ratifying convention, Major Rusk worried about dispensing with the religious test, "shudder[ing] at the idea that Roman Catholics, Papists, and Pagans might be introduced into office." Isaac Backus supported the constitutional language, remarking that "the imposing of religious tests hath been the greatest engine of tyranny in the world."[83] At the North Carolina ratifying convention, Henry Abbot warned that the elimination of religious tests "is by many thought dangerous and impolitic. They suppose that if there be no religious test required, pagans, deists, and Mahometans might obtain offices among us, and that the senators and representatives might all be pagans." James Iredell rejoined that under "the color of religious tests, the utmost cruelties have been exercised."[84] Richard Spaight said that a religious test "would enable the prevailing sect to persecute the rest."[85]

80. Joseph Story, Commentaries on the Constitution of the United States 688–89 (Ronald D. Rotunda & John E. Nowak ed. 1987).
  81. 2 Farrand 342.
  82. Id. at 468.
  83. 2 Elliot 148.
  84. 4 Elliot 192.
  85. Id. at 208.

Story emphasized that the ban on religious tests was included "to cut off for ever every pretence of any alliance between church and state in the national government." The framers knew that bigotry was "unceasingly vigilant in its strategems, to secure to itself an exclusive ascendency over the human mind; and that intolerance was ever ready to arm itself with the terrors of the civil power to exterminate those, who doubted its dogmas, or resisted its infallibility. The Catholic and the Protestant had alternately waged the most ferocious and unrelenting warfare on each other."[86]

Several state constitutions included a religious test. Delaware's constitution of 1776 required officeholders to take an oath or affirmation that they "do profess faith in God the Father, and in Jesus Christ His only Son, and in the Holy Ghost."[87] Maryland's constitution of 1776 stated that "no other test or qualification ought to be required for officeholders beyond an oath of support and fidelity to the state and a declaration of a belief in the Christian religion."[88] Pennsylvania's constitution of 1776 required officeholders to declare "I do believe in one God . . . And I do acknowledge the Scriptures of the Old and New Testament to be given by Divine inspiration." The constitution then stated: "And no further or other religious test shall ever hereafter be required of any civil officer or magistrate in this State."[89] Vermont's constitutions of 1777 and 1786 contained similar provisions, including the "no further or other religious test" language, but also required the officeholder to "own and profess the protestant religion."[90]

These provisions help explain a proposal in 1789 to amend the Constitution by adding the word "other," so that the language in Article VI would read "no other religious Test shall ever be required." In both the House and the Senate, the addition of "other" was rejected.[91] In the North Carolina ratifying convention, William Lancaster referred to these religious tests in state constitutions, and believed "it ought to be so

86. Story, Commentaries, at 690.
87. 1 Thorpe 566 (Art. 22).
88. 3 Thorpe 1690 (Art. XXXV).
89. 5 Thorpe 3085 (Sec. 10).
90. 6 Thorpe 3743 (Sec. IX), 3757 (Sec. XII). For general discussion on these state constitutional provisions, see Daniel L. Dreisbach, "The Constitution's Forgotten Religion Clause: Reflections on the Article VI Religious Test Ban," 38 J. Church & State 261 (1996), and Chester James Antieau, Arthur T. Downey, and Edward C. Roberts, Freedom from Federal Establishment: Formation and Early History of the First Amendment Religion Clauses 92–110 (1964).
91. 1 Annals of Cong. 76, 778 (1789).

in this [national] system."[92] The idea was to allow a "general" test (to apply to Christianity or Protestantism) but not a "particular" test (for specific denominations).[93]

After the effort to add "other" to Article VI failed, states began eliminating their religious tests. Delaware's constitution of 1792 removed the oath to God and Jesus Christ, prohibited a preference by law "to any religious societies, denominations, or modes of worship," and provided that "No religious test shall be required as a qualification to any office, or public trust, under this State."[94] In 1789, Georgia eliminated from its constitution the earlier requirement that legislators be Protestant.[95] South Carolina's constitution of 1778 had required legislators, the governor, the lieutenant-governor, and the privy council to be Protestant (the established state religion), but references to Protestantism are not found in the constitution of 1790.[96] The Vermont constitutions of 1777 and 1786 required lawmakers to believe in God and the Protestant religion; that requirement is excluded from the 1793 Vermont constitution.[97]

Litigation. A religious test in Maryland's constitution reached the Supreme Court in 1961. Article 37 of the Declaration of Rights provided: "No religious test ought ever to be required as a qualification for any office of profit or trust in this State, other than a declaration of belief in the existence of God."[98] The case concerned the appointment of Roy Torcaso to the office of Notary Public by the Governor of Maryland. He was denied a commission to serve because he refused to declare his belief in God. The oath and declaration began: "In the presence of Almighty God, I, Roy R. Torcaso, do solemnly promise. . . ." It concluded: "I, Roy R. Torcaso, do declare that I believe in the existence of God."[99] He claimed that the procedure violated the First and Fourteenth Amendments.

The Supreme Court pointed out that "it was largely to escape religious test oaths and declarations that a great many of the early colonists left

---

92. 4 Elliot 215.

93. Gerard V. Bradley, "The No Religious Test Clause and the Constitution of Religious Liberty: A Machine That Has Gone of Itself," 37 Case Western Reserve L. Rev. 674, 696–700 (1987).

94. 1 Thorpe 568 (Sec. 1 and 20).

95. 2 Thorpe 779 (Art. VI), 786 (Sec. 7).

96. 6 Thorpe 3249 (Art. III), 3258–65.

97. 6 Thorpe 3743 (Sec. IX), 3757 (Sec. XII), 3767 (Sec. XII).

98. 4 Swindler 450.

99. Torcaso v. Watkins, 162 A.2d 438, 440 (Md. 1960).

Europe and came here hoping to worship in their own way." Ironically, once they were in America many "turned out to be perfectly willing, when they had the power to do so, to force dissenters from their faith to take test oaths in conformity with that faith."[100] The Court stated that nothing in its prior decisions allowed government, state or federal, "to restore the historically and constitutionally discredited policy of probing religious beliefs by test oaths or limiting public offices to persons who have, or perhaps more properly profess to have, a belief in some particular kind of religious concept."[101] Neither a state nor the federal government can constitutionally force individuals to profess a belief or disbelief in any religion, impose requirements that aid religions as against nonbelievers, or aid religions based on a belief in the existence of God as against religions based on different beliefs.[102] The Court pointed to Buddhism, Taoism, Ethical Culture, and Secular Humanism as religions that do not teach "what would generally be considered a belief in the existence of God."[103] Maryland's religious test for public office unconstitutionally invaded Torcaso's "freedom of belief and religion and therefore cannot be enforced against him."[104]

Activity by the First Congress

The First Congress encountered a number of religious issues and dealt with them in accordance with the judgments of legislators, unencumbered by what judges might have decided. As David Currie notes: "It was in the legislative and executive branches, not in the courts, that the original understanding of the Constitution was forged."[105]

Congress expressed an interest in promoting religion in general with this provision of the Northwest Territory Ordinance: "Religion, morality, and knowledge, being necessary to good government and the happiness of mankind, schools and the means of education shall forever be encouraged."[106] Schools built on public lands with federal funds were expected to include religion and morality in their curriculum. A few

100. Torcaso v. Watkins, 367 U.S. 488, 490 (1961).
101. Id. at 494.
102. Id. at 488.
103. Id. at 488, n.11.
104. Id. at 496.
105. David P. Currie, The Constitution in Congress: The Federalist Period, 1789–1801, at 296 (1997).
106. 1 Stat. 52, Art. III (1789).

THE STRUGGLE FOR RELIGIOUS LIBERTY

years later, in 1796, Congress passed legislation setting aside grants of land "for the society of United Brethren for propagating the gospel among the heathen."[107] Congress would continue to provide funds to teach Christianity to Indians (Chapter 7).

CHAPLAINS

Beginning in 1774, the Continental Congress authorized Reverend Jacob Duché to open Congress with prayers.[108] He continued in that capacity for the next two years.[109] When Duché retired in October 1776, he was paid $150. Explaining that he accepted the appointment "from motives perfectly disinterested," he asked that the money be directed to the widows and children of Pennsylvania officers killed in battle.[110] Duché was replaced by other chaplains.[111] In 1788, Congress set the annual salary of chaplains at $300.[112] Chaplains were assigned to army regiments and brigades[113] and to military hospitals.[114] State conventions and legislatures appointed chaplains for the military and the legislative bodies, relying on public funds to pay them.[115]

The First Congress built on these precedents. In 1789, the Senate created a committee to prepare a system of rules governing the two Houses in cases of conference "and to take under consideration the manner of electing Chaplains."[116] The House created a similar committee and selected a chaplain.[117] The statute providing compensation for Members of Congress included a section authorizing the annual amount of $500 for each chaplain of Congress.[118]

Although Madison served on the committee that prepared a system of rules to govern the two Houses in cases of conference and to regulate the

107. 1 Stat. 491, § 5 (1796).
108. 1 Journals of the Continental Congress 26–27 (1905) (hereafter Journals).
109. 2 Journals 12–13, 22, 185; 4 Journals 303; 5 Journals 530.
110. 6 Journals 886–87, 911.
111. 6 Journals 1033, 1034; 8 Journals 756; 9 Journals 822; 27 Journals 693.
112. 34 Journals 71. See Edward Frank Humphrey, Nationalism and Religion in America, 1774–1789, at 410–15 (1924).
113. 4 Journals 61; 5 Journals 522, 789; 7 Journals 256; 8 Journals 390–91, 421, 430, 557 (Note 2), 609.
114. 8 Journals 754; 10 Journals 142.
115. Antieau, Downey & Roberts, Freedom from Federal Establishment, at 76.
116. 1 Senate Journal 10 (1789); 1 Annals of Cong. 18 (1789).
117. 1 H. Journal 11–12, 26 (1789); 1 Annals of Cong. 104–5, 233 (1789).
118. 1 Stat. 71, § 4 (1789).

appointment of chaplains,[119] and voted for the bill that funded Members of Congress and chaplains,[120] he later objected to the appointment of chaplains. The precedent seemed to him harmful and unnecessary: "It would have been a much better proof to their Constituents of their pious feeling if the members had contributed for the purpose, a pittance from their own pockets."[121] He regarded the chaplains as "a palpable violation of equal rights, as well as Constitutional principles." Individual rights were violated because religious representation in Congress was denied to such minority sects as the Roman Catholics and the Quakers. The daily devotions in Congress, Madison said, served to degrade religion by degenerating into "scanty attendance, and a tiresome formality."[122]

Christians were selected to offer prayers in Congress, but as the religious character of America diversified, other religions were included. This change occurred through the regular political process without the need for litigation. On February 1, 1860, Dr. Morris J. Raphall of Congregation B'nai Jeshurun of New York City gave the first Jewish prayer to the House of Representatives.[123] Although there was some criticism that he wore his tallit (prayer shawl) and yarmulke, a member of Congress defended his choice of ritual garb: "The Rabbi did right in adhering to his costume; he came among us to pray according to his faith. For the moment, the Hall of Congress was his Synagogue. . . . Had he yielded to our habits, so far as to come with his head uncovered, and without his vestments which a Jewish Rabbi wears at the time of solemn service, such concession to our views and feelings would also have been renouncing of that perfect equality which it was his duty as a Jew and a minister of religion to uphold."[124]

The practice of inviting a variety of religious leaders to give the prayer in Congress continues. In addition to the prayers offered by House and Senate chaplains, both chambers invite guest chaplains from a wide number of religious groups. On September 14, 2000, a Hindu priest from Ohio offered a prayer in the House of Representatives.[125] The following

119. 1 H. Journal 11–12 (1789); 1 Annals of Cong. 104–5 (1789).
120. 1 Annals of Cong. 892 (1789).
121. 9 The Writings of James Madison 100 (Hunt ed.) (letter to Edward Livingston, July 10, 1822).
122. Elizabeth Fleet, ed., "Madison's 'Detached Memoranda,'" 3 Wm. & Mary Q. 534, 558–59 (1946).
123. Cong. Globe, 36th Cong., 1st Sess. 648–49 (1860).
124. Bertrum Wallace Korn, Eventual Years and Experiences 107 (1954).
125. 146 Cong. Rec. H7579 (daily ed. September 14, 2000).

year, a Muslim Imam from Virginia offered a prayer to the House.[126] Also in 2001, the House received as its guest chaplain a leader of the Flathead Indian Reservation, which is home to the Confederated Salish and Kootenai Tribe.[127]

Military Chaplains. Until the Civil War, only Protestants were chosen to serve as military chaplains. Statutes required military chaplains to be a regular ordained minister of a "Christian denomination."[128] When war began, the largely Jewish Sixty-fifth Regiment of the Fifth Pennsylvania Cavalry had a Jewish layman serving as chaplain, but he was soon forced out because he did not fit the statutory definition.[129] Although Jews at that time were uncomfortable about objecting to public policies, the situation was not a good one and they decided to lobby the national government to change the statute. They depended on the regular political process, not the courts.

A number of metropolitan dailies joined their cause, with both Christians and Jews signing petitions that urged Congress to remove the sectarian statutory language.[130] Arnold Fischel of Congregation Shearith Israel of New York traveled to Washington, D.C., to speak to President Lincoln. Like any other citizen, he waited in line to see the President. Although Lincoln was not familiar with the issue, he read the documents that Fischel brought, listened to his argument, and responded sympathetically, telling Fischel in a letter the next day that he would "try to have a new law broad enough to cover what is desired by you in behalf of the Israelites."[131] Fischel also wrote to the Senate Committee on Military Affairs, explaining why a change in the statute would conform to the constitutional prohibition against a religious test.[132] These pressures led Congress a year later to delete "Christian denomination" and insert "some religious denomination."[133] Similar to other disputes concerning religious minorities, the regular political process worked.

126. 147 Cong. Rec. H203 (daily ed. February 7, 2001).
127. Id. at H7361 (daily ed. October 30, 2001).
128. 12 Stat. 270, § 9 (1861); 12 Stat. 288, § 7 (1861).
129. Bertrum Wallace Korn, American Jewry and the Civil War 58–60 (1951).
130. Id. at 65–68.
131. Id. at 70.
132. Jonathan D. Sarna & David G. Dalin, Religion and State in the American Jewish Tradition 130 (1997).
133. 12 Stat. 595, § 8 (1862). See also Albert Isaac Slomovitz, The Fighting Rabbis: Jewish Military Chaplains and American History 10–18 (2001 paper ed.).

As with chaplains in Congress, military chaplains reflect the changing religious population of America. Beginning in 1993, a Muslim chaplain was added to the Army. That number increased to four by 1999 and to fourteen by 2001: eight in the Army, three in the Air Force, and three in the Navy. Two of the latter serve in the Marine Corps.[134] When Congress provides chaplains for soldiers, is that an act of establishment? Yet denying soldiers access to ministers, rabbis, and other religious leaders would interfere with free exercise, especially for soldiers assigned to remote outposts. The two religion clauses—the Establishment Clause and the Free Exercise Clause—frequently overlap and compete. It is Defense Department policy "that professionally qualified chaplains shall be appointed to provide for the free exercise of religion for all members of the Military Services, their dependents, and other authorized persons."[135] To be considered for appointment as a chaplain, clergy are certified by a "DOD-recognized ecclesiastical endorsing agent" who certifies the professional qualifications of the appointee. DOD regulations establish criteria for the religious faith groups that seek to become endorsing agents.[136]

Prisons. Similarly, federal prisons provide inmates with chaplains to provide pastoral care and counseling.[137] The Bureau of Prisons provides instructions that cover religious dietary practices, opportunities to pursue religious beliefs and practices, use of inmate religious property (including rosaries, prayer beads, prayer rugs, phylacteries, and medicine pouches), access to religious books, and observance of religious holy days.[138]

Litigation. The constitutionality of legislative chaplains, both in the state legislatures and in Congress, has been challenged in court. In 1983, the Supreme Court upheld the practice of the Nebraska legislature to begin each session with a prayer by a chaplain paid by the state. The Court observed that Congress had followed the same practice "without interruption" ever since 1789, and that a precedent established by the First Congress, which drafted the Bill of Rights, "sheds light" on what the framers intended by the Establishment Clause.[139] Taking direction from the

---

134. "Military Clerics Balance Arms and Allah," New York Times, October 7, 2001, at 31.
135. 32 C.F.R. § 65.3 (7-1-00 ed.)
136. Id. at § 65.5(a)–(b).
137. 28 C.F.R. § 548.12 (7-1-99 ed.).
138. Id. at §§ 548.10–548.20; 60 Fed. Reg. 46485 (1995).
139. Marsh v. Chambers, 463 U.S. 783, 788, 790 (1983).

precedent established by Congress, the Court said "there can be no doubt that the practice of opening legislative sessions with prayer has become part of the fabric of our society."[140] In a dissent, Justice Brennan noted that the majority violated the Court's own three-part test announced in *Lemon* v. *Kurtzman* (1971). In Brennan's view, the Nebraska statute had a religious, not a secular, purpose; its principal or primary effect advanced religion; and it fostered government entanglement with religion.

While this case was being decided, a separate lawsuit concerned chaplains who worked for the U.S. Senate and the U.S. House of Representatives. In 1981, a district court held that the plaintiffs bringing the case lacked standing to sue.[141] However, the appellate court reinstated the suit and sent it back to the trial court for a decision on the merits.[142] Three weeks later the House of Representatives passed a resolution viewing with "deep concern" the appellate court decision and expressing in strong terms the constitutional power of the House "to determine the rules of its proceedings, to select officers, and otherwise to control its internal affairs." Any adverse decision from a court would imply "a lack of respect due a coordinate branch concerning matters committed to it by the Constitution." The resolution passed by a vote of 388 to zero.[143] The case was next heard by the D.C. Circuit, sitting en banc. Because of the Supreme Court's decision in the Nebraska case, the D.C. Circuit held that the complaint against the House and Senate chaplains "retains no vitality" and dismissed the case.[144]

CONSCIENTIOUS OBJECTORS

The First Congress considered giving an exemption from military service for conscientious objectors. In the militia bill of 1790, lawmakers debated exempting persons conscientiously scrupulous of bearing arms, allowing them to pay a certain amount in lieu of military service.[145] After considerable discussion, Congress decided to shift that issue to the states.[146]

140. Id. at 792.
141. Murray v. Morton, 505 F.Supp. 144 (D.D.C. 1981).
142. Murray v. Buchanan, 674 F.2d 14 (D.C. Cir. 1982). Because this panel decision was later reversed by the D.C. Circuit sitting en banc, the panel decision was printed in the advance sheets but not in the final bound version.
143. 128 Cong. Rec. 5890–96 (1982).
144. Murray v. Buchanan, 720 F.2d 689 (D.C. Cir. 1983) (en banc).
145. 1 Annals of Cong. 1869–73 (1790).
146. Id. at 1874–75.

Also, in what became the Second Amendment, the House added this provision in 1789: "But no one religiously scrupulous of bearing arms shall be compelled to render military service in person."[147] However, the Senate deleted that language.[148] This issue is explored in greater depth in Chapter 4.

The Bill of Rights

On June 8, 1789, Madison told his colleagues in the House of Representatives that he would offer a list of amendments to the Constitution. Among the amendments he suggested was language to be inserted in Article I, Section 9, between Clauses 3 and 4: "The civil rights of none shall be abridged on account of religious belief or worship, nor shall any national religion be established, nor shall the full and equal rights of conscience be in any manner, or on any pretext, infringed."[149] The prohibition of a "national religion" appeared to leave unaffected the established churches that still existed in the states. Madison also proposed other language, to be inserted in Article I, Section 10, between Clauses 1 and 2: "No State shall violate the equal rights of conscience, or the freedom of the press, or the trial by jury in criminal cases."[150] In this way, the rights of conscience would bind both the federal government and the states, but the Establishment Clause applied only to the federal government.

The House debated the religion clauses on August 15. The language, reworked by a select committee, now read: "No religion shall be established by law, nor shall the equal rights of conscience be infringed."[151] Peter Silvester (spelled Sylvester in the debate) voiced misgivings about the language, fearing "it might be thought to have a tendency to abolish religion altogether." Elbridge Gerry said it would "read better if it was, that no religious doctrine shall be established by law." Roger Sherman saw no need for the amendment because Congress "had no authority whatever delegated to them by the Constitution to make religious establishments." Daniel Carroll thought the amendment was necessary, "as many sects have concurred in opinion that they are not well secured under the present Constitution."

147. 1 S. Journal 63–64 (1789).
148. Id. at 71, 77.
149. 1 Annals of Cong. 434 (1789).
150. Id. at 435.
151. Id. at 729.

After this initial debate, Madison offered his interpretation of the language: "Congress should not establish a religion, and enforce the legal observation of it by law, nor compel men to worship God in any manner contrary to their conscience." As to the need for the language, he said that some of the state conventions looked to the power of Congress to make all laws "necessary and proper" and concluded that Congress might make laws "of such a nature as might infringe the rights of conscience, and establish a national religion." The amendment was designed to prevent such actions.

Madison now thought it advisable to change the select committee language by inserting (or reinserting) the word "national" before religion. The clause would read: "No national religion shall be established by law, nor shall the equal rights of conscience be infringed." Madison said that people appeared to fear that one sect might become preeminent, or that two strong sects would combine and compel others to conform to their creeds. Gerry did not like the term *national* because it revived the issue that had agitated delegates at the Philadelphia Convention, namely, was the Constitution establishing a federal government or a national one? Madison withdrew his motion, but observed that the words "no national religion shall be established" did not imply that the government was a national one.[152] A motion by Samuel Livermore, that the language be altered to read that Congress "shall make no laws touching religion, or infringing the rights of conscience," was adopted 31 to 20.

On August 17, members of the House considered Madison's second proposal, after some alteration of language: "No State shall infringe the equal rights of conscience, nor the freedom of speech, or of the press, nor of the right of trial by jury in criminal cases." Thomas Tucker objected on the ground that it was better to leave state governments "to themselves, and not to interfere with them more than we already do." Moving to strike the words, he said that many thought the language was "rather too much." Madison responded by saying that he conceived the language "to be the most valuable amendment in the whole list." If restrictions were to be placed on the federal government, they should be placed equally on the states. Tucker's motion was rejected, but Madison's language was changed to read: "The equal rights of conscience, the freedom of speech or of the press, and the right of trial by jury in criminal cases, shall not be infringed by any State."[153]

152. Id. at 731.
153. Id. at 755.

The House returned to the religion clauses on August 20, adopting this language: "Congress shall make no law establishing religion, or to prevent the free exercise thereof, or to infringe the rights of conscience."[154] Upon receiving the list of constitutional amendments, the Senate debated motions to alter the religion clauses.[155] After making some changes, the Senate decided to combine the clauses on religion, speech, press, assembly, and petition in this form: "Congress shall make no law establishing articles of faith or a mode of worship, or prohibiting the free exercise of religion, or abridging the freedom of speech, or the press, or the right of the people peaceably to assemble, and petition to the government for the redress of grievances."[156]

The two chambers resolved their differences and produced the language that became the First Amendment: "Congress shall make no law respecting an establishment of religion, or prohibiting a free exercise thereof, or abridging the freedom of speech, or of the press, or the right of the people peaceably to assemble, and to petition the Government for a redress of grievances." The House language that prohibited states from infringing on the rights of conscience was deleted by the Senate and never submitted to the states for ratification.

As ratified, the religion clauses represented a check on the national government, not the states. The language clearly read: "*Congress* shall make no law. . . ." However, through what has been called the Incorporation Doctrine, the Supreme Court has incrementally incorporated most of the Bill of Rights into the Due Process Clause of the Fourteenth Amendment and applied those restrictions to the states.[157] The Free Exercise Clause was applied to the states in 1940 and the Establishment Clause in 1947.[158] As interpreted by the federal courts, broad protection is granted to religious beliefs but not necessarily to religious practices. What constitutes "establishment" has turned out to be much more complex, with lawmakers, Presidents, judges, states, and the public sharply divided on what

154. Id. at 766.

155. 1 S. Journal 70 (1789).

156. Id. at 77.

157. The progress of this incorporation is presented in a table in Louis Fisher, American Constitutional Law 422–23 (2001).

158. Cantwell v. Connecticut, 310 U.S. 296, 303 (1940); Everson v. Board of Education, 330 U.S. 1, 15 (1947).

government may do in assisting religion. The outcome of that struggle has not been dictated or controlled by any of the participants, including the judiciary.

The meaning of the religion clauses in the Constitution has been confused by metaphors about the "wall of separation" between church and state. Jefferson used the wall metaphor in a statement to a committee of the Danbury Baptist Association in 1802. When the framers adopted the religion clauses of the First Amendment, he said it was their intent to build "a wall of separation between Church and State."[159] In the context of his remarks, Jefferson used the metaphor correctly, because his statement was limited to religious "opinions," the "rights of conscience," and to "natural rights." Those areas deserve a zone of individual privacy. Government has no business passing judgment on religious beliefs. But the wall does not prevent all contacts between church and state, as the letter from President Jefferson to a Baptist group clearly demonstrates.

In upholding state assistance of transportation to parochial schools in 1947, Justice Black claimed that the First Amendment "has erected a wall between church and state. That wall must be kept high and impregnable. We could not approve the slightest breach. New Jersey has not breached it here."[160] In fact, a breach did occur in that case, because the Court supported the transportation assistance. A year later, in a concurring opinion, Justice Jackson questioned the Court's reasoning and predicted correctly that the Court would make "the legal 'wall of separation between church and state' as winding as the famous serpentine wall designed by Mr. Jefferson for the University he founded."[161] Justice Reed aptly advised: "A rule of law should not be drawn from a figure of speech."[162] A complete wall between church and state is neither possible nor desirable. As explained in the next chapter, religious organizations have a right to lobby and petition government for various programs and activities, and they have done their part in enriching religious liberty and other individual freedoms.

159. 16 The Writings of Thomas Jefferson 282 (Bergh ed. 1904).
160. Everson v. Board of Education, 330 U.S. 1, 18 (1947).
161. McCollum v. Board of Education, 333 U.S. 203, 238 (1948).
162. Id. at 247.

3

THE RELIGIOUS LOBBY

Because of limitations and inadequacies in the courts, the larger political culture has had to reverse and modify judicial rulings that were too restrictive on personal liberties. Individuals and private groups feel strongly about the rights of conscience and religious liberty. Deep feelings and rich experience make it unlikely that they will passively acquiesce to the judgments of courts, legislatures, administrative bodies, or experts. Private citizens, accustomed to thinking for themselves, are not shy about testifying before legislative bodies and using other lobbying techniques, including litigation, to press their views.

Madison's Factions

Americans are used to the concept of self-government and feel comfortable about it, but for one reason or another they look unfavorably upon lobbyists and interest groups. When students ask questions that are critical about interest groups, I ask if they mean the NAACP or the ACLU. No, they don't mean *those*. After completing a talk to public administrators in Malaysia, I was peppered with questions about lobbying in America. How do those nefarious groups operate? Are their abuses checked? After about the sixth question I said, "You have lobbyists in Malaysia." They flatly denied it, but I replied that they have officials deciding policy and outside groups trying to influence the decision.

The U.S. Constitution not only accepts but invites outside pressure. The First Amendment states that Congress shall not abridge "the right of the people peaceably to assemble, and to petition the Government for a redress of grievances." If the government tried to prohibit such activities, it would be promptly branded as authoritarian and dictatorial. It is difficult to conceive of a democratic government operating in a sterile environment never contaminated by private lobbyists. In 1961, the Supreme Court noted that "the whole concept of representation depends upon the ability of the people to make their wishes known to their representatives."[1]

In Federalist No. 10, Madison analyzed factions and what to do about them. He spoke about the need "to break and control the violence of faction." The friend of popular government, he said, "never finds himself so much alarmed for their character and fate, as when he contemplates their propensity to this dangerous vice." There was great danger that governmental policy would be determined "not according to the rules of justice and the rights of the minor party, but by the superior force of an interested and overbearing majority." He worried about "the unsteadiness and injustice with which a factious spirit has tainted our public administration." By faction he meant "a number of citizens, whether amounting to a majority or minority of the whole, who are united and actuated by some common impulse of passion, or of interest, adverse to the rights of other citizens, or to the permanent and aggregate interests of the community."

This part of Madison's essay is not too convincing. Which citizens were actuated by an interest "adverse to the rights of other citizens"? Perhaps "other citizens" had interests adverse to them. Was Madison or anyone else in a position to draw up a list of groups that constituted dangerous "factions"and produce a second list of groups with an acceptable agenda? Probably not. But here Madison's analysis moves to one of the most creative and enduring models of democratic government.

He identified two methods of curing "the mischiefs of faction." One was to remove its causes, the other was to control its effects. How do you remove the cause? Two ways: government could destroy the liberty essential to its existence, or give every citizen the same opinions, passions, and interests. Neither remedy was acceptable in a democratic society. Because "liberty is to faction what air is to fire," it would make no more sense to abolish liberty than to annihilate air, which is essential to life. As to attempts to make everyone alike, not only was that "impracticable," but it would violate the "first object" of government, which is to protect the faculties that lead to differences among individuals. Factionalism is natural to humankind and cannot be avoided or eliminated.

1. Eastern Railroad Presidents Conference v. Noerr Motors, Inc., 365 U.S. 127, 137 (1961).

Unable or unwilling to control the cause of faction, Madison turns to ways of controlling its effects. In cases where a faction is less than a majority, the majority can "defeat its sinister views by regular vote." But if the faction consists of a majority, what can be done to protect the minority's interest? In a "pure democracy" consisting of few citizens, the minority remains at the mercy of the majority. In a larger republic, however, with a greater number of citizens, whose views and interests are passed through elected representatives, and where government is divided between national, state, and local levels, the minority is better protected. "Extend the sphere," Madison said, "and you take in a greater variety of parties and interests." The majority is now likely to be composed of interests that are in disagreement and will cancel or check one another.

The political system described by Madison relies primarily not on representatives with "enlightened views and virtuous sentiments" but on destructive factions neutralizing one another. Whereas the "influence of factious leaders may kindle a flame within their particular States," they will be unable to spread the conflagration to other states. "A religious sect may degenerate into a political faction in a part of the Confederacy; but the variety of sects dispersed over the entire face of it must secure the national councils against any danger from that source."

Religious Activism

Madison's assessment of factions has been borne out by America's experience. Factions, religious or otherwise, make little headway on their own. Other interests emerge to block their progress. But when religious groups join with other organizations to promote more general interests that transcend sectarianism, their contributions have been great. Religious organizations have participated in many volatile and emotionally charged issues in America, including civil rights, abortion, the Equal Rights Amendment, school prayer, and aid to parochial schools.[2] On many of these issues, religious groups have disagreed with each other and have had to revisit and often modify positions they had taken in the past. Overall, the general trend has been toward greater involvement and a growth of religious organizations that lobby on public issues. The following sections focus on religious lobbying on slavery, temperance, war, and abortion.

2. Allen D. Hertzke, Representing God in Washington: The Role of Religious Lobbies in the American Polity 5 (1988).

SLAVERY

Churches were early involved in the fight against slavery. The first printed protest against slavery in America came from a Quaker publication in 1688.[3] George Keith, a Quaker, issued a broadside against slavery in 1693.[4] Also in 1693, a Quaker meeting in Philadelphia announced a policy of buying no slaves "except to set free" and that the goal was to release slaves "after a reasonable time of service . . . and during the time they have them, to teach them to read, and give them a Christian education."[5]

Quakers expelled slave-owning Friends in 1776.[6] The previous year, a group of Philadelphia Quakers organized the country's first antislavery society.[7] About half the members of the New York Manumission Society, an antislavery group founded in 1785, were Quakers, and they made up about three-quarters of the Pennsylvania Abolition Society, founded in 1794.[8] In 1789, the General Committee of Virginia Baptists passed a resolution condemning slavery, while in 1800 the Methodist Conference called for the gradual emancipation of slaves.[9] In 1818, the General Assembly of the undivided Presbyterian Church unanimously adopted a manifesto that declared slavery "utterly inconsistent with the law of God," although also counseling against "hasty emancipation."[10]

Constitutional challenges to slavery "developed from nontechnical, popular origins that lay outside courts and legislature."[11] Antislavery societies were organized in the churches, although some clergymen defended slavery as "clearly established in the Holy Scriptures, both by precept and example."[12] Churches were typically split between the North and the

3. 2 Stokes 121. His chapter "The Church and Slavery" devotes almost 130 pages to church opposition to slavery.

4. Luke Eugene Ebersole, Church Lobbying in the Nation's Capital 2 (1951).

5. Anson Phelps Stokes & Leo Pfeffer, Church and State in the United States 281 (1964).

6. Robert Booth Fowler & Allen D. Hertzke, Religion and Politics in America: Faith, Culture, and Strategic Choices 18 (1995).

7. Sydney E. Ahlstrom, A Religious History of the American People 650 (1972).

8. Mary K. Cayton, "Social Reform from the Colonial Period through the Civil War," in 3 Encyclopedia of the American Religious Experience 1430 (Charles H. Lippy & Peter W. Williams, eds. 1988).

9. Ebersole, Church Lobbying in the Nation's Capital, at 3.

10. Ahlstrom, A Religious History of the American People, at 648.

11. William M. Wiecek, The Sources of Antislavery Constitutionalism in America, 1760–1848, at 7 (1977).

12. Michael Corbett & Julia Mitchell Corbett, Politics and Religion in the United States 95 (1999).

South. Northern Baptists deplored slavery while some Southern Baptists looked for justification to Old Testament precedents and the lack of a specific prohibition in the New Testament.[13]

In 1839, after African slaves on the *Amistad* rebelled to take over the ship, the issue of their freedom was brought to the U.S. Supreme Court. The Congregationalist members of the First Church of Christ in Farmington, Connecticut, planned to release the Africans out of jail and smuggle them into Canada if the Court ruled that they were the property of slave owners. The breakout became unnecessary when the Court decided in their favor.[14]

The Reverend George Bourne devoted his life to writing antislavery publications and helped found the American Anti-Slavery Society in 1833.[15] During this period, a number of churches were reluctant to condemn slavery. In 1836, the Presbyterian Church rejected a recommendation that slaveholders be censured, and the Methodist General Conference decided that it would not review church policy regarding discipline toward slaveholders. Other churches remained neutral on slavery.[16] Abolitionists often had an uphill battle in trying to convince northern churches to come out against slavery.[17] In 1854, when the Kansas-Nebraska bill threatened to spread slavery into the territories, 3,050 clergymen forwarded a protest to the U.S. Senate, calling slavery "a great moral wrong."[18] Antislavery sentiments solidified in the 1850s, producing "Christian Anti-Slavery Conventions" and the Church Anti-Slavery Society.[19]

The children of Lyman Beecher, a powerful Puritan preacher, made important contributions to the struggle against slavery. One of his sons, Henry Ward Beecher, used his position as minister of the Plymouth Church in Brooklyn to speak out against the evils of slavery.[20] A daughter,

13. Stokes & Pfeffer, Church and State in the United States, at 284.

14. "A New Amistad on a Mission for Freedom," Washington Post, October 6, 2001, at B9; United States v. The Amistad, 40 U.S. (15 Pet.) 518 (1842).

15. Dwight Lowell Dumond, The Antislavery Origins of the Civil War in the United States 8 (1939; republished in 1980).

16. Cayton, "Social Reform from the Colonial Period through the Civil War," at 1438.

17. John R. McKivigan, The War against Proslavery Religion: Abolitionism and the Northern Churches, 1830–1865 (1984).

18. Ebersole, Church Lobbying in the Nation's Capital, at 5.

19. Cayton, "Social Reform from the Colonial Period through the Civil War," at 1439.

20. Ebersole, Church Lobbying in the Nation's Capital, at 4.

Harriet Beecher Stowe, wrote the antislavery novel *Uncle Tom's Cabin* (1852). One study concluded: "No other groups pushed for abolition as persistently and passionately over so many years or over so broad a spectrum of citizens as did the churches and the antislavery associations they founded."[21]

TEMPERANCE

The temperance movement began in the early part of the nineteenth century. It was during that period that the consumption of alcohol in America escalated, producing devastating effects on workers, families, women, and children. The Massachusetts Society for the Suppression of Intemperance, founded in 1813, advocated moderation in the use of alcohol, not abstinence.[22] Those who supported temperance often directed their efforts to abolishing the products of distillation (hard liquor), not fermentation (wine and beer).[23] Eventually the movement turned to strict prohibition by statute or constitutional amendment.

In 1826, evangelical clergymen created the American Society for the Promotion of Temperance (ATS) and urged total abstinence.[24] Protestant reformers argued that intemperance, by "undermining man's health, impairing his reason, dulling his conscience, and obliterating his fear of God," fostered "ungodliness, immorality, disease, and death, destroying both body and soul."[25] Members of the Roman Catholic, Episcopal, and Lutheran Churches were more lenient toward drinking, although some wings of the Catholic Church supported the temperance movement.[26] Because of the use of wine for communion and seders, Catholics and Jews generally supported temperance, not prohibition.

In 1846, most of the towns and cities in New York took away the licensing of taverns and grogshops. Neal Dow was able to get the Maine

21. Paul J. Weber & W. Landis Jones, U.S. Religious Interest Groups: Institutional Profiles xviii (1994).

22. Jack S. Blocker, Jr., American Temperance Movements: Cycles of Reform 11–12 (1989).

23. Norman H. Clark, Deliver Us from Evil: An Interpretation of American Prohibition 8 (1976).

24. Blocker, American Temperance Movements, at 12.

25. James H. Timberlake, Prohibition and the Progressive Movement, 1900–1920, at 4 (1963).

26. Id. at 5.

legislature in 1851 to prohibit the manufacture and sale of "spiritous or intoxicating liquors." By 1855, similar laws had been adopted in Minnesota, Rhode Island, Massachusetts, Vermont, Michigan, Connecticut, Indiana, Delaware, Iowa, Nebraska, New York, and New Hampshire. Some of these states decided to permit wine or beer, and various artifices to allow the consumption of hard liquor.[27]

The National Temperance Society, drawing on the evangelical Christian tradition, was incorporated in 1866.[28] John Russell, a Methodist clergyman, became the principal spokesman for the Prohibition Party, founded in 1869.[29] Five years later Protestant women established the Woman's Christian Temperance Union (WCTU).[30] Howard Russell (unrelated to John Russell) built on his work as a Congregationalist minister to help found the Anti-Saloon League in 1893.[31] The League united Protestant activists across the country and made speakers available to advocate the closing of saloons. Bishop James Cannon, Jr., played a prominent role in the antisaloon movement, as did his church, the Southern Methodist.[32]

To prohibitionists, saloons provided a corrupting environment that allowed urban bosses to control immigrant voters. Saloons attracted prostitutes, gambling, and minors. The crusade against drinking, which lasted a century, has been described as "the landmark effort by churches in American politics."[33] Some of the prohibition drive had an anti-Catholic bias, with many Protestants regarding Catholic immigrants as "lower-class, illiterate, and vulnerable to evil habits."[34] The movement depended primarily on white, middle-class, rural, Protestant, and native-born citizens; southern and western states were arrayed against the eastern industrialized states.[35] However, the movement also included urban business leaders, labor leaders, physicians, teachers, and other professionals.[36]

27. Clark, Deliver Us from Evil, at 45–49.
28. K. Austin Kerr, Organized for Prohibition: A New History of the Anti-Saloon League 39–41 (1985).
29. Id. at 41–42.
30. Ruth Bordin, Woman and Temperance: The Quest for Power and Liberty, 1873–1900, at 34–36 (1981).
31. Kerr, Organized for Prohibition, at 76–89.
32. Virginius Dabney, Dry Messiah: The Life of Bishop Cannon (1949).
33. Robert Booth Fowler, Religion and Politics in America 140 (1985).
34. Clark, Deliver Us from Evil, at 88.
35. Alan P. Grimes, Democracy and the Amendments to the Constitution 83–89 (1978).
36. Clark, Deliver Us from Evil, at 11.

The Eighteenth Amendment, prohibiting liquor, cleared Congress in December 1917 and the states ratified it by January 1919. Instead of controlling crime and elevating morality by doing away with alcohol, it generated crime by producing a class of gangsters willing to supply liquor to customers anxious to have it. The Eighteenth Amendment found support in a Congress that was apportioned under the census of 1910, when a majority of Americans lived in rural areas. The censuses of 1920 and 1930 reflected a growth of urban areas in the eastern states. These population shifts provided the votes for repeal, but more important, the issue was no longer "wet" against "dry." Prohibition did not stop alcoholic consumption, although in some areas drinking declined. Congressman Manny Celler (D-N.Y.) remarked in 1933: "New York City had 26,000 saloons before prohibition; it now has over 32,000 speakeasies."[37] Ratification of the Twenty-first Amendment in 1933 put an end to the "noble experiment."

The Woman's Christian Temperance Union remains active, working to strengthen the rights and health of women and children. Still supported mainly by Protestant churches, the WCTU is a worldwide organization dedicated to educating citizens on the harmful effects of alcoholic beverages, other narcotic drugs, and tobacco.[38] In recent years, a number of groups have formed to pressure state government to impose heavier penalties on drunk drivers. Although the prohibition movement failed, temperance is still valued. No entertainer today would think of singing the once-popular lyrics, directed at the bartender, "Give me one more for my baby and one more for the road."

WAR AND PEACE

Religious groups advance various models regarding military action, ranging from holy wars, to just wars, to pacifism. At times the notion of a just war blends with a holy war. Natural law theorists from Thomas Aquinas to Hugo Grotius allowed for war in defense of religion, taking Christianity as the one true faith. Other scholars tried to limit just wars to the defense of religious liberty, rather than efforts to subjugate people with other faiths.[39]

37. 76 Cong. Rec. 4514 (1933).
38. Weber & Jones, U.S. Religious Interest Groups, at 159–60.
39. Melvin B. Endy, Jr., "War and Peace," in 3 Encyclopedia of the American Religious Experience 1410 (Charles H. Lippy & Peter W. Williams, eds. 1988).

During the Civil War, abolitionists and slave owners cited religious reasons for their positions and sought aid from the Almighty. As Lincoln noted in his Second Inaugural Address: "Both read the same Bible and pray to the same God, and each invokes His aid against the other. . . . The prayers of both could not be answered. That of neither has been answered fully." Unlike Woodrow Wilson, who would enter World War I as part of a Protestant crusade, Lincoln "stood apart from the churches and questioned their self-righteousness." He "conceived of the national mission in religious terms that were not distinctly Christian."[40]

The Spanish-American War of 1898 helped implement the philosophy of "Manifest Destiny." Under that doctrine, America had a moral obligation and a higher calling to extend Anglo-Saxon civilization to other lands, especially to bring religion to "the heathen." With mounting reports about Spanish atrocities in Cuba, the religious press "turned to proclaim a Holy War."[41] More specifically, Protestants saw the struggle as a holy war against Catholic Spain.[42]

What started out as a war over Cuba quickly spread to the Pacific, with the United States acquiring control over the Philippines, Puerto Rico, and Guam. Meeting with a group of fellow Methodists, President William McKinley explained how he decided to extend U.S. control over the Philippines. At first he didn't want any part of the territory. Later he decided that it might be appropriate to occupy parts, such as Manila and Luzon. He walked the floor of the White House "night after night until midnight," even getting down on his knees to pray for guidance. Finally, he decided it would be "cowardly and dishonorable" to return the property to Spain or to other countries, and that the people were not ready for self-rule: "There was nothing left for us to do but to take them all, and to educate the Filipinos, and uplift and civilize and Christianize them, and by God's grace do the very best we could by them, as our fellow men for whom Christ also died. And then I went to bed and went to sleep and slept soundly."[43]

Casualties were modest in the brief war between the United States and Spain. In the summer of 1914, European nations were pulled into a

---

40. Id. at 1421.
41. Walter Millis, The Martial Spirit: A Study of Our War with Spain 124 (1931).
42. Endy, War and Peace, at 1419.
43. Millis, The Martial Spirit, at 384.

war of devastating brutality and bloodshed. President Woodrow Wilson's initial policy of neutrality slowly gave way to a preference for England over Germany. Gradually, he prepared the nation for war, although in the election year of 1916 he promised to keep America out of war. His renomination at the Democratic convention was accompanied by shouts of "He Kept Us Out of War."[44] After the election, Wilson came to Congress on April 2, 1917, and asked for a declaration of war against Germany. The Senate vote was 82 to 6; the House supported the declaration 373 to 50.[45]

Religious organizations swung from neutrality to support for Wilson's involvement in war. A number of denominations, including the Scotch Presbyterians, Wesleyan Methodists, Episcopal Church, Baptists, Congregationalists, Unitarians, and Universalists, had English origins and a natural sympathy for the British cause. Catholics were generally loyal to Wilson, while Lutherans remained sympathetic to Germany.[46] Albert C. Dieffenbach, editor of *The Christian Register,* wrote in an editorial: "As Christians, of course, we say Christ approves [of the war]. But would he fight and kill? . . . There is not an opportunity to deal death to the enemy that he would shirk from or delay in seizing! He would take bayonet and grenade and bomb and rifle and do the work of deadliness against that which is the most deadly enemy of his Father's kingdom in a thousand years."[47]

Like the Spanish-American War, the war in Europe carried a crusading, moralistic spirit. William Leuchtenburg put it this way: "The United States believed that moral idealism could be extended outward, that American Christian democratic ideals could and should be universally applied. . . . The war was embraced as that final struggle where the righteous would do battle for the Lord."[48] Shailer Mathews, a scholar at the Chicago Divinity School, wrote *Patriotism and Religion* in 1918, promoting this message: "For an American to refuse to share in the present war . . . is not Christian."[49]

44. Harvey A. DeWeerd, President Wilson Fights His War: World War I and the American Intervention 21 (1968).

45. 55 Cong. Rec. 261, 412–13 (1917).

46. Ray H. Abrams, Preachers Present Arms 31–32 (1933).

47. Id. at 68.

48. William E. Leuchtenburg, The Perils of Prosperity, 1914–32, at 34 (1958).

49. Ahlstrom, A Religious History of the American People, at 885.

Looking back at World War I, it would be difficult to muster any enthusiasm for a war of unrivaled carnage, a war that brought Bolshevism to Russia, Nazism to Germany, and laid the groundwork for another world war. Taking stock of the appalling losses from 1914 to 1918, churches passed resolutions renouncing war and expressed regret for their jingoism.[50] Writing in 1934, Walter W. Van Kirk of the Federal Council of the Churches of Christ noted that Christian preachers and laymen "are saying that resort to war is contrary to the teaching of Jesus; that the churches should no longer bless war."[51]

By fighting against Nazism and fascism, World War II was easier to justify on moral grounds. After some initial opposition, religious groups offered broad support for the war, particularly after the Japanese bombed Pearl Harbor. Reinhold Niebuhr, in his periodical *Christianity and Crisis,* challenged the noninterventionist, neutral position of the Protestant weekly *Christian Century.*[52] There were ethical reasons to fight that had nothing to do with the doctrines of a particular denomination.

Military conflicts since that time—in Korea, Southeast Asia, Iraq, and Yugoslavia—produced sustained divisions within the religious community. Unlike the wars in 1898 and 1917, the goal is not to spread "civilization" to other lands but to prevent the total annihilation of society by weapons of mass destruction.[53] The result is an active peace movement among the different denominations. One of the earliest pacifist groups is the Fellowship of Reconciliation, founded in 1915. It works with Catholic Peace Fellowship, Jewish Peace Fellowship, Lutheran Peace Fellowship, Presbyterian Peace Fellowship, and Episcopal Peace Fellowship.[54] Pax Christi USA, part of Pax Christi International, was established in 1972.[55] U.S. military adventures cannot expect the same automatic flagwaving that religious groups gave to war in the past.

Evangelicals from Christian denominations have been active in sending literature to servicemen, holding religious retreats and prayer meetings,

---

50. Abrams, Preachers Present Arms, at 229–39.

51. Walter W. Van Kirk, Religion Renounces War v (1934).

52. Ray H. Abrams, "The Churches and the Clergy in World War II," 256 The Annals 110, 112–13 (1948).

53. Paul Ramsey, War and the Christian Conscience: How Shall Modern War Be Conducted Justly? (1961); William V. O'Brien, Nuclear War, Deterrence and Morality (1967).

54. Weber & Jones, U.S. Religious Interest Groups, at 78; John Ferguson, War and Peace in the World's Religions 118 (1978).

55. Weber & Jones, U.S. Religious Interest Groups, at 128.

sponsoring Bible studies, and offering evangelism training. Contact pastors are appointed to minister at military installations. Evangelicals offer these programs to counter what they see as a corrupting influence of drunkenness, prostitution, and vulgarity.[56]

ABORTION

The Supreme Court's decision in *Roe* v. *Wade* (1973) revealed how much churches differed on the morality of abortion. In addition to an amicus brief by professional associations, including obstetricians, gynecologists, and psychiatrists, which supported a woman's right to abortion, other organizations weighed in with amicus briefs. A brief prepared by Americans United for Life supported "the constitutional rights to children in the womb."[57] The National Right to Life Committee, formed to protect the life of the unborn child, filed a brief to support state statutes that restricted a mother's right to abort.[58] Planned Parenthood's briefs took the side of a woman's right to choose.[59]

The Office for Pro-Life Activities, set up in the 1960s by the U.S. Catholic Conference to challenge contraception, turned its attention to ways of overturning *Roe*.[60] The National Right to Life Committee (NRLC) was created to lobby legislatures to limit abortions and to deny public funding. The Religious Coalition for Abortion Rights (RCAR), composed of Protestant, Jewish, and other faith groups, was formed in 1973 to respond to Catholic efforts to overturn *Roe*.

One of the first actions by groups opposed to *Roe* was to deny public funds for abortion. Congress passed that restriction (the Hyde Amendment) in 1976 and the Court upheld it in 1980.[61] Filing a brief in opposition to the Hyde Amendment was the National Council of Churches of Christ, representing an aggregate membership of forty million, the American Ethical Union, and the National Organization for Women.[62] Joining the American Ethical Union were other religious organizations,

56. Anne C. Loveland, American Evangelicals and the U.S. Military, 1942–1993, at 1–2, 8–9, 16–21 (1996).
57. 75 Landmark Briefs 355 (1975).
58. Id. at 489–562.
59. Id. at 681–780.
60. A. James Reichley, Religion in American Public Life 292–93 (1985).
61. Harris v. McRae, 448 U.S. 297 (1980).
62. 115 Landmark Briefs 498, 599, 634 (1981).

including the United Methodist Church, Catholics for a Free Choice, Church of the Brethren, and Union of American Hebrew Congregations.

Other Supreme Court cases on abortion illustrate the same pattern, with religious groups lining up on one side or the other. *Webster* v. *Reproductive Health Services* (1989) attracted briefs by the American Jewish Congress, Americans United for Separation of Church and State, Catholics United for Life, the Knights of Columbus, the Lutheran Church, the National Right to Life Committee, and the Rutherford Institute.[63] An even longer list of religious organizations filed briefs in *Planned Parenthood* v. *Casey* (1992), which reversed the trimester analysis of *Roe*.[64]

Roe led to the creation of a number of militant, confrontational groups. Operation Rescue had its beginning in 1984 as Project Life when Randall Terry, a seminary student, and his wife urged women entering abortion clinics to have their babies.[65] As the movement developed, it began blocking entrances to abortion clinics and harassing clinic workers. Antiabortion activities have killed several doctors and clinic employees, prompting the Justice Department to create an antiabortion violence task force.[66] In 1994, Congress passed the Freedom of Access to Clinic Entrances Act (FACE). Missionaries to the Preborn, founded in 1990, organized protests outside clinics that performed abortions.[67]

Some clergy invite intervention by government to restrict abortion, while others object to any role for government and favor private choice.[68] Polls indicate that Presbyterians, Episcopalians, and Jews generally support unconditional choice on abortion, but those religious communities are split among various positions.[69] Catholic bishops, strongly pro-life, question their ability to influence the views of Catholics in the general

63. Landmark Briefs, vol. 183 (1990).

64. Landmark Briefs (1993). No volume number was assigned because the volume on *Casey* was made available separately from the series.

65. Weber & Jones, U.S. Religious Interest Groups, at 126.

66. Faye D. Ginsburg, Contested Lives: The Abortion Debate in an American Community xii–xiii (1998 ed.).

67. Laura R. Olson, Filled with Spirit and Power: Protestant Clergy in Politics 84 (2000).

68. Id. at 85–95.

69. Hertzke, Representing God in Washington, at 124; Elizabeth Adell Cook, Ted G. Jelen & Clyde Wilcox, Between Two Absolutes: Public Opinion of the Politics of Abortion 93–130 (1992).

population.[70] After initially opposing the legalization of birth control measures, bishops acquiesced on that issue and continued to speak out against abortion.[71]

In several decisions, Justice Scalia has commented on the impact of private lobbying on the Court. After the Court decided *Webster* in 1989, he remarked: "We can now look forward to at least another Term with carts full of mail from the public, and streets full of demonstrators, urging us—their unelected and life-tenured judges who have been awarded these extraordinary, undemocratic characteristics precisely in order that we might follow the law despite the popular will—to follow their popular will."[72] Whether public pressure should influence the Court is a normative matter that can be answered in many ways, but there seems little doubt—as a factual matter—that the deep and ongoing public opposition to *Roe* led the Court in 1992 to abandon some central tenets of that decision, such as the trimester analysis.[73]

Organizing for Action

As Kenneth Wald reminds us, separation of church and state "does not mean the segregation of religion from politics."[74] Issues of religion and morality provoke people and groups to vigorously advocate their legal and constitutional positions. The Court accepts the legitimacy of lobbying by church groups: "Of course, churches as much as secular bodies and private citizens have that right."[75] As with other tax-exempt institutions under Section 501 (c)(3), churches and other religious groups are prohibited from participating in, or intervening in (including the publishing or

70. Corbett & Corbett, Politics and Religion in the United States, at 366. See also Richard J. Gelm, Politics and Religious Authority: American Catholics Since the Second Vatican Council 65–97 (1994).

71. Mary C. Segers, "The Bishops, Birth Control, and Abortion Policy: 1950–1985," in Mary C. Segers, ed., Church Polity and American Politics: Issues in Contemporary American Catholicism 215–31 (1990).

72. Webster v. Reproductive Health Services, 492 U.S. 490, 535 (1989).

73. Planned Parenthood v. Casey, 505 U.S. 833 (1992). See Neal Devins, Shaping Constitutional Values: Elected Government, the Supreme Court, and the Abortion Debate (1996); Barbara Hinkson Craig & David M. O'Brien, Abortion and American Politics (1993).

74. Kenneth D. Wald, Religion and Politics in the United States 124 (1997).

75. Walz v. Tax Commission, 397 U.S. 664, 670 (1970).

distribution of statements), "any political campaign on behalf of (or in opposition to) any candidate for public office."[76] This language, offered as an amendment by Senator Lyndon B. Johnson in 1954, became law.[77] The prohibition against endorsing or opposing political candidates is frequently flouted by ministers and other religious leaders, with little risk of losing their tax-exempt status. Only rarely has the IRS enforced this provision. Some members of Congress are debating language that would remove the prohibition.[78]

RELIGIOUS INTEREST GROUPS

The intensity of church lobbying, on all three branches, has increased dramatically. In 1950, there were approximately sixteen major religious lobbies in Washington, D.C.: ten Protestant, two Catholic, and four interdenominational.[79] By 1985 that number had climbed to "at least eighty and the list is growing."[80] In the 1990s, the estimate of the number of religious lobbies reached "at least one hundred."[81] A 1994 compilation of U.S. religious interest groups lists 120 organizations.[82]

These groups often coalesce to form a strikingly powerful political force, savvy and experienced in the ways of directing legislative, executive, and judicial agendas. Religious groups were part of the successful effort to enact the Civil Rights Act of 1964.[83] Senator Hubert Humphrey, a pivotal force behind this statute, said that without the clergy, "we couldn't have possibly passed this bill."[84] Other studies give credit to the churches but also to other groups, such as blacks and organized labor.[85] Church

76. 26 U.S.C. 501(c) (3) (1994).

77. 100 Cong. Rec. 9604 (1954); 68A Stat. 163 (1954).

78. "Churches on Rights Seek Right to Back Candidates," New York Times, February 3, 2002, at 18.

79. Ebersole, Church Lobbying in the Nation's Capital, at 24–56. Also descriptive of church lobbies in 1968: Richard E. Morgan, The Politics of Religious Conflict: Church and State in America 48–68 (1968).

80. Allen D. Hertzke, "The Role of Religious Lobbies," in Charles W. Dunn, ed., Religion in American Politics 123 (1989).

81. Fowler & Hertzke, Religion and Politics in America, at 54.

82. Weber & Jones, U.S. Religious Interest Groups (1994).

83. Reichley, Religion in American Public Life, at 246–50.

84. Robert D. Loevy, ed., The Civil Rights Act of 1964: The Passage of the Law That Ended Racial Segregation 89 (1997).

85. James F. Findlay, "Religion and Politics in the Sixties: The Churches and the Civil Rights Act of 1964," 77 J. Am. Hist. 66, 88–89 (1990); James F. Findlay, Church

lobbies were key participants in the passage of the Elementary and Secondary Education Act of 1965, which provided federal funds to both public and private schools.[86] The constitutional issue of church-state separation was surmounted by arguing that the funds would benefit children, not schools.[87]

The growth in sophisticated lobbying by religious groups is reflected in amicus curiae filings with the Supreme Court. Religious groups successful in legislative and executive arenas realize that they must participate "in *every* major playing field, including the courts, if they are going to count" in America.[88] During the period from 1928 to 1940, amicus briefs were prepared for 14.3 percent of the church-state cases. For a more recent period, from 1986 to 1992, the participation rate is 100 percent.[89]

Religious organizations often oppose Court rulings and help enact legislation that fosters greater religious freedom. Religious organizations can also be effective in mobilizing their strength to *defend* Court decisions. In 1962, the Court held that a New York "Regents' Prayer" was unconstitutional because government should not compose an official prayer for minors in public schools.[90] The public outcry to the decision was so intense that pressure quickly built to pass a constitutional amendment to nullify the Court's ruling. However, that movement stalled when congressional hearings revealed broad support by Protestant, Catholic, and Jewish organizations for the decision.[91] Two decades later, when President Ronald Reagan urged a constitutional amendment to permit school prayer, Protestant and Jewish groups joined to oppose the amendment.[92]

JEWISH LOBBYING

The section on chaplains in Chapter 2 describes the successful effort of Jews in 1861 to lobby for a broader statutory definition of military

---

People in the Struggle: The National Council of Churches and the Black Freedom Movement, 1950–1970, at 7 (1993).

86. James L. Adams, The Growing Church Lobby in Washington 89–100 (1970).

87. Id. at 89–90, 106.

88. Fowler & Hertzke, Religion and Politics in America, at 202 (emphasis in original).

89. Lee Epstein, "Interest Group Litigation during the Rehnquist Court Era," 9 J. Law & Pol. 639, 685 (1993). See also Leo Pfeffer, "Amici in Church-State Litigation," 44 Law & Contemp. Prob. 83 (Spring 1981).

90. Engel v. Vitale, 370 U.S. 421 (1962).

91. Louis Fisher, American Constitutional Law 681–82 (4th ed. 2001).

92. Hertzke, Representing God in Washington, at 166–67, 179.

chaplains. With the turn of the twentieth century, American Jews created permanent organizations to articulate and advance their interests. In response to a series of pogroms against Jews in Russia, several prominent German-Jewish leaders established the American Jewish Committee (AJC) in 1906. They lobbied against the adoption of a literacy test for immigrants and pressed for reforms that would allow a greater number of Jews to enter the country from eastern and southern Europe. These leaders met regularly with Presidents and lawmakers in an effort to craft legislative and diplomatic solutions.[93]

Louis Marshall, the key strategist for the AJC, felt uncomfortable about creating an organization that might be looked upon by others as indicating that Jews have "interests different from those of other American citizens."[94] Ever since their arrival in America beginning in the 1830s, German Jews had taken efforts not to appear too conspicuous or politically influential. They worried that the creation of an identifiable Jewish lobbying group might provoke anti-Semitism. However, at the organizational meeting it was agreed that American Jews were best informed about the conditions of Jews in Europe and could provide reliable and useful information for the government.[95] The AJC constitution declared: "The purpose of this committee is to prevent infringement of the civil and religious rights of Jews, and to alleviate the consequences of persecution."[96]

In 1913, following the anti-Semitism surrounding Georgia's prosecution of Leo Frank, charged with the murder of a thirteen-year-old girl, B'nai B'rith created the Anti-Defamation League (ADL). An armed mob took Frank out of jail and hanged him. In 1986, the Georgia Board of Pardons and Paroles gave Frank a posthumous pardon. With other Jewish organizations, the ADL became active not only in litigation but also in generating broad public and legislative interest in methods of reducing religious discrimination.[97]

Although the AJC performed important work in opening immigration

93. Naomi W. Cohen, Encounter with Emancipation: The German Jews in the United States, 1830–1914, at 220–46 (1984).

94. Judith S. Goldstein, The Politics of Ethnic Pressure: The American Jewish Committee Fight against Immigration Restriction, 1906–1917, at 55 (1990).

95. Id. at 56.

96. Id. at 57. See also Naomi W. Cohen, Not Free to Desist: The American Jewish Committee, 1906–1966 (1972).

97. Gregg Ivers, To Build a Wall: American Jews and the Separation of Church and State 56–63 (1995).

to Russian Jews and easing their arrival, the strains between German and Russian Jews were deep and nearly unbridgeable. German Jews perfected their English, followed Reform Judaism, opposed Zionism, and shunned radical politics. Russian Jews spoke Yiddish, practiced anything from Orthodox Judaism to atheism, advocated a Jewish state in Palestine, and were prominent in socialist and communist organizations. Objecting to the elitist, closed nature of the AJC, Russian Jews set up their own organization in 1918: the American Jewish Congress.

Whereas Marshall was reluctant to use litigation to advance Jewish interests, preferring discrete lobbying over public confrontations,[98] the American Jewish Congress did not hesitate to seek remedies from the courts. In time, they created the Commission on Law and Social Action (CLSA) to handle litigation strategy.[99] Both organizations, however, have joined major church-state cases, with the American Jewish Congress somewhat more active than the American Jewish Committee. When the AJ Committee intervenes in these cases, they are apt to work closely with non-Jewish religious organizations.[100]

Reform and Conservative Jews support separation of church and state to a greater extent than Orthodox Jews.[101] In a case involving the grant of public funds to parochial schools, the AJ Congress, the AJ Committee, and the ADL submitted a brief urging the Court to deny aid that would assist religious instruction.[102] Yet a brief prepared by the National Commission on Law and Public Affairs (COLPA), representing the Orthodox Jewish community and its system of Jewish day schools, supported equal funding for public and religious school.[103] A similar split is seen in a lawsuit challenging the authority of New York to create a separate school district for the Hasidic Satmar sect. The AJ Congress wrote a brief in opposition to the special school district, as did a separate brief by the AJ Committee and the ADL.[104] COLPA submitted a brief in support of the Satmar school.[105] Finally, an AJ Committee brief argued

98. Id. at 37, 40.
99. Id. at 21, 64.
100. Id. at 201–2.
101. Gregg Ivers, "Religious Organizations as Constitutional Litigants," 25 Polity 243, 250–51 (1992).
102. 259 Landmark Briefs 434–74; Agostini v. Felton, 521 U.S. 203 (1997).
103. 259 Landmark Briefs 692–702.
104. 228 Landmark Briefs 420–500, 501–42; Board of Ed. of Kiryas Joel v. Grumet, 512 U.S. 687 (1994).
105. 228 Landmark Briefs 717–51.

that a government display of a crèche or menorah would violate the Establishment Clause; COLPA's brief denied that such displays would violate the Constitution.[106]

Following the Court's decision in *Cantwell* v. *Connecticut* (1940), Jewish organizational activity in church-state matters "shifted ever more from the legislatures toward the courts."[107] To the extent that Jewish organizations relied on judicial decisions over legislative remedies, they assumed "the limitations of majoritarian politics in the church-state arena." Yet by hoping to accomplish their aims with "one precise judicial stroke," they also risked judicial decisions "that can dash a group's collective hopes."[108] An attorney for the American Jewish Congress expressed dismay over recent church-state decisions by the Supreme Court: "No one has any idea what this Court will do. . . . The Court's decisions do not make us feel comfortable to invest in a major test case."[109]

THE CHRISTIAN RIGHT

The Christian Right, composed primarily of evangelical Protestant groups with a conservative agenda, found its voice in the 1970s. Instead of church activists coming from mainline religious institutions, evangelists and fundamentalists tested their political strength and leverage. The Moral Majority, created in 1979 by Jerry Falwell and Robert J. Billings, attracted so much attention that a year later Paul M. Weyrich spoke confidently about "Christianizing America."[110] People for the American Way (PAW) was established in 1980 to counter the Christian Right.

The Christian Right found its energy in reaction to Supreme Court decisions on school prayer, Bible reading in the schools, and abortion. Reflecting their defense of traditional values, conservative evangelicals also opposed the use of "offensive" books in public schools, gay rights, and the Equal Rights Amendment.[111] Those forces led to the creation of the

106. 189 Landmark Briefs 323–62, 363–82; Allegheny County v. Greater Pittsburgh ACLU, 492 U.S. 573 (1989).

107. Jonathan D. Sarna & David G. Dalin, Religion and State in the American Jewish Experience 228 (1997).

108. Ivers, To Build a Wall, at 5.

109. Id. at 212.

110. Bill Keller, "Evangelical Conservatives Move from Pews to Polls, But Can They Sway Congress?" CQ Weekly Report, September 6, 1980, at 2629.

111. Wald, Religion and Politics in the United States, at 223–25.

Moral Majority by Jerry Falwell. Minister of a large Baptist church in Lynchburg, Virginia, Falwell was an established television evangelist. Within a short time, the Moral Majority had chapters in all fifty states.

The Moral Majority helped elect Ronald Reagan as President in 1980 and defeat five of six liberal Senators, shifting control of the Senate to the Republican Party. Those results may have come less from the Moral Majority than from disenchantment with Jimmy Carter and the vulnerability of liberal Senators in conservative states.[112] Although Christian Right activists were appointed to major posts within the Reagan administration, many were disappointed that Reagan offered primarily symbolic gestures (such as an occasional speech for school prayer), while devoting most of his time and energy to satisfying the agenda of economic conservatives (tax cuts) and foreign policy conservatives (increased defense spending).[113]

The decentralized nature of the Moral Majority meant that the national organization had to spend a lot of time disassociating itself from misguided initiatives launched by state chapters. A Maryland chapter wanted to ban "anatomically correct" cookies from public sale, while in Indiana the Moral Majority pushed for legislation to allow parents to spank their children or even whip them.[114] By 1987, the Moral Majority had run out of money and leadership.

Pat Robertson's 1987–1988 campaign for President marked another publicized effort to "Christianize" America.[115] Robertson, an ordained Baptist minister from Virginia, announced on October 1, 1987, his bid for the Republican nomination for President. With his Christian Broadcasting Network and *The 700 Club* television show, he was well known among the evangelical community and enjoyed a strong financial base. However, his campaign foundered in part because other televangelist figures such as Jim Bakker, Oral Roberts, and Jimmy Swaggert were hit with embarrassing scandals. In an effort to isolate himself from them

112. Corbett & Corbett, Politics and Religion in the United States, at 369; Richard G. Hutcheson, Jr., God in the White House: How Religion Has Changed the Modern Presidency 155–59 (1988).

113. Clyde Wilcox, Onward Christian Soldiers? The Religious Right in American Politics 89 (2000).

114. Mark J. Rozell & Clyde Wilcox, Second Coming: The New Christian Right in Virginia Politics 35 (1996).

115. Bob Benenson, "Robertson's Cause Endures Despite His Defeat," CQ Weekly Report, May 14, 1988, at 1267.

and defuse concerns about theocratic intentions, Robertson resigned his Baptist ministry and stepped down as chairman of the Christian Broadcasting Network. He began referring to himself as a "Christian businessman" rather than a TV evangelist, but a series of campaign gaffes pushed his ratings down.[116] Robertson had to drop a libel suit against Congressman Pete McCloskey, who claimed that Robertson bragged that his father had kept him out of combat in the Korean War.[117]

Unable to mobilize and unite religiously conservative Christians, Robertson bowed out of the race and supported George Bush, who had been endorsed by Falwell. Although Robertson spent large sums of money, he managed to win only a few caucuses and straw polls. He failed to win a single primary, even in Virginia. The following year, in 1989, he launched the Christian Coalition. Successes have been primarily at the grassroots area, such as training local activists to run for school boards and city councils. Even at that level, however, initiatives by Christian activists are often neutralized by organizations like the National Education Association.[118] Americans for Separation of Church and State, People for the American Way, and other liberal organizations also mobilized their forces to check the Christian Right.

In 1990, Robertson founded the American Center for Law and Justice (ACLJ) to serve as the public interest law firm for the Christian Coalition. The ACLJ has taken a number of cases to the Supreme Court on issues of abortion clinics, equal access, school prayer, and distribution of religious literature at airports. It has pledged to "tear down" the "fictitious wall" of separation promoted by the "ACLU and its left-wing allies."[119]

Some of the fervent speeches by Christian Right leaders at the 1992 Republican national convention may have damaged Bush's reelection effort. An intolerant, mean-spirited quality seemed to pervade the convention. Many voters were concerned that the Christian Right had "captured"

116. Id. at 1268; Kenneth D. Wald, "Ministering to the Nation: The Campaigns of Jesse Jackson and Pat Robertson," in Emmett H. Buell, Jr., & Lee Sigelman, eds., Nominating the President 119–49 (1991).

117. Allen D. Hertzke, Echoes of Discontent: Jesse Jackson, Pat Robertson, and the Resurgence of Populism 81, 148 (1993); Clyde Wilcox, God's Warriors: The Christian Right in Twentieth-Century America 147 (1992).

118. Wilcox, Onward Christian Soldiers, at 84.

119. Gregg Ivers, "Please God, Save This Honorable Court: The Emergence of the Conservative Religious Bar," in Paul S. Herrnson et al., eds., The Interest Group Connection 297 (1998).

the Republican Party.[120] Ralph Reed, executive director of the Christian Coalition, recognized the need to alter the organization's image. Speaking in September 1993, he said he wanted to put "a friendlier face on what we are."[121]

In 1994, the Christian Coalition helped the Republicans take control of both Houses of Congress.[122] For the first time in forty years, the Republicans ran the House of Representatives. The Christian Coalition put its muscle behind the House Republican "Contract with America," but discovered, as did Speaker Newt Gingrich, the difficulty of moving controversial legislation through the system of checks and balances. The Senate had very different notions about the value of the Contract, while President Bill Clinton stood prepared with his veto power to stop unacceptable bills. The legislative record was modest.

Republicans retained control of Congress in the 1996 and 1998 elections, but the Christian Right was disappointed with the electoral record of their candidates and the marginal progress on issues. Evangelicals had been difficult to mobilize and direct.[123] In the transition from the Moral Majority to Christian Coalition, conservatives learned to tone down "word of God" appeals by using more secular language, like "family values." Instead of citing Scripture, the appeal is more to "rights, equality, and opportunity."[124] The goal to "Christianize" America was replaced by softer and less threatening rhetoric to accommodate the religious pluralism of the United States. Ralph Reed told a Jewish audience in 1995 that his organization stood for "a nation that is not officially Christian, Jewish, or Muslim. A nation where the separation of church and state is complete and inviolable."[125]

120. Wald, Religion and Politics in the United States, at 230.

121. Kenneth Jost, "Religion and Politics," CQ Researcher, October 14, 1994, at 896.

122. John C. Green, "The Christian Right and the 1994 Elections: An Overview," in Mark J. Rozell & Clyde Wilcox, eds., God at the Grass Roots: The Christian Right in the 1994 Elections 1–18 (1995).

123. Mark J. Rozell & Clyde Wilcox, eds., God at the Grass Roots, 1996; The Christian Right in the American Elections (1997); John C. Green, Mark J. Rozell & Clyde Wilcox, eds., Prayers in the Precincts: The Christian Right in the 1998 Elections (2000).

124. Matthew C. Moen, "From Revolution to Evolution: The Changing Nature of the Christian Right," in Steve Bruce, Peter Kivisto & William H. Swatos, Jr., eds., The Rapture of Politics 130 (1995); Matthew C. Moen, The Transformation of the Christian Right (1992); Mark J. Rozell & Clyde Wilcox, "Pragmatism and Its Discontents: The Evolution of the Christian Right in the United States," in Madeleine Cousineau, ed., Religion in a Changing World 193–201 (1998).

125. Wald, Religion and Politics in the United States, at 237.

The Christian Right played an important role in the election of George W. Bush in 2000, delivering a large bloc of votes in key states and spending large sums of money to defeat John McCain in the primaries.[126] What the Christian Right will get from the Bush administration is uncertain. School vouchers are an important part of the Christian Right agenda, but it proved to be too divisive for legislative action in 2001. Greater progress seemed likely in adopting some kind of "faith-based initiative," but a number of factors combined to limit legislative success (see Chapter 9).

GROUP POLITICAL STRATEGIES

The goals of the Christian Right to "Christianize" America never materialized for a number of reasons, primarily the great variety of religious organizations and beliefs in the United States. The framers saw clearly that the main protection to religious freedom would be the prevalence of many religious denominations. The greater the number of sects, the less likelihood that one would dominate. At the Virginia ratifying convention, James Madison said that if there were "a majority of one sect, a bill of rights would be a poor protection for liberty. Happily for the states, they enjoy the utmost freedom of religion. This freedom arises from that multiplicity of sects which pervades America, and which is the best and only security for religious liberty in any society; for where there is such variety of sects, there cannot be a majority of any one sect to oppress and persecute the rest."[127]

Religious groups in America are influential and powerful when they join with other groups for a broader cause, such as civil rights or the Religious Freedom Restoration Act of 1993. When they seek to advance specific religious doctrines and impose their creed on other citizens, they unleash a system of counterbalances and opposing groups that seek to neutralize their goals.

Among religious groups, there has been a marked shift in attitudes about seeking relief in the courts for constitutional injuries. A study in 1990 remarked: "Recent scholarship on the nexus between religion and politics has suggested that Congress has replaced the judiciary as the

126. Mark J. Rozell, "The Christian Right: Evolution, Expansion, Contraction," presented at the Ethics and Public Policy conference, "Evangelicals and American Public Life," Cape Elizabeth, Maine, June 17–19, 2001.
127. 3 Elliot 330.

center of the political stage in the area of church-state policymaking, pulling to it the resources and attention of religious lobbies."[128] Battles over church-state relations in America, "historically the domain of the court, have moved in recent years to the Congress."[129] Instead of the "minoritarian politics" of the courts, religious groups engage in "the majoritarian or consensus-seeking politics of the Congress."[130] This strategy was adopted by other groups in the 1990s. The American Civil Liberties Union (ACLU), which had used litigation extensively to further its interests, now said: "Congress is increasingly asked to look at these [constitutional] issues because there is nobody else. It is now the court of last resort."[131]

Justice Thurgood Marshall reflected on the efforts of organized groups to lobby for constitutional rights. Far from expressing concern about these bare-knuckled struggles, he regarded the political process as of more fundamental importance than the operation of the courts: "No matter how solemn and profound the declarations of principle contained in our charter of government, no matter how dedicated and independent our judiciary, true justice can only be obtained through the actions of committed individuals, individuals acting both independently and through organized groups."[132]

128. Gregg Ivers, "Organized Religion and the Supreme Court," 32 J. Church & State 775, 778–79 (1990). See also James E. Wood, "Church Lobbying and Public Policy," 28 J. Church & State 183 (1986).

129. Hertzke, Representing God in Washington, at 161.

130. Id.

131. W. John Moore, "In Whose Court?" National Journal, October 5, 1991, at 2400.

132. Thurgood Marshall, "Group Action in the Pursuit of Justice," 44 N.Y.U. L. Rev. 661, 662 (1969).

4

CONSCIENTIOUS OBJECTORS

Individuals give both religious and ethical reasons for refusing to serve in the military. Although conscientious objection is associated with a number of Christian churches, drawing from biblical sources that range from the Ten Commandments ("Thou shalt not kill") to the Sermon on the Mount (Matthew 5:3–11), opposition to war has had a more universal appeal. Ethical objectors rely on a personal and not necessarily religious moral code, while societies have long distinguished between just and unjust wars. Some conscientious objectors oppose a particular military action; others resist all types of warfare.

The first governmental institution in the United States to recognize the rights of conscientious objectors was the legislature, not the courts. Judges came late to this constitutional issue, offering rulings that upheld or developed what had already been set down in statutes and state constitutions. Under pressure from religious organizations and other groups, lawmakers were the ones to carve out exemptions for those who refused to bear arms for religious or ethical reasons. Those exemptions have been gradually widened to accommodate legislative language proposed by religious groups. Presidents and executive officials have played important roles in protecting conscientious objectors, as have the states.

The Colonies and Early State Governments

In requiring citizens to serve in the militia, colonies and early state governments made exceptions for individuals who presented religious objections. Massachusetts in 1661, Rhode Island in 1673, and Pennsylvania in 1757 passed legislation to allow conscientious objectors to perform noncombatant services. For example, the Pennsylvania law provided that all "Quakers, Mennonists, Moravians, and others conscientiously scrupulous of bearing arms" were entitled, upon the call to arms, to assist by extinguishing fires, suppressing the insurrection of slaves and other persons, caring for the wounded, and performing other services.[1] In 1757, a Quaker named John Woolman in New Jersey refused to pay taxes to support the French and Indian war as "contrary to my conscience," even though he knew that his decision "might be construed into an act of disloyalty."[2] When the Assembly of Pennsylvania passed legislation in 1775 to create a militia, it recognized that "many of the good people of this Province are conscientiously scrupulous of bearing of arms," and counseled those willing to join the militia to "bear a tender and brotherly regard toward this class of their fellow-subjects and Countrymen." At the same time, the Assembly asked the "nonassociators" to "cheerfully assist, in proportion to their abilities," the efforts of those engaged in the common defense.[3]

On July 18, 1775, the Continental Congress debated plans to put the militia "into a proper state of defence." It recommended that all able-bodied men, between sixteen and fifty years of age, form themselves into regular companies of militia. Each soldier was to be furnished a musket, bayonet, cartridge-box, and other military equipment. The Congress then announced: "As there are some people, who, from religious principles, cannot bear arms in any case, this Congress intend no violence to their consciences, but earnestly recommend it to them, to contribute liberally in this time of universal calamity, to the relief of their distressed brethren in the several colonies, and to do all other services to their oppressed Country, which they can consistently with their religious principles."[4] The Schwenkfelders, a Protestant sect, refused on conscience to take up arms during the Revolution, but announced that they would "gladly and willingly bear our due share of the common civil taxes and burdens excepting the bearing of arms and weapons."[5]

After the Declaration of Independence, a number of state constitutions specifically recognized the rights of conscientious objectors. The 1776 constitution of Pennsylvania provided: "Nor can any man who is conscientiously scrupulous of bearing arms, be justly compelled thereto, if he

1. U.S. Selective Service System, Conscientious Objection (Special Monograph No. 11, Vol. I) 30 (1950).

2. Lillian Schlissel, ed., Conscience in America: A Documentary History of Conscientious Objection in America, 1757–1967, at 34, 36 (1968).

3. U.S. Selective Service System, at 33.

4. 2 Journals of the Continental Congress 189 (1905).

5. Schlissel, Conscience in America, at 39–40.

will pay such equivalent."[6] The Vermont Constitution of 1777 stated that no one "conscientiously scrupulous of bearing arms, [may] be justly compelled thereto."[7] The New Hampshire Constitution of 1784 contained language similar to Pennsylvania's.[8] The Maine Constitution of 1819 identified the religious sects entitled to exemption: "Persons of the denomination of Quakers and Shakers . . . may be exempted from military duty; but no other person . . . shall be so exempted, unless he shall pay an equivalent, to be fixed by law."[9]

The First Congress

On June 8, 1789, during debate in the House of Representatives, James Madison offered a list of amendments to the Constitution. They were to be passed first by Congress and submitted to the states for ratification. Included among his recommendations: "The right of the people to keep and bear arms shall not be infringed; a well armed and well regulated militia being the best security of a free country: but no person religiously scrupulous of bearing arms shall be compelled to render military service in person."[10] As the debate continued, the language of what would become the Second Amendment shifted somewhat: "A well regulated militia, composed of the body of the people, being the best security of a free state, the right of the people to keep and bear arms shall not be infringed; but no person religiously scrupulous shall be compelled to bear arms."[11]

Elbridge Gerry of Massachusetts disliked the exception for religious belief, warning that it would weaken the establishment of a reliable militia. The clause "would give an opportunity to the people in power to destroy the Constitution itself. They can declare who are those religiously scrupulous, and prevent them from bearing arms." He wanted the language confined to persons belonging to a "religious sect scrupulous of bearing arms." James Jackson, from Georgia, thought that Gerry exaggerated the danger. He didn't expect that "all the people of the United States would turn Quakers or Moravians." However, for those who chose not to participate in the militia, he suggested this final clause: "upon paying an

6. Pa. Const. of 1776, VIII; 8 Swindler 278.
7. Vt. Const. of 1777, Ch. I, IX; 9 Swindler 490.
8. N.H. Const. of 1784, Art. I, XIII; 6 Swindler 345.
9. Me. Const. of 1819, Art. VII, Sec. 5; 4 Swindler 323.
10. 1 Annals of Cong. 434 (1789).
11. Id. at 749.

equivalent, to be established by law."[12] Egbert Benson of New York wanted the exception for religious objectors eliminated, preferring to leave it to the "benevolence" of the legislature to grant this privilege by statute. He conceded that objections to military service "may be a religious persuasion, but it is no natural right, and therefore ought to be left to the discretion of the Government." His motion to delete the language failed, 22 to 24.[13]

On August 20, Thomas Scott of Pennsylvania objected to the exemption for persons religiously scrupulous. Like Gerry, he feared that it would lead to difficulties in creating a dependable militia, eventually producing what legislators liked least: a standing army.[14] Scott was not bothered by those he knew to be religiously scrupulous; his concerns were those "who are of no religion." Elias Boudinot of New Jersey supported the religious exception. How could the country depend on men who were conscientious objectors, he asked. How could the country compel them to bear arms, "when, according to their religious principles, they would rather die than use them?"[15]

The House accepted this language: "A well regulated militia, composed of the body of the people, being the best security of a free state, the right of the people to keep and bear arms, shall not be infringed, but no one religiously scrupulous of bearing arms shall be compelled to render military service in person."[16] However, when the Senate acted on the Second Amendment it deleted the religious exemption.[17]

The next year, during debate on the militia bill, members of Congress again considered a religious exemption for the armed forces. On December 17, Congress received a petition from the Quakers, "praying an exemption from militia duties and penalties on that account."[18] Aedanus Burke of South Carolina said it was contrary to the interest of the militia to establish so many exemptions, and gave notice that he would move to reduce them. He also remarked that it was not "consonant with the principle of justice to make those conscientiously scrupulous of bearing arms pay for not acting against the voice of their conscience." Citizens boasted

12. Id. at 750.
13. Id. at 751.
14. Id. at 766–67.
15. Id. at 767.
16. 1 Senate Journal 63–64 (1789).
17. Id. at 71, 77.
18. 2 Annals of Cong. 1859 (1790).

that America was the land of liberty, "and yet we are going to make a respectable class of citizens pay for a right to a free exercise of their religious principles."[19] James Jackson asked how Congress would identify the individuals who were really conscientiously scrupulous. No tribunal had been created "to make them swear to their scruples." Other sects, besides the Quakers, were "averse to bearing arms." If Congress did not require compensation from the exempted, "it will lay the axe to the root of the militia."[20]

As the debate continued on December 22, Burke said he would exempt the people called Quakers "and all persons religiously scrupulous of bearing arms." Jackson cautioned that the effect of this privilege "would be to make the whole community turn Quakers." Anyone exempted "ought to pay a full equivalent on every principle of justice and equity." John Vining of Delaware, defending the contributions of Quakers to American liberties, agreed that "an equivalent might be assessed on these people without difficulty, and which, from their numbers, supposed to be one-twentieth part of the people, would amount to a sum sufficient to support a militia."[21]

Madison moved to insert among the exemptions "persons conscientiously scrupulous of bearing arms." Unlike other legislators, he did not restrict the exemption to particular religious denominations, but placed the emphasis on conscience. He praised the Quakers in this regard, pointing out that when they had it "in their power to establish their religion by law they did not." As to Jackson's apprehension that the entire country would convert to Quakerism, Madison said he did not believe that Americans "would hypocritically renounce their principles, their conscience, and their God, for the sake of enjoying the exemption."[22] William Giles of Virginia spoke out against the exemption for Quakers. Every individual had an obligation to contribute to the protection of society, "and it is a violation of moral duty to withhold this personal service." Everyone who receives the protection of the laws "ought to contribute his proportion to the support of the laws." What criteria, he asked, would determine whether someone operated under the principle of conscience?[23]

19. Id. at 1865.
20. Id.
21. Id. at 1869–70.
22. Id. at 1871–72.
23. Id. at 1872–73.

On December 23, Madison offered language providing an exemption for "all persons religiously scrupulous of bearing arms, who shall make a declaration of the same before a civil magistrate, . . . but be liable to a penalty of _____ dollars."[24] On the following day, a majority of lawmakers seemed inclined to leave the issue to the states. Benjamin Bourn of Rhode Island pointed out that Madison's language would be more burdensome than provided in several states, which exempted Quakers not only from military duty but also from all fines and penalties. As examples he gave New Hampshire, Massachusetts, Rhode Island, and Connecticut. In the end, the House dropped the matter in the laps of the states.[25]

Civil War Exemptions

Congress did not rely on conscription during the American Revolution, the War of 1812, or the Mexican War. The country depended on volunteers and state militia to do the fighting. Without national legislation, conscientious objectors had to rely on state laws and state constitutions for their protection. To defend their rights of religious liberty and conscience, they looked to lawmakers, not judges. The first national effort to draft soldiers came with the Civil War, starting with the Confederate Congress in April 1862 and continuing a year later with Congress.

During debate in Congress on the 1863 conscription bill, Senator Ira Harris of New York proposed that all persons "who, being from scruples of conscience averse to bearing arms, are by the constitution of any State excused therefrom."[26] Some persons, he noted, were so opposed to bearing arms that they would not even pay a fine. Henry Wilson of Massachusetts wanted the amendment modified to read "the constitution or law of any State," because some states recognized the exemption for Shakers and Quakers in law but not the constitution. Daniel Clark of New Hampshire agreed, noting that his state constitution did not excuse a Shaker but the law did. Clark further argued that if Quakers and Shakers were excused from military service, "they will pour out of their subsistence to aid the country, and their blessings to help your cause. They had better be excused."[27] After several Senators raised objections to the amendment, Harris withdrew it.

24. Id. at 1874.
25. Id. at 1875.
26. Cong. Globe, 37th Cong., 3d Sess. 994 (1863).
27. Id.

In the House, Thaddeus Stevens of Pennsylvania worried about late converts. He wanted individuals to declare on oath or affirmation that they had been conscientiously scrupulous against bearing arms "for more than _____ years."[28] He later filled in the blank with "one year" and accepted language making it three years, yet his amendment was rejected, 18 to 95.[29] An amendment by Senator Lazarus Powell of Kentucky directed any drafted person "conscientiously unable to perform military service or pay commutation," by reason of "sincere and religious scruples," to apply to a federal judge. If the petition appeared to be "honest and true," and if the petitioner had maintained a consistent position in opposition to military service on religious grounds, the judge could relieve the person of statutory penalties. However, the exempted person would be required to contribute toward "any public hospital or charitable service, a peace offering in accordance with his means." That amendment failed, 8 to 32.[30]

The bill that became law made no mention of conscientious objectors. All able-bodied male citizens and all persons of foreign birth who declared on oath their intention to become citizens, between the ages of twenty and forty-five, "are hereby declared to constitute the national forces, and shall be liable to perform military duty in the service of the United States when called out by the President for that purpose."[31] Certain persons were excepted or made exempt from the statute, but there was no exemption for individuals with religious objections. However, Quakers and other individuals could avail themselves of another section of the statute. Any person drafted and notified to appear may "furnish an acceptable substitute to take his place in the draft" or may pay to such person, as the Secretary of War may authorize to receive it, a sum not exceeding $300. The person furnishing the substitute or paying the money "shall be discharged from further liability under that draft."[32]

Quakers in the North faced a difficult dilemma. They wanted to help in the fight against slavery, which they had long opposed, but simultaneously held "a conscientious conviction that war was the wrong way to do it."[33] Many Quakers joined the military service and fought and died

28. Id. at 1261.
29. Id. at 1292.
30. Id. at 1389–90.
31. 12 Stat. 731 (1863).
32. Id. at 733, § 13.
33. Edward Needles Wright, Conscientious Objectors in the Civil War 15–16 (1931).

alongside their fellowmen. Those who refused the draft regarded the payment of $300 as the equivalent of military service. The Society of Friends drafted the following language that individual Quakers could present to draft boards:

> The undersigned is informed that his name is included in a list of persons reported to be drafted in _____ for service in the Army of the United States.
>
> He respectfully represents that he is a member of the Religious Society of Friends and is conscientiously scrupulous against bearing arms or being otherwise concerned in war, and on this ground he cannot conform himself to the draft, procure a substitute, pay the $300 provided by the law, or any other sum as a commutation for military service, and he respectfully asks to be released therefrom.[34]

Other religious organizations appealed to Congress and President Lincoln for relief, indicating their willingness to serve as chaplains and nurses.[35] The Judge Advocate General of the Army released a circular stating that persons having conscientious scruples in regard to bearing arms were not on that account exempt. The only way to be released for military service was to pay the $300. Toward the end of 1863, Secretary of War Edwin Stanton tried to devise a compromise that would satisfy both the government and the Quakers. With great ingenuity, he proposed a Special Fund for the benefit of freed slaves. Any Quaker who paid $300 into that account would be exempt from military service.[36] That kind of creative proposal could not have come from a judge.

Quakers met with members of Congress to seek a legislative solution. On January 14, 1864, Senator Wilson offered an amendment to give members of "religious denominations conscientiously opposed to the bearing of arms" some options. They could be drafted as noncombatants and assigned to duty in the hospitals or to the care of freedmen, or they could pay $300 to individuals designated by the Secretary of War, to be applied to the benefit of sick and wounded soldiers.[37] Senator Henry Anthony of Rhode Island spoke of the impracticality of trying to draft conscientious objectors: "I cannot show you and you cannot show me one

34. Id. at 69–70.
35. Id. at 70–71.
36. Id. at 72.
37. Cong. Globe, 38th Cong., 1st Sess. 204 (1864).

single efficient man that has been added to the Army by the impressment of men conscientiously scrupulous against bearing arms."[38] As enacted into law on February 24, 1864, the new statutory language provided that

> members of religious denominations, who shall by oath or affirmation declare that they are conscientiously opposed to the bearing of arms, and who are prohibited from doing so by the rules and articles of faith and practice of said religious denominations, shall, when drafted into the military service, be considered noncombatants, and shall be assigned by the Secretary of War to duty in the hospitals, or to the care of freedmen, or shall pay the sum of three hundred dollars to such person as the Secretary of War shall designate to receive it, to be applied to the benefit of the sick and wounded soldiers: *Provided,* That no person shall be entitled to the benefit of the provisions of this section unless his declaration of conscientious scruples against bearing arms shall be supported by satisfactory evidence that his deportment has been uniformly consistent with such declaration.[39]

These protections for religious minorities did not come from the courts. Quakers and other religious groups instinctively turned to the President, executive officers, and to members of Congress for relief. It was through the regular political process that their rights were recognized and finally safeguarded with statutory language. While Quakers appreciated the motivation behind the 1864 statute, some continued to oppose any contribution to the war effort, including making payments, assisting in hospitals, or serving freedmen.[40] On June 27, 1864, in debate on the next conscription bill, Representative Thaddeus Stevens offered this language: "That the law with regard to persons conscientiously opposed to bearing arms shall not be altered or affected by this act, except so far as it regards the amount of money to be paid for exemptions."[41] After some change in the wording, Stevens's amendment was agreed to, 79 to 64.[42] Further modification produced this curious statutory language: "Nothing contained in this act shall be constructed to alter, or in any way affect, the provisions of the seventeenth section of an act approved February twenty-fourth, eighteen hundred and sixty-four, entitled 'An act to

38. Id. at 205.
39. 13 Stat. 9, § 17 (1864).
40. Wright, Conscientious Objectors in the Civil War, at 83–84.
41. Cong. Globe, 38th Cong., 1st Sess. 3316 (1864).
42. Id. at 3354–55.

amend an act entitled "an act for enrolling and calling out the national forces, and for other purposes,"' approved March third, eighteen hundred and sixty-three."[43]

However strange the statutory language, the administration interpreted it in light of Stevens's intent. For the duration of the war, the administration "respected more and more the wishes of those conscientiously opposed to bearing arms, by not forcing them into any kind of service against their will."[44] President Lincoln, urged to force Quakers, Mennonites, and other conscientious objectors into the Army, replied: "No, I will not do that. These people do not believe in war. People who do not believe in war make poor soldiers. Besides, the attitude of these people has always been against slavery. If all our people held the same views about slavery as these people there would be no war. . . . We will leave them on their farms where they are at home and where they will make their contributions better than they would with a gun."[45]

World War I Experiences

America's entry into World War I in 1917 ushered in a new period of treatment for conscientious objectors. Unlike the conscription statutes for the Civil War, Congress did not allow citizens to hire substitutes or pay a commutation fee. Moreover, the rights of conscientious objectors were recognized from the start, with distinctions drawn between combatant and noncombatant duties. The National Defense Act of 1916 identified various exemptions from military duties, including exemption from military service in a noncombatant capacity for all persons of religious belief "if the conscientious holding of such belief by such person shall be established under such regulations as the President shall prescribe." However, "no person so exempted shall be exempt from militia service in any capacity that the President shall declare to be noncombatant."[46]

Throughout the lengthy House and Senate debates on this bill, legislators did not discuss the provision for conscientious objectors. The religious exemption was by now well established. In the bill reported on March 6, 1916, by the House Committee on Military Affairs, the section on conscientious objectors did not require membership in a religious

43. 13 Stat. 380, § 10 (1864).
44. Wright, Conscientious Objectors in the Civil War, at 86.
45. Selective Service System, Conscientious Objection, at 42–43.
46. 39 Stat. 197, § 59 (1916).

group. It read: "All persons who because of religious beliefs are exempted by the laws of the respective States and Territories shall be exempt from militia duty without regard to age."[47] Later versions of the bill distinguished between combatant and noncombatant duties.[48]

After the United States entered World War I in April 1917, Congress passed legislation authorizing President Wilson to increase the military establishment. Section 4 of the statute, containing the religious exemption, required membership in a religious organization. Nothing in the Act was to be construed

> to require or compel any person to serve in any of the forces herein provided for who is found to be a member of any well-recognized religious sect or organization at present organized and existing and whose existing creed or principles forbid its members to participate in war in any form and whose religious convictions are against war or participation therein in accordance with the creed or principles of said religious organizations, but no person so exempted shall be exempted from service in any capacity that the President shall declare to be noncombatant.[49]

During debate in the Senate on April 28, 1917, Charles Thomas of Colorado objected to the reported bill because it exempted only conscientious objectors who were members of a "well-recognized religious sect . . . whose existing creed or principles forbid its members to participate in war in any form." He could see no reason for not exempting individuals who were opposed to war on religious grounds but did not belong to such sects.[50] He offered broader coverage: "Nothing in this act contained shall be construed to require or compel service in any of the forces herein provided for by any person who is conscientiously opposed to engaging in such service."[51] Senator Robert LaFollette of Wisconsin offered substitute language to incorporate Thomas's amendment but include a procedure of tribunals to review the application of conscientious objectors. However, LaFollette got off track by referring to as many as ten

47. H.R. 12766, 64th Cong., 1st Sess. 49 [lines 8–10], as reported by the House Committee on Military Affairs.

48. See H. Rept. No. 695, 64th Cong., 1st Sess. 38 (1916), and S. Doc. No. 442, 64th Cong., 1st Sess. 38 (1916).

49. 40 Stat. 78, § 4 (1917).

50. 55 Cong. Rec. 1473 (1917).

51. Id.

million U.S. citizens of German or Austrian birth, or German or Austrian parentage, who would not want "to fight against their own kith and kin."[52] Several Senators protested that "our ancestors fought our own blood in the War of the Revolution."[53] LaFollette's substitute was rejected by voice vote.[54] The Senate then returned to the Thomas amendment, with a different system of selecting local tribunals, but that amendment was rejected as well.[55]

A similar debate occurred in the House. Edward Keating of Colorado praised the bill for "very properly recogniz[ing] the organized conscience of the Nation."[56] However, his amendment would go further by recognizing "the unorganized conscience of the Nation," exempting "any person who is conscientiously opposed" to engaging in military service, whether a member or not of an organized religion. Such persons would be liable to draft and assigned by the President to various kinds of civil service, including agriculture, forestry, reclamation of waste land, highway construction and repair, public education, and prison work. To qualify for the exemption, an individual would have to convince the members of a local board that he was a conscientious objector.[57] Keating's amendment lost on a vote of 31 to 152.[58] Other amendments relating to conscientious objectors, offered by Charles Sloan of Nebraska and Fiorello LaGuardia of New York, were also rejected.[59] The accompanying committee reports did not elaborate on the religious exemption section.[60]

Selective service regulations in 1917 stated that any registrant found by a local board to be a member of "any well-recognized religious sect or organization organized and existing May 18, 1917," and whose "then existing creed or principles" opposed war or participation in war, shall be furnished a certificate that he can only be required to serve in a capacity declared by the President to be noncombatant.[61]

52. Id. at 1476.
53. Id. at 1477 (statement of Senator McCumber).
54. Id. at 1478.
55. Id. at 1478–79.
56. 55 Cong. Rec. 1528 (1917).
57. Id. at 1529.
58. Id. at 1530.
59. Id. at 1533.
60. H. Rept. No. 17, 65th Cong., 1st sess. (1917); H. Rept. No. 49, 65th Cong., 1st Sess. (1917); H. Rept. No. 52, 65th Cong., 1st Sess. (1917); H. Rept. No. 53, 65th Cong., 1st Sess. (1917).
61. Schlissel, Conscience in America, at 133.

On March 20, 1918, President Wilson issued an executive order setting forth guidelines for the kinds of noncombatant service to be performed by conscientious objectors. These duties included service in the Medical Corps, the Quartermaster Corps, and the engineer service. Section 3 of the order broadened the category of conscientious objectors to include those "who profess religious or other conscientious scruples." Because of Wilson's broader definition, conscientious objectors were called either the "religious objector" or the "individual objector."[62] Persons who objected to participating in war because of conscientious scruples, but failed to receive certification as members of a religious sect or organization, would serve in noncombatant positions. Sentences imposed by courts-martial would include confinement in Disciplinary Barracks but not in a penitentiary.[63]

Harlan F. Stone, who would later serve on the U.S. Supreme Court as Associate Justice and Chief Justice, wrote an article in 1919 describing his experience as a member of a Board of Inquiry responsible for reviewing the claims of drafted men who refused military service on grounds of conscience. For someone slated within six years to sit on the Court to dispense justice, his harsh language is astonishing. Doing little to conceal his contempt for those he interviewed, he dismissed most as low in average mentality, "sublime egoists," "glib talkers," "loose-thinking," "wild-talking," "muddle-headed," and even described some as "bovine-faced."[64] He did describe the remarkable case of Richard L. Stierheim, who was drafted and sent overseas, where he refused to perform military service and eventually deserted. After capture, he was tried by court-martial and sentenced to death. While awaiting execution, he volunteered to enter No Man's Land, at risk of his life, to rescue the wounded. Without assistance, he rescued six men under machine-gun fire. He later volunteered to return to No Man's Land to bury the dead. His sentence was remitted and he was assigned noncombatant duties.[65]

Of those who claimed the status of conscientious objector, 3,989 requested exemption also from noncombatant duty. Ninety-nine agreed to go to France to assist in reconstruction activities, 1,200 worked on farms,

62. Walter Guest Kellogg, The Conscientious Objector 22 (1919).

63. Executive Order 2823 (March 20, 1918).

64. Harlan F. Stone, "The Conscientious Objector," 21 Colum. Univ. Q. 253, 260, 262, 264–65, 266, 269 (1919).

65. Id. at 261. A much more balanced treatment of conscientious objectors during World War I is by the chairman of the Board of Inquiry: Walter Guest Kellogg, The Conscientious Objector (1919).

and other arrangements were made, leaving 503 who were given prison sentences. Of that number, 17 were sentenced to death, 142 received a life sentence, and the rest served terms from five years to twenty-five years or longer. After the war, their sentences were commuted and no one was executed. The last prisoner was released in November 1920.[66] Roger Baldwin, director of the American Union Against Militarism, notified the draft board on October 18, 1918, that he would refuse induction. He served one year in prison. In 1920, with John Dewey and others, he formed the American Civil Liberties Union.[67]

The 1917 draft law was challenged in court on a number of grounds, including the argument that the exemption for conscientious objectors was repugnant to the First Amendment by establishing or interfering with religion. Writing for a unanimous Court in 1918, Chief Justice White found no merit to the complaint. He said "we pass without anything but statement" the claim of establishment or interference "because we think its unsoundness is too apparent to require us to do more."[68]

Also in 1918, the Second Circuit decided the case of Louis Fraina and Edward Ralph Cheyney, convicted of conspiring to commit an offense against the United States by aiding and abetting others to evade the requirements of the Selective Service Act. At a public meeting they urged resistance to the war and handed out a pamphlet entitled "Conscientious Objectors," written by Fraina. He told the audience that the conscription law recognized only conscientious objectors affiliated with recognized religious groups, such as the Quakers. He insisted that nonmembers deserved exemption on the basis of their individual conscience:

> But since when must a man necessarily belong to a church, belong to a creed, a recognized creed, before he can have a conscience? . . . The government, in making conscientious objection to war a part of religion or creed, is placing a premium upon religion. It is placing a premium upon the superstitions of religion, it is placing a premium upon the passive attitude of the religion of the Quakers. . . .
>
> Now, the nonreligious conscientious objector is a distinctly different type. The nonreligious conscientious objector is one of the people, a social being, and as such has an objection to war. I do not object to war because my father was a Quaker and I inherited his

---

66. Pacifist Handbook 12–13 (Fellowship of Reconciliation, 1939).
67. Schlissel, Conscience in America, at 142.
68. Selective Draft Law Cases, 245 U.S. 366, 389–90 (1918).

religion. I object to war because I have acquired my conscientious convictions, I have acquired the objection by experience, by thinking, action, and I have felt it flow into my conscience and my life.[69]

Although Fraina's conviction was affirmed, the issue he raised remained part of the public debate. Linking conscientious objection solely to membership in established churches would soon be found unacceptable to religious organizations and to Congress.

Broadening the Exemption in 1940

Congress next confronted the conscientious objector exemption when it passed the Selective Training and Service Act of 1940, as part of the preparation for World War II. Much had changed in recent decades. More American churches supported the right of their members to object to participation in wars. Church members were encouraged to follow their own consciences, even in the face of persecution or prosecution. Individuals understood that they could be conscientious objectors even without membership in a religious organization.[70]

When the bill was introduced on June 21, 1940, and referred to the House Committee on Military Affairs, it limited the exemption for conscientious objectors to persons who were members "of any well recognized religious sect whose creed or principles forbid its members to participate in war in any form."[71] This phrase was lifted from the 1917 statute. A companion bill in the Senate, introduced the previous day, adopted the same language.[72] As the bill moved through committee, it dropped the reference to religious organizations. For example, as reported from the Senate Committee on Military Affairs, the exemption covered any person who by religious training and belief is conscientiously opposed to participating in war in any form.[73]

The language changed because of testimony received from religious organizations. The broader coverage was first suggested by two Quakers during House hearings and in a meeting at the War Department.[74]

69. Fraina v. United States, 255 F. 28, 31 (2d Cir. 1918).
70. 3 Stokes 293–95.
71. H.R. 10132, 76th Cong., 3d Sess. 8 (1940).
72. S. 4164, 76th Cong., 3d Sess. 8 (1940).
73. S. Rept. No. 2002, 76th Cong., 3d Sess. 3 (1940).
74. Julien Cornell, The Conscientious Objector and the Law 7, 12 (1943). See also Selective Service System, Conscientious Objection, at 70–79.

Raymond Wilson, a Quaker, told the House Military Affairs Committee that the statutory phrase "well-recognized religious sect" would benefit Quakers "but we do not believe that they have any right of preferential treatment. We want the consideration on the basis of conscience rather than on the basis of membership."[75] Harold Evans, representing the Religious Society of Friends, made the same point to the Senate Military Affairs Committee.[76]

The language in the bill as introduced was restrictive in two senses. Not only did an individual seeking classification as conscientious objector have to be a member of a well-recognized religious sect, it had to be one "whose creed or principles forbid its members to participate in war in any form." Dorothy Day, editor of the *Catholic Worker*, explained to the Senate Military Affairs Committee that the legislative language would cover Quakers and Mennonites but not Catholics: "After all it is not part of our creed."[77] Amos Horst, a Mennonite, asked the House Military Affairs Committee to change the bill to cover "any person" conscientiously opposed to participating in war.[78] Other religious organizations, including the Methodist Episcopal Church, the Northern Baptist Convention, and the Congregational Church, wanted the exemption to cover individuals, not members of particular sects.[79] Many other religious bodies took similar positions.[80]

C. S. Longacre, representing the Seventh-Day Adventists, crystallized the issue for the House Military Affairs Committee: "Our constitution does not recognize church creeds. It recognizes the rights of individual consciences."[81] Subsequent versions of the bill from the House committee and the conference committee retained this emphasis on individual conscience.[82] The 1940 statute contains a list of exemptions, including anyone who, "by reason of religious training and belief, is conscientiously opposed to participation in war in any form." Unlike the language of the World War I statutes, it was not necessary to be a member of a religious

75. National Service Board for Religious Objectors, Congress Looks at the Conscientious Objector 15 (1943). See also his testimony reproduced at 74–75.
76. Id. at 28.
77. Id. at 24.
78. Id. at 74.
79. Id. at 75.
80. Id. at 86–89.
81. Id. at 71.
82. H. Rept. No. 2903, 76th Cong., 3d Sess. 5 (1940); H. Rept. No. 2937, 76th Cong., 3d Sess. 5, 17–18 (1940).

organization. Options included noncombatant service as defined by the President. If the individual opposed noncombatant service, he could be assigned to work "of national importance under civilian direction."[83]

By the end of 1944, about eight thousand conscientious objectors served in the Civilian Public Service. Officially it was supervised by the Selective Service. In fact, it functioned under the administration of the historic peace churches. The operation cost the churches about $4.5 million. The men in the camps received no wages and were expected to contribute $30 a month. When they worked on farms or in hospitals, they received $15 a month. A number of conscientious objectors sent to prison were released after the war.[84]

In 1945, the Supreme Court reviewed Illinois's refusal to admit an individual to the bar. His application to practice law was rejected after stating his inability to take the required oath to support the state constitution because of conscientious scruples that prevented him from serving in the state militia in time of war. The Court rejected his claim that exclusion from the bar violated due process. It argued that if refusal to take such an oath barred an alien from national citizenship, as the Court had held in 1931,[85] Illinois could insist that an officer charged with the administration of justice take an oath to support the state constitution, including a willingness to perform military service.[86] Black dissented, joined by Douglas, Murphy, and Rutledge.

The following year, the Court revisited its position that aliens may be denied citizenship if they are unwilling to bear arms. The case involved a Seventh-Day Adventist who objected on religious grounds to combatant service but stated a willingness to serve in a noncombatant status. Writing for a 5 to 3 majority, Justice Douglas said that the individual's religious scruples would not have disqualified him from becoming a member of Congress or holding other public offices. Treating the matter as one of statutory construction, Douglas said that the oath required for public officers is "in no material respect" different from that prescribed for aliens. He concluded that there was no suggestion that Congress intended to set a stricter standard for aliens seeking citizenship than for individuals in

83. 54 Stat. 889, § 5(g) (1940).

84. 3 Stokes 306. For a study of the 1940 law and its implementation, see Mulford Q. Sibley & Philip E. Jacob, Conscription of Conscience: The American State and the Conscientious Objector, 1940–1947 (1952).

85. United States v. Macintosh, 283 U.S. 605 (1931).

86. In re Summers, 325 U.S. 561, 573 (1945).

public office. Pointing to previous conscription statutes that had made accommodations for citizens with religious scruples, he emphasized the respect shown by Congress over the years "for the conscience of those having religious scruples against bearing arms."[87]

Belief in a Supreme Being

Congress and the judiciary became involved in another issue: whether the conscientious objector exemption required belief in a "Supreme Being." The 1940 law had created disagreement about the meaning of "religious training and belief." General Lewis B. Hershey, Director of Selective Service, issued an opinion stating that a conscientious objector would have to recognize "some source of all existence which is divine because it is the source of all things."[88] The first case to challenge that definition came from Mathias Kauten, whose claim to be a conscientious objector was rejected by an Appeal Board on the ground that his opposition to the war was philosophical and political, not religious. He admitted to being either an atheist or an agnostic.[89]

The Second Circuit affirmed the Appeal Board, ruling that his objections were based "on philosophical and political considerations applicable to this war rather than on 'religious training and belief.'"[90] The Second Circuit decided that Congress, in granting the religious exemption, "intended to satisfy the consciences of the very limited class we have described and not to give exemption to the great number of persons who might object to a particular war on philosophical or political grounds."[91] At the same time, the Second Circuit toyed with a definition of religion that did not seem to require belief in a deity. It spoke about "a response of the individual to an inward mentor, call it conscience or God, that is for many persons at the present time the equivalent of what has always been thought a religious impulse."[92] This more generous definition of religious belief appears in subsequent decisions by the Second Circuit.[93]

87. Girouard v. United States, 328 U.S. 61, 66–67 (1946), overruling United States v. Macintosh, 283 U.S. 605 (1931) and United States v. Bland, 283 U.S. 636 (1931).
88. Cornell, The Conscientious Objector and the Law, at 13.
89. United States v. Kauten, 133 F.2d 703, 707 n. 2 (2d Cir. 1943).
90. Id. at 707–08.
91. Id. at 708.
92. Id.
93. United States v. Downer, 135 F.2d 521 (2d Cir. 1943); United States v. Badt, 141 F.2d 845 (2d Cir. 1944).

The Ninth Circuit, however, adopted a more traditional definition of religion. Herman Berman, who asked to be classified as a conscientious objector, was classified as 1-A and ordered to an induction center. The Ninth Circuit held that his conscientious social belief and moralistic philosophy did not satisfy the statutory exemption: "His philosophy and moral and social policy without the concept of deity cannot be said to be religion in the sense of that term as it is used in the statute."[94] Moreover, the court found insufficient evidence to show that his "way of life" or objections to war related to any "religious training or belief."[95]

Congress now had an opportunity to revisit this issue. It could take its cues from the Second Circuit, the Ninth Circuit, or devise an entirely different standard. Legislation in 1948 seemed to reflect the position of the Ninth Circuit. The religious exemption for conscientious objectors defined "religious training and belief" to mean "an individual's belief in a relation to a Supreme Being involving duties superior to those arising from any human relation, but does not include essentially political, sociological, or philosophical views or a merely personal moral code."[96] In reporting the bill, the Senate Committee on Armed Services cited the Ninth Circuit opinion.[97] Floor amendments addressed the issue of conscientious objectors, but only with regard to the procedures to be used in reviewing their claims.[98] The requirement that an individual's religious belief be related to a Supreme Being was not discussed.

From 1955 to 1965, the Supreme Court dealt with several conscientious objector cases, eventually addressing the statutory requirement of a belief in a Supreme Being. In a 1955 case, the claim of a Jehovah's Witness to be a conscientious objector had been rejected by an Appeal Board. The Court found that his inconsistent statements and failure to produce evidence of prior pacifist positions cast doubt on the sincerity of his claim and justified the board's decision.[99] Also in 1955, the Court reviewed the case of another Jehovah's Witness whose claim to be a conscientious objector was rejected by the Justice Department because he stated that he was already "in the Army of Christ Jesus serving as a soldier." The depart-

94. Berman v. United States, 156 F.2d 377, 381 (9th Cir. 1946), cert. denied, 329 U.S. 795 (1946).

95. Id.

96. 62 Stat. 613 (1948).

97. S. Rept. No. 1268, 80th Cong., 2d Sess. 14 (1948).

98. 94 Cong. Rec. 7277–79, 7303–07 (1948).

99. Witmer v. United States, 348 U.S. 375, 382–83 (1955).

ment took that as evidence that he was not opposed to "participation in war in any form," as required by statute.[100] The Court rejected that interpretation, concluding that Congress did not have in mind theocratic wars or one's willingness to fight at Armageddon.[101]

The case in 1965 dealt directly with belief in "a Supreme Being." If Congress was in fact offering a legal benefit to one type of conscientious objector—those who professed belief in a Supreme Being— and that term was equivalent to God, the statute was on shaky ground. Not every religion is theistic. Could Congress extend the exemption for conscientious objectors to some religions but not to others? Surely it couldn't extend it to Protestants but not Catholics, or vice versa. Could it prefer theistic over nontheistic religions? Probably not. In 1961, in striking down a requirement that a notary public take an oath affirming a belief in God, the Court ruled that government may not "aid those religions based on a belief in the existence of God as against those religions founded on different beliefs."[102]

Rather than confront Congress on its constitutional authority to draft the law as it did and possibly invalidate the statutory provision, the Court resorted to some judicial legerdemain in defining "a Supreme Being." First, it concluded that when Congress used the expression "Supreme Being" rather than "God," it was "merely clarifying the meaning of religious training and belief so as to embrace all religions and to exclude essentially political, sociological, or philosophical views." The next step was to decide what might fit under "all religions." As to that issue, the Court said that "the test of belief 'in a relation to a Supreme Being' is whether a given belief that is sincere and meaningful occupies a place in the life of its possessor parallel to that filled by the orthodox belief in God of one who clearly qualifies for the exemption." In other words, "a Supreme Being" could be some force outside oneself, even if not a traditional deity. In urging this broader view, the Court underscored the complexity of religion in America:

> Over 250 sects inhabit our land. Some believe in a purely personal God, some in a supernatural deity; others think of religion as a way of life envisioning as its ultimate goal the day when all men can live together in perfect understanding and peace. There are those who think of God as the depth of our being; others, such as the Buddhists,

100. Sicurella v. United States, 348 U.S. 385, 386–88 (1955).
101. Id. at 390.
102. Torcaso v. Watkins, 367 U.S. 488, 495 (1961).

strive for a state of lasting rest through self-denial and inner purifi-
cation; in Hindu philosophy, the Supreme Being is the transcenden-
tal reality which is truth, knowledge and bliss.[103]

The Court pointed to the striking parallel between language in the 1948
law and Chief Justice Hughes's dissent in *United States* v. *Macintosh* (1931).
The statute spoke of "an individual's belief in a relation to a Supreme
Being involving duties superior to those arising from any human relation."
Hughes wrote: "The essence of religion is belief in a relation to God involving duties superior to those arising from any human relation."[104] Having established this connection, the Court proceeded to say that Congress
"must have had in mind" the admonitions of Hughes when he noted that
the word "God" had many meanings for the faithful: "Putting aside dogmas with their particular conceptions of deity, freedom of conscience itself
implies respect for an innate conviction of paramount duty. The battle for
religious liberty has been fought and won with respect to religious beliefs
and practices, which are not in conflict with good order, upon the very
ground of the supremacy of conscience within its proper field."[105]

The Court seemed to accept the Second Circuit's position in *Kauten*
(treating conscience as roughly synonymous with God) rather than the
more restrictive definition developed by the Ninth Circuit in *Berman*.
The Court acknowledged that Senate Report No. 1268 expressly cited
Berman, but that "might mean a number of things." For example, instead
of citing *Berman* "for what it said 'religious belief' was, Congress cited it
for what it said 'religious belief' was not," namely the exclusion of conscientious objectors who depended solely on political, social, or philosophical grounds. Both the Second and Ninth Circuits had agreed on that
point. Then why did Congress add the phrase "a Supreme Being" and cite
Berman? The Court explains that the Ninth Circuit itself (although using
"God" instead of "Supreme Being") depended on Hughes's dissenting
language.[106] Finally, the Court said it was "perfectly reasonable" for Congress to cite *Berman*, since it denied cert in that case but not in *Kauten*.[107]

Under the Court's interpretation, individuals are entitled to be classified

103. United States v. Seeger, 380 U.S. 163, 174–175 (1965).

104. United States v. Macintosh, 283 U.S. 605, 633–34 (1931) (Hughes, C.J., dissenting).

105. United States v. Seeger, 380 U.S. at 176 (citing United States v. Macintosh, 282
U.S. at 634).

106. Id. at 178.

107. Id. at 179.

as conscientious objectors if they profess a "religious belief" and do not depend solely on a "personal moral code." The issue of "a Supreme Being" disappears. In fact, the Court quotes favorably from Paul Tillich that if the word *God* has little meaning to an individual, it is enough to "speak of the depths of your life, of the source of your being, of your ultimate concern, *of what you take seriously without any reservation.*"[108] A concurrence by Justice Douglas concedes that the Court did a lot of stretching, but "it is no more so than other instances where we have gone to extremes to construe an Act of Congress to save it from demise on constitutional grounds."[109] There were no dissents.

In 1967, Congress revisited the issue and removed the statute's definition of religious training and belief ("an individual's belief in a relation to a Supreme Being involving duties superior to those arising from any human relation").[110] What the Court in effect deleted, Congress deleted in fact. In reporting the Military Selective Service Act of 1967, the House Armed Services Committee noted *Seeger* and the controversy that had ensued. The committee decided to eliminate the language that had caused so much trouble.[111]

Current National Policy

In subsequent cases, the Court continued to fine-tune the exemption for conscientious objectors. In 1970 it upheld the claim of someone who could neither affirm nor deny a belief in "a Supreme Being."[112] A year later it examined the statutory restriction to individuals opposed "to participation in war in any form." In so doing, it denied relief to those who objected in particular to the Vietnam War.[113] The Court may have had good institutional (and political) reasons for not challenging Congress on that point, but the objection to particular wars and not all wars is central to traditional efforts to distinguish between just and unjust wars.[114]

108. Id. at 187 (emphasis in original).
109. Id. at 188.
110. 81 Stat. 104 (1967).
111. H. Rept. No. 267, 90th Cong., 1st Sess. 31, 61 (1967); H. Rept. No. 346, 90th Cong., 1st Sess. 15 (1967).
112. Welsh v. United States, 398 U.S. 333, 337 (1970).
113. Gillette v. United States, 401 U.S. 437 (1971).
114. Joseph E. Capizzi, "Selective Conscientious Objection in the United States," 38 J. Church & State 339 (1996); Kent Greenawalt, "All or Nothing at All: The Defeat of Selective Conscientious Objection," 1971 Sup. Ct. Rev. 31.

Among the cases reviewed was the application of Cassius Clay (Muhammad Ali) for the status of conscientious objector.[115]

The 1948 law eliminated the 1940 option for "work of national importance under civilian direction." That alternative was restored in 1951, with passage of the Universal Military Training and Service Act. Instead of being inducted and performing noncombatant work, a conscientious objector could be deferred from military service and directed to perform "such civilian work contributing to the maintenance of the national health, safety, or interest as the local board may deem appropriate."[116] A number of organizations had lobbied Congress to find a more "constructive" role for conscientious objectors than to have them sit in jail.[117]

Under current law, persons may not be subject to combatant training and service if, by reason of "religious training and belief," they are "conscientiously opposed to participation in war in any form." The *term religious training and belief* "does not include essentially political, sociological, or philosophical views, or a merely personal code." Individuals who receive exemption from combatant training and service shall be assigned to noncombatant service as defined by the President. If the person is found to be conscientiously opposed to participation in noncombatant service, in lieu of induction that person is subject to such regulations as the President may prescribe, "such civilian work contributing to the maintenance of the national health, safety, or interest" as the Director of Selective Service may deem appropriate.[118]

The law on conscientious objectors reflects several centuries of commitment and understanding by individuals, religious groups, and elected officials. Political actors, not judges, created the exemption and recognized the legitimacy of individual conscience. Religious organizations were responsible for enacting the initial exemption and also the gradual broadening of the definition so that it came to include not only members of "well-recognized" religions but also those who did not belong to any religious group. Courts were not a part of this dialogue until recent decades, and their contribution was not in creating the exemption or even sanctioning its legitimacy but rather in refining its meaning.

115. Clay v. United States, 403 U.S. 698 (1971).
116. 65 Stat. 86 (amending § 456(j)) (1951); H. Rept. No. 535, 82d Cong., 1st Sess. 19–20 (1951).
117. 1951 CQ Almanac, at 289.
118. 50 App. U.S.C. § 456(j) (1994).

5

FLAG SALUTES AND YARMULKES

Decisions by the Supreme Court in 1940 on a compulsory flag-salute case and again in 1986 on the wearing of yarmulkes in the military offer some instructive lessons. In neither case did the Court have the "final voice" on the meaning of religious liberty. Citizens and elected officials did not passively accept the two rulings as either binding or intelligent. The condemnation was swift and sure. So intense was the criticism in the first case that the Court reversed itself three years later. The 1986 decision was countermanded a year later in a statute enacted by Congress. In both cases, the larger political system insisted on a policy more protective of religious freedoms than had been announced by the Court.

Compulsory Flag Salute

In 1940 and again in 1943, the Supreme Court reviewed cases brought by Jehovah's Witnesses who opposed, on religious grounds, a compulsory flag salute. The first decision upheld the salute; the second struck it down. The opinion by Justice Jackson in 1943 is no doubt eloquent in upholding the interests of a beleaguered religious minority, but the real credit for safeguarding the constitutional rights of the Witnesses belongs to all the individuals and associations in the country who denounced the 1940 ruling and refused to accept it as national policy. It frequently happens that public opinion is more discerning than judicial rulings. William Howard Taft, during his service as a federal judge, wrote: "If the law is but the essence of common sense, the protest of many average men may evidence a defect in a judicial conclusion though based on the nicest legal reasoning and profoundest learning."[1]

1. William Howard Taft, "Criticisms of the Federal Judiciary," 29 Am. L. Rev. 641, 643 (1895).

The first flag-salute statute appeared in Kansas in 1907. Over time, other states passed legislation to compel schoolchildren to salute the flag. The Jehovah's Witnesses, relying on a literal interpretation of the Bible, believed that saluting a secular symbol violated their religious beliefs.[2] The Witnesses attracted some enemies by aggressively proselytizing for their views. One scholar referred to them as "a sect distinguished by great religious zeal and astonishing powers of annoyance."[3] For example, the Witnesses referred to the Roman Catholic Church as the "harlot."[4]

THE 1940 OPINION

The compulsory flag salute survived a number of early test cases,[5] but in 1937 a federal district judge in Pennsylvania found this type of statute unconstitutional. The case involved the refusal of two children, Lillian Gobitas (thirteen years old) and her brother William (twelve), to salute the flag because of their religious beliefs as Jehovah's Witnesses. The family name would be incorrectly spelled "Gobitis" throughout the litigation.[6] The school regarded Lillian's and William's refusal as an act of insubordination and expelled them from school. Their father was financially unable to pay for their education at a private school.

The judge ruled that if someone on the basis of sincere religious beliefs defied a statute, the individual's right would prevail unless the state demonstrated that the statute was necessary for the public safety, health, morals, property, or personal rights.[7] Concerned that other courts had given insufficient weight to the value of religious liberty, he appealed to his

---

2. "Thou shalt not make unto thee any graven image, or any likeness of any thing that is in heaven above, or that is in the earth beneath, or that is in the water under the earth. Thou shalt not bow down thyself to them, nor serve them" (Exodus 20:4–5).

3. Zechariah Chafee, Jr., Free Speech in the United States 399 (1941).

4. Shawn Francis Peters, Judging Jehovah's Witnesses: Religious Persecution and the Dawn of the Rights Revolution 19 (2000).

5. Leoles v. Landers, 192 S.E. 218 (Ga. 1937), dismissed for want of substantial federal question, 302 U.S. 656 U.S. (1937); Hering v. State Board of Education, 189 A. 629 (N.J. 1937), dismissed for want of substantial federal question, 303 U.S. 624 (1938); Gabrielli v. Knickerbocker, 82 P.2d 391 (Cal. 1938), dismissed for want of jurisdiction, 306 U.S. 621 (1939); Johnson v. Deerfield, 25 F.Supp. 918 (D. Mass. 1939), aff'd, 306 U.S. 621 (1939).

6. Peters, Judging Jehovah's Witnesses, at 19.

7. Gobitis v. Minersville School Dist., 21 F.Supp. 581, 584 (E.D. Pa. 1937).

state's heritage. The state constitution provided that "all men have a natural and indefeasible right to worship Almighty God according to the dictates of their own consciences; . . . no human authority can, in any case whatever, control or interfere with the rights of conscience." The judge noted that William Penn, the founder of Pennsylvania, was expelled from Oxford University "for his refusal for conscience' sake to comply with regulations not essentially dissimilar [to the compulsory flag salute], and suffered, more than once, imprisonment in England because of his religious convictions. The commonwealth he founded was intended as a haven for all those persecuted for conscience' sake."[8] Taking note of the religious intolerance that was "again rearing its ugly head in other parts of the world," as in Nazi Germany, he regarded it as "of the utmost importance that the liberties guaranteed to our citizens by the fundamental law be preserved from all encroachment."[9]

His decision was upheld by the Third Circuit.[10] The Supreme Court agreed to hear the case, but before issuing a ruling it decided another Jehovah's Witness case. A Witness had been prosecuted for violating a state law that prohibited the solicitation of money, services, and subscriptions "of any valuable thing" unless approved in advance by a public official. Jesse Cantwell went from house to house to solicit money, sell books, and play records on a portable phonograph. Some of the records included attacks on Roman Catholics. A unanimous Court struck down the state law as a violation on the free exercise of religion. The Court also held that the religion clauses of the First Amendment applied to the states.[11]

Two weeks later, the Court handed down its decision in the flag-salute case. In their brief, the plaintiffs pointed out that the "form of salute is very much like that of the Nazi regime in Germany."[12] Yet instead of understanding the need for religious diversity and individual rights, many Americans turned with venom against minority sects. As the German army raced across Europe in the spring of 1940, American communities feared "Fifth Column" activities. On May 23, a mob in Del Rio, Texas, attacked three Witnesses thought to be Nazi agents. On June 2, the Gallup

8. Id. at 585.

9. Id. at 586. See also Gobitis v. Minersville School Dist., 24 F.Supp. 271 (E.D. Pa. 1938).

10. Minersville School Dist. v. Gobitis, 108 F.2d 683 (3d Cir. 1939).

11. Cantwell v. Connecticut, 310 U.S. 296, 303 (1940).

12. Respondents' Brief, Minersville School Dist. v. Gobitis, at 3; 37 Landmark Briefs 375.

Poll reported that 65 percent of the people believed that Germany would attack the United States.[13] A front page headline in the *New York Times* on June 1 announced that the war in Europe "Imperils Whole World."[14] Two days later, in the midst of this emotional frenzy, the Court released its opinion upholding the compulsory flag salute.

The Justices seemed to give little consideration to the political consequences that would come from their ruling. Studies on what took place in conference describe the flag-salute decision as a "case study in judicial misperceptions and breakdown in communication among the Justices."[15] In summarizing the basic issues at stake, Chief Justice Hughes had no doubt about the authority of states to impose a compulsory flag salute, and apparently no one in the conference opposed him.[16] Allison Dunham, Justice Stone's law clerk, recalled that Stone went into the conference with an intent to vote in favor of religious liberty, but failed to indicate at the conference his misgivings, nor did he circulate his dissent in time for it to have any effect on possible allies.[17] Unaware of any opposition to Hughes's position in conference, Justices Black, Douglas, and Murphy added their names to the majority opinion. By the time they saw Stone's dissent, they felt, as relative newcomers, that it was too late to desert the majority and join Stone.[18] Murphy's initial instinct was to write a dissenting opinion, but he held his tongue because he saw no other Justices on his side.[19]

Writing for an 8 to 1 majority, Justice Frankfurter leaned heavily on two premises: liberty requires unifying sentiments, and national unity promotes national security.[20] For Frankfurter, whose family immigrated to the United States when he was twelve years old, the flag salute was sacrosanct, a symbol of the assimilationist ideal he embraced.[21] Consequently,

13. Francis H. Heller, "A Turning Point for Religious Liberty," 29 Va. L. Rev. 440, 447 (1943)

14. Robert S. Peck, "A Wrenching Reversal," 5 Constitution 51, 53 (1993).

15. Alice Fleetwood Bartee, Cases Lost, Causes Won 53 (1984).

16. 2 Merlo J. Pusey, Charles Evans Hughes 728–29 (1952).

17. Alpheus Thomas Mason, Harlan Fiske Stone: Pillar of the Law 528, asterisked footnote (1956).

18. William O. Douglas, The Court Years, 1939–75: The Autobiography of William O. Douglas 45 (1981).

19. J. Woodford Howard, Jr., Mr. Justice Murphy: A Political Biography 251 (1968).

20. Minersville School District v. Gobitis, 310 U.S. 586 (1940).

21. Richard Danzig, "Justice Frankfurter's Opinions in the Flag Salute Cases: Blending Logic and Psychologic in Constitution Decisionmaking," 36 Stan. L. Rev. 675, 696–97 (1984).

when the Witnesses—who cited sixty-one biblical passages in their Supreme Court brief—called upon the Justices to embrace religious pluralism, Frankfurter concluded that their proper course was to present their case "in the forum of public opinion and before legislative assemblies rather than to transfer such a contest to the judicial arena."[22] That is, Frankfurter instructed them that the safeguards for religious liberty were political, not judicial. Justice Stone's dissent attacked a number of Frankfurter's arguments, especially his doctrine of judicial self-restraint. To defer to legislative judgment and the democratic process, said Stone, "seems to me no less than the surrender of the constitutional protection of the liberty of small minorities to the popular will."[23]

PUBLIC REACTION

Frankfurter's decision was excoriated by law journals, the press, and religious organizations. The *New Republic*, which Frankfurter helped found, warned that the country was "in great danger of adopting Hitler's philosophy in the effort to oppose Hitler's legions," and accused the Court of coming "dangerously close to being a victim of [war] hysteria."[24] In a subsequent wrap-up of the Court's work, the *New Republic* noted derisively: "Already Mr. Justice Frankfurter has been heroically saving America from a couple of school children whose devotion to Jehovah would have been compromised by a salute to the flag."[25] Mark DeWolfe Howe called Frankfurter's decision "a disheartening omen of the Court's unwillingness when chauvinism is loose in the land to safeguard the dissenter."[26]

Thirty-one of thirty-nine law reviews that discussed the decision did so critically. Newspapers accused the Court of violating constitutional rights and buckling under popular hysteria.[27] Editorials in 171 newspapers condemned Frankfurter's opinion.[28] A study of the flag-salute cases concluded: "The plain fact was that *[Gobitis]* had not settled the flag-salute

22. 310 U.S. at 600.
23. Id. at 606.
24. "Frankfurter v. Stone," The New Republic, vol. 102, at 843–44 (June 24, 1940).
25. Walton Hamilton & George Braden, "The Supreme Court Today," The New Republic, vol. 103, at 180 (August 5, 1940).
26. Mark DeWolfe Howe, The Garden and the Wilderness: Religion and Government in American Constitutional History 111 (1965).
27. David R. Manwaring, Render Unto Caesar: The Flag-Salute Controversy 158–60 (1962); Heller, "A Turning Point for Religious Liberty," 29 Va. L. Rev. at 452–53.
28. Alpheus Thomas Mason, Harlan Fiske Stone: Pillar of the Law 532 (1956).

controversy; if anything, it had made it worse. The press, both lay and legal, had shown outspoken hostility. The case had had small and *decreasing* influence as a legal precedent. Expressions of displeasure came even from the Department of Justice. The only tangible results of the decision appeared to be persecution and violence."[29]

Frankfurter's decision was followed by a wave of violence against Witnesses across the country. John Noonan writes: "Planned by no central authority, unintended by the Supreme Court, overshadowed by World War II, the legal and illegal persecution of Witnesses from 1941 to 1943 was the greatest outbreak of religious intolerance in twentieth-century America."[30] Within weeks of the decision, hundreds of attacks were reported by the Justice Department. In the two years following Frankfurter's ruling, Justice officials spoke of "an uninterrupted record of violence and persecution of the Witnesses. Almost without exception, the flag and the flag salute can be found as the percussion cap that set off those acts."[31]

Roman Catholics, although often the prime target of attacks from Jehovah's Witnesses, found particularly offensive Frankfurter's remark that "the courtroom is not the arena for debating issues of educational policy."[32] A Catholic writer objected that if Frankfurter's theory had been applied in a 1925 case, regarding the power of the state to outlaw private schools, "today there would not be a single private school in Oregon."[33]

Justices Black, Douglas, and Murphy, part of Frankfurter's 8–1 majority, soon regretted their votes. Douglas explained that the three Justices joined Frankfurter because he was "indeed learned in constitutional law and we were inclined to take him at face value."[34] They initially regarded Frankfurter as a "flaming liberal," but were quickly disillusioned by his decision in the flag-salute case.[35] A few months after the decision,

29. Manwaring, Render Unto Caesar, at 251 (emphasis in original).

30. John T. Noonan, Jr., The Believer and the Powers That Are 251 (1987). Vigilante assaults on Witnesses are described in Peters, Judging Jehovah's Witnesses, at 1–8, 72–123.

31. Victor W. Rotnem & F. G. Folsom, Jr., "Recent Restrictions Upon Religious Liberty," 36 Am. Pol. Sci. Rev. 1053, 1062 (1942).

32. 310 U.S. at 598.

33. Manwaring, Render Unto Caesar, at 156; Pierce v. Society of Sisters, 268 U.S. 510 (1925).

34. Douglas, The Court Years, at 44.

35. Mr. Justice and Mrs. Black: The Memoirs of Hugo L. Black and Elizabeth Black 72 (1986).

Douglas told Frankfurter that Black was having second thoughts. Sarcastically, Frankfurter asked whether Black had spent the summer reading the Constitution. "No," Douglas replied, "he has been reading the papers."[36]

THE STATES REFUSE TO FOLLOW

Several state courts found Frankfurter's opinion unacceptable. Reliance on state constitutional law provided greater protection to religious liberty than could be obtained from the U.S. Supreme Court. In New Hampshire, children of Jehovah's Witnesses were suspended from public school because they refused to salute the American flag. By so acting, they were judged delinquent, taken from their family, and placed in a state industrial school. In 1941, the Supreme Court of New Hampshire deplored the breaking up of a family for "no more than the conscientious acts of the children, based upon the religious teachings of their parents."[37] In holding that the children were not delinquent within the meaning of state law, the court urged legislative and administrative authorities to seek an accommodation that would not violate the religious scruples of the students.

School authorities in New Jersey, after expelling the children of Jehovah's Witnesses for refusing to salute the flag, then chose to convict their parents of being disorderly persons because they had not kept their children in regular attendance at school! In 1942, the Supreme Court of New Jersey found no evidence that the parents refused to keep their children in school, quoting approvingly from another decision: "The flag is dishonored by a salute by a child in reluctant and terrified obedience to a command of secular authority which clashes with the dictates of conscience."[38]

In Kansas, the children of Jehovah's Witnesses were punished for not saluting the flag. When the parents sought alternative schooling to protect the religious beliefs of their children, the state found them guilty of violating the compulsory education statute. School authorities justified this policy under the authority of *Gobitis*. The Supreme Court of Kansas held that *Gobitis* merely stood for the proposition that if a flag-salute regulation was valid in Pennsylvania it was not invalid under the U.S.

36. H. N. Hirsch, The Enigma of Felix Frankfurter 152 (1981).
37. State v. Lefebvre, 20 A.2d 185, 187 (N.H. 1941).
38. In re Latrecchia, 26 A.2d 881, 882 (N.J. 1942).

Constitution. The court then pointed to the detailed language of the Kansas Bill of Rights: "The right to worship God according to the dictates of conscience shall never be infringed; nor shall any person be compelled to attend or support any form of worship; nor shall any control of or interference with the rights of conscience be permitted."[39] Under state law, the compulsory flag-salute was not valid in Kansas.

Early in 1943, the Supreme Court of Washington reversed lower court decisions that had labeled children of Jehovah's Witnesses "delinquent" because they refused to salute the flag. The children had been taken from the custody of their parents. The court noted that the state constitution provided greater protection for religious freedom than found in the First Amendment of the U.S. Constitution. The state constitution provided: "Absolute freedom of conscience in all matters of religious sentiment, belief and worship, shall be guaranteed to every individual, and no one shall be molested or be disturbed in person or property on account of religion."[40] After casting doubt on the continued vitality of Gobitis, the court concluded that the state constitution controlled the case, not rulings of the U.S. Supreme Court: "Under all the circumstances, that opinion [Gobitis] can scarcely be deemed to have become authoritative. In any event, it is for this court to construe and apply the portion of our state constitution above quoted."[41]

This nationwide debate had a profound impact on the U.S. Supreme Court. In 1942, Justices Black, Douglas, and Murphy publicly apologized for their votes in Gobitis. They now announced that it had been "wrongly decided."[42] Frankfurter remarked bitterly that his opinion in Gobitis was "okayed by those great libertarians until they heard from the people."[43] Deserted by Black, Douglas, and Murphy, Frankfurter was left with a bare 5–4 majority. The margin was even shakier because two members of the Gobitis majority had been replaced by Wiley Rutledge and Robert H. Jackson. The original 8 to 1 majority evaporated so rapidly that a three-judge federal court in 1942 determined that Gobitis was no longer binding, even though it had yet to be overruled. The court calculated that of the seven remaining Justices on the Supreme Court who had participated in Gobitis, "four have given public expression to the view that it is

39. State v. Smith, 127 P.2d 518, 522 (Kans. 1942).
40. Bolling v. Superior Court for Clallam County, 133 P.2d 803, 806 (Wash. 1943).
41. Id. at 809.
42. Jones v. Opelika, 316 U.S. 584, 624 (1942).
43. Joseph P. Lash, From the Diaries of Felix Frankfurter 70 (1975).

unsound."[44] Moreover, opinions by Rutledge while serving on the D.C. Circuit suggested that he would likely join Stone, Black, Douglas, and Murphy in overturning *Gobitis*.[45]

Legislation that Congress passed in 1942, to codify existing rules and customs for the display and use of the American flag, also shook the foundations of *Gobitis*. Language in the bill indicated a preference for avoiding rigidly enforced flag salutes. After stating that in pledging allegiance to the flag a citizen would extend the right hand, palm upward, toward the flag, the statute further provided: "However, civilians will always show full respect to the flag when the pledge is given by merely standing at attention, men removing the headdress."[46] As interpreted by the Justice Department, this statute challenged the merits of *Gobitis* and undercut the requirement for the compulsory flag salute. The Department had been informed that Jehovah's Witnesses would have no objection to standing at attention during the flag-salute exercise.[47] In this way they could demonstrate their love of country without violating their religious beliefs. The Justice Department sent out a memo to all U.S. Attorneys, asking them to call to the attention of local authorities the more flexible standard adopted by Congress.[48]

THE COURT SWINGS AROUND

When the flag-salute issue returned to the Supreme Court, this time involving a West Virginia case, a brief by the ACLU noted that Congress had entered the field by passing legislation. Of "great importance," said the brief, "is the fact that Congress did not deem it wise, or see fit, to impose any penalties for failure to salute the flag."[49] During oral argument, counsel for the expelled students offered this candid assessment of *Gobitis:* "There cannot be found in the law a more unstatesmanlike decision, except possibly the Dred Scott decision." He urged the Court to

44. Barnette v. West Virginia State Board of Ed., 47 F.Supp. 251, 253 (S.D. W.Va. 1942) (three-judge court).

45. Busey v. District of Columbia, 129 F.2d 24, 38 (D.C. Cir. 1942).

46. 56 Stat. 380, § 7 (1942).

47. Rotnem & Folsom, Jr., "Recent Restrictions Upon Religious Liberty," 36 Am. Pol. Sci. Rev. at 1064.

48. Manwaring, Render Unto Caesar, at 188–89.

49. Brief for American Civil Liberties Union, Amicus Curiae, West Virginia State Board of Education v. Barnette; 40 Landmark Briefs 177–78.

reverse itself, reminding the Justices that "it is human to err and divine to forgive."[50] The Justice Department did not participate in the case.

The Supreme Court overruled *Gobitis* in 1943, almost three years to the date that it was announced. Only Justices Roberts and Reed agreed with Frankfurter that *Gobitis* was properly decided.[51] Justice Jackson, for a 6 to 3 majority, wrote a powerful and moving defense of religious freedom and the Bill of Rights, but credit for the liberalized decision belongs to those who refused to accept the Court's 1940 pronouncements on the meaning of the Constitution, minority rights, and religious liberty.

The flag salute remains a contentious issue in some communities. After the terrorist attacks on September 11, 2001, officials in Wisconsin voted to allow public schools to offer the Pledge of Allegiance as a means of promoting national unity and patriotism.[52] The New York City Board of Education adopted a resolution requiring all public schools to lead students in the Pledge of Allegiance at the beginning of each school day. The resolution specified that students and staff members shall not be compelled to participate or be subject to discipline if they choose not to participate. The requirement to cite the pledge had been largely ignored over the past three decades because of opposition to the Vietnam War. School Chancellor Harold O. Levy cautioned that the decision to pledge allegiance should not be an occasion for intolerance.[53] Although the pledge was popular in many school districts, some schools in the Upper West Side of Manhattan avoided routine recitation.[54]

The Yarmulke Case

Religious interests, more often than not, fare well in the political marketplace. One manifestation of this phenomenon is the willingness of lawmakers to exempt religious interests from statutory and regulatory requirements. Many of these political accommodations are examined in Chapter 9. A particularly vivid illustration of the power of religious interests to

50. 11 LW 3279 (1943).

51. West Virginia State Board of Education v. Barnette, 319 U.S. 624 (1943).

52. "In Shift, School Can Use Pledge to Flag," New York Times, October 17, 2001, at A12.

53. "New York Schools to Require Recitation of Pledge of Allegiance," October 18, 2001, at A20.

54. "Pledge, Indivisible, with Meaning for All," New York Times, October 23, 2001, at A19.

obtain legislative protection is the congressional response to a 1986 Supreme Court decision upholding an Air Force regulation that had prohibited an observant Jew in the military from wearing a skullcap (yarmulke) while on duty. The Court's opinion unleashed a political storm, prompting Congress to intervene within a year to repair the damage.

THE AIR FORCE INVOKES REGULATION

Simcha Goldman, an Orthodox Jew and ordained rabbi, served as a Captain in the U.S. Air Force and was assigned to a mental health clinic where he worked as a clinical psychologist. While in uniform and on duty, he wore a yarmulke at all times. Orthodox Jewish religious practice requires a Jewish male to keep his head covered. Over a three-and-a-half-year period, Goldman wore a yarmulke while in uniform without incident.

Matters changed on May 8, 1981, when the Air Force informed Goldman that wearing a yarmulke violated the military dress code, and he could not wear it indoors while in uniform except while working at the regional hospital. His counsel asked the Air Force to permit an exception but was turned down. On June 23, the Air Force ordered Goldman to stop wearing a yarmulke anywhere while in uniform, including at the regional hospital. Because of the dispute over the yarmulke, a previously positive recommendation for Goldman was withdrawn and replaced by a negative one. He was threatened with court-martial if he continued to wear a yarmulke while in uniform.

Why, after three and a half years, did Goldman's wearing of a yarmulke provoke an incident? In April 1981, the month before he was warned about wearing the yarmulke, he appeared at a court-martial proceeding to testify on behalf of the defense (and therefore against the Air Force). The action against Goldman therefore appeared to have a retaliatory motive.[55]

LITIGATION

After exhausting administrative remedies, Goldman's attorney went to court to enjoin the Secretary of Defense and the Secretary of the Air Force from preventing Goldman from wearing his yarmulke. A district

---

55. Goldman v. Weinberger, 475 U.S. 503, 511 (1986) (concurrence by Justice Stevens, joined by Justices White and Powell).

court decided that Goldman was entitled to a preliminary injunction because he was likely to prevail in claiming that the Air Force regulation violated the First Amendment's free exercise clause. The judge noted that
the dispute involved a departmental regulation, not a statute passed "by a
coequal branch of government."[56] In short, the court was not butting
heads with Congress. The judge appeared to make light of the Pentagon's
position that allowing Goldman to wear his yarmulke "will crush the
spirit of uniformity, which in turn will weaken the will and fighting ability of the Air Force."[57]

On the heels of this decision, another Orthodox Jew challenged the
Air Force policy on yarmulkes. A district judge from the same circuit
sided with the Air Force, concluding that departures from uniformity
would adversely affect "the promotion of teamwork, counteract pride and
motivation, and undermine discipline and morale, all to the detriment of
the substantial compelling governmental interest of maintaining an efficient Air Force."[58]

These two conflicting decisions reached the D.C. Circuit. Almost
three years elapsed before it issued a ruling on Goldman's case. All three
judges on the panel agreed that the Air Force was justified in adopting
and enforcing its regulation, notwithstanding Goldman's First Amendment rights.[59] The Air Force argued that Jewish law does not require the
covering of the head during work. Goldman conceded that some devout
Orthodox Jews do not feel obliged to cover their heads at all times.[60] The
Air Force said that if it accommodated Goldman on his yarmulke, other
military personnel would offer religious reasons to use turbans, robes, face
and body paint, shorn hair, unshorn hair, badges, rings, amulets, brace-
lets, jodhpurs, and symbolic daggers.[61]

The D.C. Circuit voted against a motion to rehear the case en banc.
Three judges, with quite familiar names, dissented from this denial of a
rehearing. Judge Kenneth Starr, later Solicitor General in the Bush administration and independent counsel for the Whitewater investigation,
said that the panel's decision in the Goldman case "does considerable

---

56. Goldman v. Secretary of Defense, 530 F.Supp. 12, 15 (D.D.C. 1981).
57. Id. at 16.
58. Bitterman v. Secretary of Defense, 553 F.Supp. 719, 725 (D.D.C. 1982).
59. Goldman v. Secretary of Defense, 734 F.2d 1531, 1535 (D.C. Cir. 1984).
60. Id. at 1537.
61. Id. at 1539.

violence to the bulwark of freedom guaranteed by the Free Exercise Clause."[62] Judges Ruth Bader Ginsburg and Antonin Scalia, now on the Supreme Court, said that the military's order to Goldman not to wear his yarmulke suggested "callous indifference" to Goldman's religious faith and ran counter to the American tradition of accommodating spiritual needs.[63]

The decision by the D.C. Circuit triggered legislative action in Congress. As an amendment to the defense authorization bill in 1984, Representative Stephen Solarz proposed that members of the armed forces may wear unobtrusive religious headgear, such as a skullcap, if religious observances or practices require the wearing of such headgear. Under this amendment, offered for a one-year trial period, the Defense Department could prohibit the headgear if it interfered with the performance of military duties.[64] Although Representative William Dickinson warned that "we are flying in the face of a court decision just made," the amendment was accepted.[65] The conferees decided to eliminate the House amendment but required the Defense Department to report on changes in service regulations that would promote the free expression of religion to the greatest extent possible consistent with the requirements of military discipline.[66] This lengthy study, touching on a broad range of issues, concluded that courts would most likely defer to the military services regarding the wearing of yarmulkes.[67]

THE SUPREME COURT WEIGHS IN

The Supreme Court accepted Goldman's case for review. The brief submitted by Solicitor General Charles Fried, supporting the Defense Department regulation, argued that Goldman's position would force the military to choose between "virtual abandonment of its uniform regulations and constitutionally impermissible line drawing."[68] The entire purpose of uniform standards "would be defeated if individuals were allowed

---

62. Goldman v. Secretary of Defense, 739 F.2d 657, 658 (D.C. Cir. 1984).

63. Id. at 660.

64. 130 Cong. Rec. 14295 (1984).

65. Id. at 14298.

66. H. Rept. No. 98–1080, 98th Cong., 2d Sess. 293–94 (1984); 98 Stat. 2532–33, § 554 (1984).

67. Joint Service Study on Religious Matters 21, 25 (March 1985).

68. Brief for the Respondents, Goldman v. Weinberger, No. 84–1097, U.S. Supreme Court, October Term, 1985, at 19.

exemptions." To disregard the government's interests in favor of exceptions made on a case-by-case basis "would make a mockery of the military's compelling interest in uniformity."[69] Fried said that the standard for evaluating religious liberty in the civilian sector had no application to the military.[70]

During oral argument in 1986, some Justices appeared to be uncomfortable about second-guessing military regulations. Justice Rehnquist pointed out to Nathan Lewin, Goldman's attorney, that the religious liberty cases he had cited for support came from civilian life: "We've never applied that sort of balancing test where the military has been involved, have we?" Lewin acknowledged that was true.[71] Oral argument wandered a bit when Justice White asked whether Goldman could satisfy his religious belief by wearing a toupee. Lewin conceded that a toupee would suffice, but his client wouldn't be interested because "he's not bald." Trying to turn the tables, Lewin said that "on someone who has a full head of hair, wearing a toupee would look somewhat strange." White was fully prepared: "It doesn't in the courtrooms in London where they are required to wear a wig."[72]

Kathryn Oberly of the Justice Department advised the Court to stay out of the battle and leave the dispute to the elected branches: "If Congress thinks that further accom[m]odation is either required or desirable it can legislate it."[73] In the event that Congress made a mistake it would be relatively easy to correct it with new legislation, but if the Court tried to constitutionalize mandatory exceptions to the uniform requirements, it would be "far more difficult for what might turn out to be a mistake in judgment about the effect on discipline and morale to be corrected."[74]

The Supreme Court, divided 5 to 4, held that the First Amendment did not prohibit the Air Force regulation even though Goldman's religious belief required the wearing of a yarmulke. The Court accepted the judgment of the Air Force that the outfitting of military personnel in standardized uniforms "encourages the subordination of personal preferences and identities in favor of the overall group mission."[75] For the

69. Id. at 49–50.
70. Id. at 20–28.
71. Oral argument, Goldman v. Weinberger, U.S. Supreme Court, January 14, 1986, at 5.
72. Id. at 21–24.
73. Id. at 45.
74. Id.
75. Goldman v. Weinberger, 475 U.S. 503, 508 (1986).

Court, the values of uniformity, hierarchy, unity, discipline, and obedience justified the regulation.

The majority of five included Justices Stevens, White, and Powell. In a separate concurrence, those three agreed that the Air Force had reason to pursue a single standard (visibility of religious apparel) because otherwise the military would have to contend with a variety of religious claims: wearing of a yarmulke by an Orthodox Jew, a turban by a Sikh, a saffron robe by a Satchidananda Ashram-Integral Yogi, dreadlocks by a Rastafarian, and so forth. An exception for yarmulkes, they said, would represent a risky departure from the basic principle of uniformity.[76]

In his dissent, Justice Brennan (joined by Justice Marshall) presented conflicting views on which branch of government is responsible for protecting individual rights. First he claimed that the Court's decision represented an abdication of its role "as principal expositor of the Constitution and protector of individual liberties in favor of credulous deference to unsupported assertions of military necessity."[77] Yet later he acknowledged that other parts of government also protect religious freedom: "Guardianship of this precious liberty is not the exclusive domain of federal courts. It is the responsibility as well of the States and of the other branches of the Federal Government."[78] His concluding sentence pointed toward the remedy: "The Court and the military have refused these servicemen their constitutional rights; we must hope that Congress will correct this wrong."[79]

CONGRESS ENTERS THE PICTURE

There was never any doubt about the authority of Congress to tell the Air Force to change its regulation. The Constitution provides that Congress shall "make rules for the Government and Regulation of the land and naval Forces."[80] Within two weeks of the Court's decision, legislation was introduced to permit members of the armed forces to wear items of apparel not part of the official uniform. Members of the military could wear any "neat, conservative, and unobtrusive" item of apparel to satisfy the tenets of a religious belief. The Secretary of the military service could

76. Id. at 512–13.
77. Id. at 514.
78. Id. at 523.
79. Id. at 524.
80. U.S. Const., art. I, § 8, cl. 14.

prohibit the wearing of the item after determining that it "significantly interferes with the performance of the member's military duties."[81]

In the defense authorization bill, which Congress passes each year, the House Armed Services Committee included a provision regarding the wearing of neat and conservative religious apparel by members of the armed forces while in uniform. The phrase "neat and conservative" was lifted from military service regulations. In acknowledging the importance of uniformity, cohesion, and esprit, the committee denied that the wearing of yarmulkes or turbans "would necessarily threaten good order, discipline, or morale in the armed forces."[82]

This provision remained in the bill as passed by the House but lost narrowly in the Senate. An amendment to permit members of the military to wear, under certain circumstances, religious apparel not part of the official uniform, was tabled by a vote of 51 to 49.[83] Senator Barry Goldwater, chairman of the Senate Armed Services Committee, strongly opposed the amendment. He warned that Muslims would be allowed to wear the dress and gear of a Muslim, Hopi Indians would wear a red band around their head ("That is religion, too."), and other Indians would want to wear feather headdresses.[84] His blunt advice: "If you are not happy in uniform, get out of uniform. Join something else."[85] When the bill reached conference, the conferees dropped the House provision, which the military services strongly opposed.[86]

The following year, the House again added language to permit the wearing of neat and conservative religious apparel by the military while in uniform, provided it did not interfere with the performance of military duties. No one spoke against the amendment. Senate debate was more spirited, but this time the provision passed 55 to 42. The Senate's reversal reflected some switches by Senators and the results of the 1986 elections. Six Senators (Boschwitz, Burdick, Danforth, Domenici, Harkin, and Rockefeller) switched from favoring the 1986 tabling motion to favoring the 1987 amendment. Eight new Senators (Adams, Breaux, Daschle,

81. 132 Cong. Rec. 6655 (1986) (Senator Alfonse D'Amato); id. at 7042, 7211 (Senator Frank Lautenberg).

82. H. Rept. No. 99–718, 99th Cong., 2d Sess. 200, 488 (1986). See also 132 Cong. Rec. 20644 (1986).

83. 132 Cong. Rec. 19808 (1986).

84. Id. at 19802.

85. Id. at 19803.

86. H. Rept. No. 1001, 99th Cong., 2d Sess. 474 (1986); 1986 CQ Almanac, at 485.

Graham, Karnes, Mikulski, Reid, and Wirth) voted for the 1987 amendment. Other adjustments brought the final tally to 55.[87]

Lobbying against the Senate amendment was fierce. The American Legion, with over 2.5 million members, and the Military Coalition, representing sixteen of the largest organizations for military personnel, opposed the amendment.[88] In a letter, Secretary of Defense Caspar Weinberger spelled out the reasons for rejecting the amendment, as did a document called a "twenty-star letter." The latter was signed by the Chairman of the Joint Chiefs of Staff, the Army Chief of Staff, the Air Force Chief of Staff, the Commandant of the Marine Corps, and the Acting Chief of Naval Operations: five officers with four stars each! A twenty-star letter against an amendment in a defense authorization bill is heavy artillery![89]

As the debate progressed, Senator Brock Adams said that the issue "should never have gone to the courts and never come before the Congress." In the past, he pointed out, the military services had been able to accommodate individuals on a case-by-case basis. These informal agreements seemed to serve everyone's interest. In announcing support for the amendment, he remarked how shocked he was by the intensity of lobbying: "I have had more calls from constituents on this issue than I had on SDI [Strategic Defense Initiative]; I had more requests for visits from DOD [Department of Defense] on this issue than I did on a comprehensive test ban."[90]

The statutory language allows members of the armed forces to wear an item of religious apparel while in uniform. The Secretary of a service may prohibit the wearing of an item of religious apparel when the Secretary determines that it would interfere with the performance of the member's military duties, or if the Secretary determines that the item is not neat and conservative. The statute applies only to the wearing of religious apparel that is part of the observance of religious faith practiced by the member.[91]

---

87. Senators Gore and Simon, who opposed the 1986 tabling motion, did not vote on the 1987 amendment. Senators Byrd, Nickles, and Johnston switched from opposing the 1986 tabling motion to opposing the 1987 amendment. Three Senators who opposed the 1986 tabling motion did not return in 1987 (Mathias, Hart, and Hawkins).

88. 133 Cong. Rec. 25251 (1987) (remarks by Senator Murkowski).

89. Id. at 25256.

90. Id. at 25258.

91. 101 Stat. 1086–87, § 508 (1987).

What happened with the compulsory flag salute and the Air Force regulation on yarmulkes illustrates the breadth and richness of constitutional debate in the United States. In neither case did the Supreme Court dictate or decide the final meaning of religious liberty. The first decision was opposed by newspapers, religious organizations, state courts, and Congress. This political climate produced a Court reversal three years later. The second decision was so unacceptable that Congress passed legislation within a year to secure a more expansive definition of religious freedom. In both cases, the regular political process assumed responsibility for protecting religious liberties that were unobtainable from the Court.

6

SCHOOL PRAYER

The 1962 Supreme Court decision on school prayer, *Engel* v. *Vitale,* sent shock waves across the country. Irate members of Congress responded with a number of restrictive measures, including constitutional amendments to overturn the ruling and legislation to remove the Court's jurisdiction to hear such cases. However, with most religious organizations rallying behind the decision, these court-curbing efforts were repeatedly rejected. School prayer remains a prominent, deeply divisive issue, but the battleground has shifted to such alternatives as voluntary prayer, a "moment of silence," giving religious groups equal access to schools and universities, and other initiatives, all of which leave *Engel* unscathed.

Misunderstanding the Ruling

Much of the inflammatory rhetoric that greeted *Engel* reflected ignorance, misconceptions, and deliberate distortion of the Court's decision. Some of the confusion flowed from the clumsy and tactless way it was written and presented. At bottom, the Court held that New York's "Regents' Prayer" was unconstitutional because "it is no part of the business of government to compose official prayers for any group of the American people to recite as a part of a religious program carried by government."[1] The Court did not rule against prayer. Justices sometimes have a tin ear, but they know enough not to try to prevent children from praying in school. What they did was to rule against the government's involvement in drafting a prayer to be said by students compelled to attend school.

1. Engel v. Vitale, 370 U.S. 421, 425 (1962). New York law directed that the following prayer be said aloud by each class of a public school at the beginning of the day: "Almighty God, we acknowledge our dependence upon Thee, and we beg Thy blessings upon us, our parents, our teachers, and our Country."

123

The program, as modified and approved by state courts, did not require all students to recite the prayer. It permitted students "who wish to do so to remain silent or be excused from the room."[2] This procedure appeared to make the prayer discretionary, not compulsory, but Black noted that when the "power, prestige and financial support of government is placed behind a particular religious belief, the indirect coercive pressure upon religious minorities to conform to the prevailing officially approved religion is plain."[3] It would take unusual confidence for a child to remain silent or ask to be excused from the room. Justice Douglas, in his concurrence, seemed not to appreciate the student's dilemma: "As I read this regulation, a child is free to stand or not stand, to recite or not recite, without fear of reprisal or even comment by the teacher or any other school official."[4]

Despite all the anger directed at the Court and *Engel*, the country has consistently accepted and supported the basic principles embedded in the ruling. *The New York Times* reported the decision correctly with this headline: "Supreme Court Outlaws Official School Prayers in Regents Case Decision."[5] The story by Anthony Lewis explained in the first two paragraphs that the constitutional deficiency flowed from the drafting of the prayer by the New York Board of Regents.[6] The *Washington Post-Times Herald* was less careful with its headline, "Public School Prayer Outlawed," and yet the lead paragraph brought the case back to its fundamentals: "The Supreme Court struck down the saying of official prayers in the public schools as unconstitutional yesterday."[7] Other newspapers displayed headlines that were grossly misleading: "No Praying in Schools, Court Rules" *(Indianapolis News)*, "Possible End to Christian, Jewish Holy Day Activity in Public Schools as Court Bans N.Y. Prayer" *(Baltimore Sun)*, "Supreme Court Outlaws Prayers in Public Schools" *(Detroit Free Press)*, and "No Prayers in Schools, Supreme Court Orders" *(Dallas Morning News)*.[8]

If one follows the development of the case, there was never hostility to

---

2. Id. at 430.
3. Id. at 431.
4. Id. at 438.
5. New York Times, June 26, 1962, at 1.
6. Id.
7. Washington Post–Herald Tribune, June 26, 1962, at 1.
8. Chester A. Newland, "Press Coverage of the United States Supreme Court," 17 West. Pol. Q. 15, 29 (1964).

religion or to prayer. During oral argument, the attorney for the plaintiffs opposing the Regents' Prayer strongly endorsed religion and prayer. He told the Justices: "I come here not as an antagonist of religion; . . . my clients are deeply religious people; . . . I say prayer is good. My clients say prayer is good."[9] In writing for the majority, Justice Black tried to steer clear of any animosity toward religion:

> It has been argued that to apply the Constitution in such a way as to prohibit state laws respecting an establishment of religious services in public schools is to indicate a hostility toward religion or toward prayer. Nothing, of course, could be more wrong. The history of man is inseparable from the history of religion. . . . It is neither sacrilegious nor antireligious to say that each separate government in this country should stay out of the business of writing or sanctioning official prayers and leave that purely religious function to the people themselves and to those the people choose to look to for religious guidance.[10]

However, Douglas's concurrence invited unfortunate and unnecessary speculations. He suggested that the decision might prohibit other ceremonial observations of a religious nature, such as the Court's traditional invocation when it convenes and the offering of a daily prayer by a chaplain in Congress. Those conjectures, totally unrelated to the issue before the Court, helped fuel public confusion and outrage. Stewart's dissent also strayed far afield. He did not want to deny school children their "wish" to recite the prayer or to interfere with those "who want to begin their day by joining in prayer." The dispute before the Court had nothing to do with the desire of children to pray on their own initiative. It was the constitutionality of a state composing an official prayer for minors in public schools. After reading the decision, constitutional law scholar Philip Kurland had the impression of the majority "walking on eggs and of the two minority Justices stamping after them."[11]

By making concrete "what might otherwise have been dismissed as idle speculation,"[12] critics of *Engel* were encouraged to distort what the Court

9. 56 Landmark Briefs 1038.

10. 370 U.S. at 433–35.

11. Philip B. Kurland, "The Regents' Prayer Case: 'Full of Sound and Fury, Signifying . . . ,'" 1962 Sup. Ct. Rev. 1, 13 (1962).

12. William M. Beaney & Edward N. Beiser, "Prayer and Politics: The Impact of Engel and Schempp on the Political Process," 13 J. Pub. L. 475, 479 (1964).

had held. For example, Douglas's concurrence became the focal point of congressional hearings, held shortly after the decision. "Again and again witnesses pointed to it as an example of what the Court would do in the future."[13] More striking, the prayer case was grossly misrepresented by the President of the American Bar Association, who weighed in with the far-fetched claim that the decision would require elimination of the motto "In God We Trust" from all coins.[14] That issue was never before the Court, either expressly or by implication. The public impression never recovered from these irresponsible readings.

Members of Congress helped fan the flames. Senator Sam J. Ervin, Jr. (D-N.C.) announced that the Court "has held that God is unconstitutional." Even in their most ambitious and enterprising rulings, Justices do not reach that far. Thomas Abernathy (D-Miss.) urged legislative action against the Court "to calm the power grab of these power-drunken men." Mendel Rivers (D-S.C.) railed against "this bold, malicious, atheistic and sacrilegious twist of this unpredictable group of uncontrolled despots." To W. R. Raleigh Hull, Jr. (D-Mo.), the Court had subverted the rights of Americans "to protect some fancied rights of a minority of citizens, in some instances Communists, murderers, rapists and similar scum." William Arthur Winstead (D-Miss.) wondered whether the Court "is trying to drive God and religion out of our schools and even out of our heritage."[15] George William Andrews (D-Ala.) touched all the rhetorical bases: "They put the Negroes in to the schools and now they have driven God out of them."[16]

Two days after *Engel*, President Kennedy was asked at a news conference for his opinion of the ruling. Recognizing that some people disagreed with the decision and others agreed with it, he said "it is important for us if we are going to maintain our constitutional principle that we support the Supreme Court decisions even when we may not agree with them." He also pointed to "a very easy remedy and that is to pray ourselves." The decision was a "welcome reminder" to American families to pray more at home, attend church "with a good deal more fidelity," and "make the true meaning of prayer much more important in the lives of all

13. Id. at 479.
14. Newland, "Press Coverage of the United States Supreme Court," 17 West. Pol. Q. at 28.
15. 108 Cong. Rec. 11709, 11718, 11732, 12227, 12342 (1962).
16. Kurland, "The Regents' Prayer Case," 1962 Sup. Ct. Rev. at 3.

our children." He urged citizens to "support the Constitution and the responsibility of the Supreme Court in interpreting it, which is theirs, and given to them by the Constitution."[17]

THE DRIVE FOR A CONSTITUTIONAL AMENDMENT

Some legislative responses to *Engel* had a frivolous or juvenile quality, such as a House amendment (rejected 47 to 66) to use appropriated funds to purchase Bibles for "the personal use of each justice."[18] The House voted to place above the Speaker's desk the motto "In God We Trust." In justifying this action, William Randall of Missouri advised his colleagues: "We have given perhaps not directly but yet in a not so subtle way our answer to the recent decision of the U.S. Supreme Court order banning the regents prayer from the New York schools."[19]

Pressure mounted for more serious threats, such as a constitutional amendment to permit school prayer. The day following *Engel,* Representative Frank Becker (R-N.Y.) introduced this constitutional amendment: "Prayers may be offered in the course of any program in any public school or other public place in the United States."[20] That language did not directly challenge the Court's decision, which was restricted to the government's role in *composing* prayer and using coercion. Becker's language a year later, drafted with other members, was even more in line with *Engel:* "Nothing in this Constitution shall be deemed to prohibit the offering, reading from, or listening to prayers or biblical scriptures, if participation therein is on a voluntary basis, in any governmental or public school, institution, or place."[21] *Engel* focused on *compulsory* prayer.

One month after the Court's decision, the Senate Judiciary Committee held two days of hearings to explore the issue of prayers in public schools. Careless language in Douglas's concurrence supplied lawmakers with ammunition to attack the Court. For example, Senator Kenneth Keating (R-N.Y.) said that Douglas indicated that the principles of the majority decision "would invalidate every reference to religion in governmental activities, including the marshal's supplication at the beginning of every

17. Public Papers of the Presidents, 1962, at 510–11.
18. 108 Cong. Rec. 14360–61 (1962).
19. Id. at 21102.
20. H. J. Res. 752, 87th Cong., 2d Sess. (1962).
21. 109 Cong. Rec. 16700 (1963).

session of the Supreme Court—'God save the United States and this honorable Court.'"[22] Obviously that was not the case. The Court's decision was directed toward compulsory prayers for children in public schools, not ceremonial references to God made in courtrooms or Congress. The Douglas concurrence featured prominently in statements made by other Senators critical of the Court.[23] The hearings allowed critics of the decision to fulminate and voice their disgust, but no steps were taken to challenge the Court. The committee did not issue a final report, nor did it propose remedial legislation.[24]

When the House Judiciary Committee finally held hearings in 1964 on a constitutional amendment to reverse the Court, most of the religious organizations testified in favor of *Engel*. They understood that their united opposition to the amendment would make it "respectable" and "safe" for legislators to vote against Becker's proposal. With one religious leader after another testifying against the amendment, Becker and his supporters were in no position to argue that only the Godless opposed them.[25] Protestant and Jewish groups generally found fault with the amendment; Catholic leaders were divided.[26] Dr. Edwin H. Tuller, speaking on behalf of the National Council of Churches (representing about forty million Americans), told the committee that public institutions belong to all citizens, "whatever their religious beliefs or lack of them, and that it was not right for a majority to impose religious practices on the minority in public institutions."[27] The leaders of a number of Jewish groups strongly supported the Court's decision and opposed the constitutional amendments introduced to override the Court.[28] Prominent legal scholars testified against the amendment.

In 1966, the Senate debated this constitutional amendment offered by Everett Dirksen, Republican of Illinois: "Nothing contained in this Constitution shall prohibit the authority administering any school, school system, educational institution or other public building supported in whole or in part through the expenditure of public funds from providing

22. "Prayers in Public Schools and Other Matters," hearings before the Senate Committee on the Judiciary, 87th Cong., 2d Sess. 17 (1962).

23. Id. at 20, 23, 27, 35–36, 38, 42.

24. Beaney & Beiser, "Prayer and Politics," 13 J. Pub. L. at 480.

25. Id. at 497, 499–500.

26. 1964 CQ Almanac 399.

27. "School Prayers" (Part I), hearings before the House Committee on the Judiciary, 88th Cong., 2d Sess. 656 (1964).

28. Id. (Part II), at 1627–31; id. (Part III), at 1996–2000, 2013–22.

for or permitting the voluntary participation by students or others in prayer. Nothing contained in this article shall authorize any such authority to prescribe the form or content of any prayer."[29] The amendment was obviously drafted with great care to avoid a collision with *Engel*. Nevertheless, a number of religious leaders testified in opposition to the amendment and sent telegrams against it.[30] Dirksen's amendment only attracted a vote of 49 to 37, or nine votes short of the necessary two-thirds.[31]

Over the next three decades, several hundred constitutional amendments were introduced to permit school prayer. Not one succeeded.[32] Even when opponents of the Court drafted these amendments, they never disturbed *Engel's* fundamental principle that government should not compose school prayers and compel students to recite them. For example, the Republican Platform in 1964 offered constitutional language to permit individuals and groups "who choose to do so to exercise their religion freely in public places, provided religious exercises are not *prepared or prescribed* by the state or political subdivision thereof and no person's participation therein is coerced, thus preserving the traditional separation of church and state."[33]

JURISDICTION STRIPPING

Article III of the Constitution provides that the Supreme Court "shall have appellate jurisdiction, both as to Law and Fact, with such exceptions, and under such Regulations as the Congress shall make." There have been several efforts by members of Congress to strip the federal courts of jurisdiction to hear school prayer cases. All of these initiatives failed. On the day following the Court's decision in *Engel*, Representative Mendel Rivers (D-S.C.) said it was time for Congress to exercise its authority "to drastically restrict and limit the appellate jurisdiction of this court which flaunts its authority in our very faces and it flaunts its authority because we have permitted them to run rampant over us."[34] A month

29. 112 Cong. Rec. 23555 (1966).

30. Id. at 23534, 23541, 23546; 1966 CQ Almanac at 513, 514–15.

31. 112 Cong. Rec. at 23556.

32. John R. Vile, Encyclopedia of Constitutional Amendments, Proposed Amendments, and Amending Issues 237–39 (1996).

33. 2 Donald Bruce Johnson, National Party Platforms, 1960–1976, at 683 (1978) (emphasis added).

34. 108 Cong. Rec. 11732 (1962).

later, Representative Howard Smith (D-Va.) also urged Congress to limit the Court's appellate jurisdiction in cases related to school prayer.[35]

Senator Jesse Helms (R-N.C.) took the lead in promoting this type of court-stripping bill. In 1974, he introduced legislation to limit the jurisdiction of the Supreme Court and district courts to enter any judgment, decree, or order that would deny or restrict, as unconstitutional, voluntary prayer in any public school.[36] Since his bill focused on voluntary prayer, it did not attempt to overturn *Engel*. Helms pointed out the advantages of his approach. Whereas a constitutional amendment requires a two-thirds vote in each House of Congress and ratification by three-fourths of the states, congressional regulation of appellate jurisdiction needs only a simple majority of both Houses.[37] Procedurally that is correct, but Congress has thus far refused to limit appellate jurisdiction on school prayer cases.

Over the next decade, Congress debated the merits of what became known as the "Helms Amendment": legislation to return state-sponsored voluntary prayer to the public schools by denying jurisdiction to the Supreme Court and lower federal courts.[38] On April 5, 1979, during action on a bill to establish a Department of Education, the Senate accepted his amendment to remove the jurisdiction of federal courts over "any Act interpreting, applying, or enforcing a State statute, ordinance, rule, or regulation, which relates to voluntary prayers in public schools and public buildings." The vote was 47 to 37. There was surprisingly little debate, but the dispute returned with full force several days later.[39]

On April 9, Senator Byrd offered to place the Helms amendment on a bill to eliminate the mandatory jurisdiction of the Supreme Court. Senator Kennedy, implying that the amendment had breezed through four days earlier because there had been inadequate notice, described the opposition to the Helms amendment by a number of religious groups, including the Baptist Joint Committee on Public Affairs, the Lutheran Council, United Presbyterian Church, Church of the Brethren, American Jewish Congress, United Church of Christ, Unitarian Universalist Association, and the United Methodist Church.[40] Helms responded with

35. Id. at 13591–93.
36. 120 Cong. Rec. 30720 (1974).
37. Id. at 30721.
38. 121 Cong. Rec. 870 (1975); 124 Cong. Rec. 4342 (1978).
39. 125 Cong. Rec. 7577–81 (1979).
40. Id. at 7632.

a list of 441 churches that supported his amendment.[41] On this go-round, the Byrd (Helms) amendment passed, 51 to 40, and the bill regarding mandatory jurisdiction also passed, 61 to 30.[42] However, because the House took no action on the bill, the Helms amendment died with it.

The Senate then took votes to reconsider the Helms amendment that had been added to the Education Department bill. Byrd explained that he had voted for the amendment on April 5 but opposed it now, in part because it would endanger passage of the education bill.[43] After much parliamentary maneuvering and a series of roll-call votes, Byrd offered a motion to table the Helms amendment, and his motion carried, 53 to 40.[44] Thirteen Senators who supported the Helms amendment on April 5 voted to table it on April 9.[45] Although the Senate had twice accepted the Helms amendment, the practical effect was nil.

Helms encountered resistance from the Reagan administration. In 1982, Attorney General William French Smith advised the Senate Judiciary Committee that Congress could not, consistent with the Constitution, make "exceptions" to Supreme Court jurisdiction that would "intrude upon the core functions" of the Supreme Court.[46] When Edwin Meese appeared before the committee in 1984 as Attorney General–designate, he was asked about jurisdiction-stripping bills covering such issues as school prayer, busing, and abortion. He agreed that it would be "improper for the Congress to attempt to diminish or take away the core functions of the Supreme Court." When pressed as to whether it was merely improper but also constitutionally impermissible, he said it would be both.[47] Moreover, if such legislation were passed, he would recommend a veto.[48]

In 1982, the Conference of Chief Justices of State Courts opposed jurisdiction-stripping initiatives because they would result in fifty distinct and unreviewable interpretations of federal constitutional protections.[49] The practical problems of withdrawing jurisdiction are substantial. If

41. Id. at 7640.
42. Id. at 7644, 7648.
43. Id. at 7649–50.
44. Id. at 7657.
45. 1979 CQ Almanac 396, 9-S, 10-S.
46. "Nomination of Edwin Meese III," hearings before the Senate Committee on the Judiciary, 98th Cong., 2d Sess. 184 (1984).
47. Id. at 185.
48. Id. at 186.
49. 128 Cong. Rec. 689 (1982).

Congress withdrew appellate jurisdiction from the federal courts, all questions of federal law (including constitutional disputes) would be decided
by the states. If Congress withdrew jurisdiction only from the Supreme
Court, constitutional questions would be left to the federal courts and
whatever conflicting decisions they produced. If Congress withdrew jurisdiction in selected areas, such as school prayer, "the tradition of stare deci-
sis could lead the lower federal and state courts to follow the Supreme
Court decisions [such as *Engel*] that originally prompted the congressional
contraction."[50] The result would be new rigidity in constitutional analysis.

In 1985, Helms argued that "religious liberty is too important to leave
exclusively in the hands of judicial elites more concerned about imposing
their own political views on the Nation than in objectively interpreting
the words of the Constitution."[51] Opponents of his amendment acknowledged that the Constitution gives Congress authority over appellate jurisdiction, but wondered how to place limits on that power. If Congress
stripped the Court of the power to hear cases regarding school prayer,
Senator Pat Moynihan (D-N.Y.) asked: "Do we next strip it of the power
to take issues concerning free speech? Do we strip it of the power to consider all first amendment rights, freedom of the press, religion, and assembly, and then move to the right of the search and seizure?"[52] On this
occasion, the Senate tabled the Helms amendment, 62 to 36.[53] In 1988,
the Senate tabled it by an even bigger margin, 71 to 20.[54]

Reagan Initiatives

The effort to undo the school prayer decision fell largely to the Moral
Majority, Christian Coalition, and other members of the so-called Religious Right. Outraged by the Court's school prayer and abortion decisions, these groups "came to feel that American society and American
culture were turning against them" and tried to gain power through the
Republican Party.[55] By coming "out of the pews into the polls," as Jerry

50. Ralph A. Rossum, "Congress, the Constitution, and the Appellate Jurisdiction of
the Supreme Court: The Letter and the Spirit of the Exceptions Clause," 24 Wm. &
Mary L. Rev. 385, 424 (1983).
51. 131 Cong. Rec. 23175 (1985).
52. Id. at 23172.
53. Id. at 23210.
54. 134 Cong. Rec. 19748 (1988).
55. Peter L. Berger, "Democracy and the Religious Right," Commentary, January
1997, at 55.

Falwell put it, Republicans worked hard at securing the vote of "these Christian people."[56] In the 1980 presidential campaign, Ronald Reagan advocated school prayer, creationism, and tax breaks for religious schools. Once elected, he took steps to repay his debt to the Religious Right. During his eight years in office, Reagan made extensive use of the arsenal of weapons available to a President in his support for school prayer, including bully pulpit speeches, court briefs and arguments, appointments, legislative proposals, and vetoes. None of these initiatives threatened *Engel.*

Although Reagan lost no time in stating that the Supreme Court had "ruled wrongly" on school prayer,[57] and announced in his 1983 State of the Union Message that "God should never have been expelled from America's classrooms,"[58] his administration never squarely confronted the Court on *Engel.* His first Attorney General, William French Smith, said it was "false" to believe that his department favored the return of school prayer. Instead, Justice lawyers merely argued "that a statute permitting a moment of silence in school did not offend the Constitution."[59] In 1983, a federal district judge directly challenged *Engel* by ruling in favor of the constitutionality of state-mandated spoken prayers in Alabama public schools. Solicitor General Charles Fried described the judge's order as "truly harebrained." When some Justice officials debated whether to enter the case in support of the judge's decision, Fried regarded the strategy "as a kamikaze mission in which only the pilot would get killed."[60] By the time Justice filed a brief with the Supreme Court in December 1983, Solicitor General Rex Lee simply asked the Justices to "take a fresh look" at school prayer, and only in the sense of permitting a moment of silence or voluntary prayer.[61]

Reagan's bark exceeded his bite. While his administration sought to expand opportunities for religious expression in the schools, Reagan never embraced state-mandated school prayers. In 1982, remarking that "God should [never] have been expelled from the classroom," he proposed this constitutional amendment: "Nothing in this Constitution shall

56. "Anatomy of a Landslide," Time, November 17, 1980, at 31.
57. Public Papers of the Presidents, 1981, at 958.
58. Public Papers of the Presidents, 1983, I, at 106–07.
59. William French Smith, Law & Justice in the Reagan Administration: Memoirs of an Attorney General 129–30 (1991).
60. Charles Fried, Order and Law 29–30 (1991).
61. Brief for the United States as Amicus Curiae, Wallace v. Jaffree, at 15–16; 155 Landmark Briefs 124–25.

be construed to prohibit individual or group prayer in public schools or other public institutions. No person shall be required by the United States or by any State to participate in prayer."[62] This language did not repudiate *Engel*. Over the years, Reagan sought to advance issues crucial to fiscal/social conservatives: the balanced budget amendment, the item veto, rights for the unborn, and voluntary prayer. But his campaign for a constitutional amendment on voluntary prayer failed in 1984.

The House had considered voluntary prayer before, voting 240 to 163 in 1971 for an amendment to permit voluntary prayer or meditation in public buildings. The vote fell 28 votes shy of the two-thirds needed. The Senate effort in 1984 produced a vote of 56 to 44, 11 votes short. While the Senate Judiciary Committee, by a vote of 14 to 3, concluded that the amendment was necessary to "provide a formal, structured opportunity during the school-day when each student can silently speak to his Creator,"[63] continued disagreements among religious interests led to the amendment's defeat. A joint letter of opposition to the amendment was submitted by a coalition of religious organizations, including American Baptist Churches in the USA, American Jewish Committee, American Jewish Congress, Seventh-Day Adventists, Lutheran Church in America, Presbyterian Church in the USA, United Church of Christ, United Methodist Church, and United Presbyterian Church in the USA.[64]

After the 1984 effort, only one other school prayer amendment reached the floor for a vote. In June 1998, at the urging of the Christian Coalition, the House of Representatives debated this language: "To secure the people's right to acknowledge God according to the dictates of conscience: The people's right to pray and to recognize their religious beliefs, heritage, or traditions on public property, including schools, shall not be infringed. The Government shall not require any person to join in prayer or other religious activity, initiate or designate school prayers, discriminate against religion, or deny equal access to a benefit on account of religion."[65] This language left *Engel* in place. The government was not to "initiate or designate school prayers." The amendment failed on a vote of 224 to 203, or 61 votes short.[66]

---

62. Public Papers of the Presidents, 1982, I, 603, 647–48.
63. S. Rept. No. 98–347, 98th Cong., 2d Sess. 38 (1984).
64. James E. Wood, Jr., "Equal Access: A New Direction in American Public Education," 27 J. Church & State 5, 8 (1985).
65. 144 Cong. Rec. H4078 (daily ed. June 4, 1998).
66. Id. at H4112.

Equal Access Act

Court-stripping bills and constitutional amendments represent only part of the congressional response to *Engel*. In a 1981 case, a state university allowed student secular groups to meet in university buildings but denied the same privilege to student religious groups. The university reasoned that giving permission to the latter would violate the Establishment Clause. The Supreme Court, voting 8–1, disagreed. State efforts to comply with the Establishment Clause do not permit discrimination against the religious speech of the student group seeking access to buildings for their meetings.[67]

This decision triggered congressional hearings in 1983, focusing on legislation that would require student religious groups to be afforded the same rights as other student groups to meet on school grounds. Groups testifying against the bill included the ACLU, the Unitarian Universalists Association of Churches in North America, the Anti-Defamation League of B'nai B'rith, the American Jewish Congress, and the Baptist Joint Committee on Public Affairs. Testifying in favor of the legislation: the National Council of the Church of Christ in the United States of America, and the Catholic League for Religious and Civil Rights.[68]

The bill picked up support after the defeat of a constitutional amendment (S. J. Res. 73) designed to permit organized, recited prayer in the public schools. Like other amendments, this one did not try to overturn *Engel*: "Nothing in this Constitution shall be construed to prohibit individual or group prayer in public schools or other public institutions. No person shall be required by the United States or any state to participate in prayer. Neither the United States nor any state shall compose the words of any prayer to be said in public schools."[69] With defeat of this amendment, the bill for equal access emerged as the next-best option. The bill passed with strong support in the Senate (88 to 11) and attracted a substantial majority in the House (337 to 77).[70]

The Equal Access Act states that it shall be unlawful for any public

67. Widmar v. Vincent, 454 U.S. 263 (1981).

68. "Equal Access: A First Amendment Question," hearings before the Senate Committee on the Judiciary, 98th Cong., 1st Sess. (1983). Testimony by religious groups also appears in "Hearings on the Equal Access Act," hearings before the House Committee on Education and Labor, 98th Cong., 1st Sess. (1983).

69. 1984 CQ Almanac 246.

70. 130 Cong. Rec. 19252, 20951 (1984).

secondary school that receives federal funds "to deny equal access or a fair opportunity to, or discriminate against, any students who wish to conduct a meeting within that limited open forum on the basis of religious, political, philosophical, or other content of the speech at such meetings. The statute defines "limited open forum" to cover situations where a school grants an opportunity for one or more "noncurriculum related" student groups to meet on school premises during noninstructional time. These meetings must be voluntary and student-initiated, without sponsorship by the school, the government, or its agents or employees. The legislation is not to be construed to authorize the United States or any state to influence the form or content of any prayer or other religious activity.[71]

Congress usually provides guidelines in committee reports and other documents to indicate how it wants a statute implemented. In the case of the Equal Access Act, this legislative history was absent because the final version of the legislation was added as an amendment to the Emergency Math/Science Education Act.[72] The church groups that participated in the drafting of the Equal Access Act were worried that school officials, acting out of fear and ignorance, would conclude that "any religious activity, however voluntary or student initiated, could be challenged in the courts, necessitating payment of costly legal fees."[73] To minimize that bureaucratic behavior, church groups joined with school administrators, the ACLU, and the National Educational Association in drafting guidelines for principals and teachers. These guidelines were placed in the *Congressional Record*.[74] In 1990, the Supreme Court upheld the Equal Access Act against challenges that it violated the Establishment Clause. Eight Justices agreed that, in this case, a public high school had allowed such clubs as Subsurfers and a chess group to meet after school and should not have prohibited a Christian club from meeting.[75] Some religious groups, including the American Jewish Committee and the Council on Religious Freedom, filed briefs arguing that the statute violated the Establishment Clause. Reaching the same conclusion was a brief submitted by the Anti-Defamation League of B'nai

71. 98 Stat. 1302–4 (1984).

72. 130 Cong. Rec. 32315 (1984) (statement by Rep. Bonker).

73. Hertzke, Representing God in Washington, at 163.

74. 130 Cong. Rec. 32066–6, 32315–18 (1984). See Hertzke, Representing God in Washington, at 172–75.

75. Westside Community Bd. of Ed. v. Mergens, 496 U.S. 226 (1990).

B'rith, the ACLU, the National Coalition for Public Education and Religious Liberty, and other groups. Briefs supporting the use of public schools for religious clubs were prepared by the Knights of Columbus and the U.S. Catholic Conference.[76]

The Court had held earlier that high school students may form religious groups and meet in schoolrooms.[77] In 1993, the Court ruled that if states permit school property to be used after hours for social, civic, and recreational purposes, they may not discriminate on the basis of religious viewpoint.[78] The Christian Legal Society, the U.S. Catholic Conference, the Baptist Joint Committee on Public Affairs, and several other church groups supported the school's film series with religious content.[79] The National Jewish Commission on Law and Public Affairs (COLPA) also argued that an organization may not be denied access to school property merely because it intends to engage in religious expression.[80]

Building on these cases, the Court in 1995 held that the University of Virginia denied students their right of free speech when it helped finance the printing of student publications but withheld payment from "Wide Awake," a Christian newspaper. The university argued that funding the newspaper would have violated the Establishment Clause, but a 5–4 majority ruled that no violation exists when a university subsidizes publications on a religion-neutral basis. The Court found it significant that the financial assistance came from student fees rather than from a tax levied by the state, but admitted that the payment of student fees is also mandatory.[81]

The most recent extension of this principle of neutrality came in 2001, when the Court ruled that public schools must open their doors to after-school religious activities. The 6–3 decision applied to elementary schools the same principle that had been applied to public high schools and universities.[82] A large number of briefs submitted by religious groups supported this broader access. These organizations include COLPA, twenty theologians and scholars of religion, the Christian Legal Society, the Union of Orthodox Jewish Congregations of America, the National

76. 195 Landmark Briefs 420, 457, 496, 551.
77. Bender v. Williamsport Area School Dist., 475 U.S. 534 (1986).
78. Lamb's Chapel v. Center Moriches School Dist., 508 U.S. 384 (1993).
79. 217 Landmark Briefs 291.
80. Id. at 365.
81. Rosenberger v. University of Virginia, 515 U.S. 819 (1995).
82. Good News Club v. Milford Central School, 121 S.Ct. 2093 (2001).

Council of Churches, the Baptist Joint Committee on Public Affairs, and the General Conference of Seventh-Day Adventists. Briefs opposed to after-school religious meetings were filed by the Anti-Defamation League, Hadassah, National Coalition for Public Education and Religious Liberty, the National Council of Jewish Women, the American Jewish Congress, Americans United for Separation of Church and State, and the American Jewish Committee.

Local Noncompliance

Congressional actions are only part of the story on school prayer. Much depends on the extent of local community compliance with the 1962 decision. Several studies at the end of the 1960s revealed that the Court's ruling had reduced the amount of school-sponsored prayer in public schools but had not eliminated it. Outright defiance was commonplace. In small towns in Pennsylvania, teachers still led their classes in a recitation of the Lord's Prayer. A study in 1966 indicated that nearly 13 percent of the nation's public schools and almost 50 percent of the South's continued to have devotional readings.[83] An article in 1984 indicated that students in some public schools were still beginning each day with a prayer.[84]

School superintendents and teachers could safely ignore the Court's decision in many areas because local prosecutors, raised nearby, were unlikely to use their resources to force compliance with an unpopular decision. School authorities could assume that *Engel* only outlawed state-prescribed prayers and left intact the teacher's discretion to lead the class in prayer. Also, local leaders usually like to avoid conflict.[85] If no one complains about prayer in the classroom, nothing is likely to happen. Classroom practices can be expected to continue unchanged unless public officials provide guidance for change. In many communities, state and local officials decided not to issue any opinion, instruction, or memorandum on procedures for implementing *Engel*.[86]

83. Ben E. Franklin, "Pennsylvanians Lead School Prayer Revolt," New York Times, March 26, 1969, at 1.

84. "Prayer in Many Schoolrooms Continues Despite '62 Ruling," New York Times, March 11, 1984, at 1.

85. Kenneth M. Dolbeare & Phillip E. Hammond, The School Prayer Decisions: From Court Policy to Local Practice 7 (1971).

86. Id. at 51.

Moment of Silence

Some state lawmakers looked for alternative religious exercises in public schools to blunt the force of *Engel*. By the 1980s, more than twenty states had enacted "moment of silence" statutes.[87] A number of states filed amicus briefs defending these and other laws. For example, in a 1985 case, attorneys general from Arizona, Delaware, Indiana, Louisiana, Oklahoma, and Virginia filed an amicus brief in support of moment of silence laws.[88] In 1985, the Supreme Court decided 6–3 that Alabama's one-minute period of silence in all public schools "for meditation or voluntary prayer" violated the Constitution because the purpose of the statute was to advance religion.[89] Although the statute appeared on its surface to have a secular purpose, the legislative history made it clear that the intent was to promote prayer.

The lesson that states drew from the Court's opinion was that if they wanted a successful "moment of silence" law, they should keep quiet about religious objectives during legislative debate and the implementation phase. After Virginia enacted a minute of silence statute, to take effect in the fall of 2000, the state's Education Department advised school districts to avoid telling students that they have the option to pray. The guidelines issued by the state Superintendent of Public Instruction merely recommended that a teacher or principal announce: "As we begin another day, let us pause for a moment of silence."[90] After some legislators criticized the tepidness of this recommendation, the state Attorney General said that teachers should feel free to mention prayer.[91]

The Fourth Circuit, covering Virginia, Maryland, West Virginia, South Carolina, and North Carolina, upheld the Virginia statute. Writing for a 2 to 1 majority, Judge Paul Niemeyer ruled that Virginia "has introduced at most a minor and nonintrusive accommodation of religion." Just as this "short period of quiet serves the religious interests of those

87. Note, "The Unconstitutionality of State Statutes Authorizing Moments of Silence in the Public Schools," 96 Harv. L. Rev. 1874, 1874 n.1 (1983). See also David Z. Seide, "Daily Moments of Silence in Public Schools: A Constitutional Analysis," 58 N.Y.U. L. Rev. 364 (1983).
88. Brief of the States' Attorneys General as Amici Curiae, Wallace v. Jaffree; 155 Landmark Briefs 559.
89. Wallace v. Jaffree, 472 U.S. 38 (1985).
90. "Don't Raise Prayer Issue, Schools Told," Washington Post, June 14, 2000, at A1.
91. "Schools Get New Advice on Prayer," Washington Post, June 17, 2000, at B1.

students who wish to pray silently, it serves the secular interests of those who do not wish to do so."[92] On October 29, 2001, the Supreme Court decided not to review the Fourth Circuit ruling.[93]

Clinton's 1995 Memo

Much has changed since the *Engel* decision in 1962. Because of the Equal Access Act and other legislative initiatives, there are many opportunities for students to pray and study religion in public schools. In 1995, at a high school in Virginia, President Clinton recounted his years in junior high school, when school prayer and Bible reading were "as common as apple pie in my hometown." Yet he later came to recognize that Jews in the classroom "were probably deeply offended by half the stuff we were saying or doing or maybe made to feel inferior." He also wondered whether Catholic students were always comfortable with these religious activities. Because of the diversity of religions within a classroom, he agreed with the decision in *Engel* to prohibit government-prescribed prayers.[94]

However, he also told the students that religion need not be kept out of schools. If a student is told he cannot wear a yarmulke, the government has an obligation to advise the school that the child has that right. If a student is told she cannot bring a Bible to school, "we have to tell the school, no, the law guarantees her the right to bring the Bible to school." Similarly, students can read the Bible silently in study hall and publicize their religious groups in the same manner as nonreligious groups.[95] Students can pray privately and individually, can say grace before lunch, and at times pray out loud together. Nothing prohibits teachers from discussing religion and its contributions to history. Clinton said that if students "can wear T-shirts advertising sports teams, rock groups, or politicians, they can also wear T-shirts that promote religion."[96]

On the same day, Clinton issued a memorandum to his Secretary of Education and Attorney General, setting forth general principles for reli-

---

92. Brown v. Gilmour, 258 F.3d 265, 278, 281 (4th Cir. 2001).
93. 70 LW 3315 (2001); see "Va. Minute of Silence Survives Test in High Court," *Washington Post*, October 30, 2001, at B1.
94. Public Papers of the Presidents, 1995, II, at 1078.
95. Id. at 1080.
96. Id. at 1081.

gious expression in public schools. In part, the memo was designed to take some of the steam out of a proposed school prayer amendment. In this memo, Clinton said that nothing in the First Amendment "converts our public schools into religion-free zones, or requires all religious expression to be left behind at the schoolhouse door." Students have the right to engage in individual or group prayer and religious discussion during the school day. They may "read their Bibles or other scriptures, say grace before meals, and pray before tests to the same extent that they may engage in comparable non-disruptive activities." In informal settings, such as cafeterias and hallways, students may pray and discuss their religious views. They may attempt to persuade their peers about religious topics. They may participate in events, before and after school, with religious content. School officials may neither discourage nor encourage these activities. Although public schools may not provide religious instruction, "they may talk *about* religion, including the Bible or other scripture," and take into account religious influences on art, music, literature, and social studies.[97]

Studies indicate that students in public schools are active in prayer clubs and other religious activities. When classes are over at a high school, student members of a Christian club may meet in the home economics room. During the next ninety minutes, they bow their heads in prayer, listen to a youth minister stress the importance of knowing Jesus, and are reminded to read their Bibles every morning. There are approximately ten thousand Christian clubs active in secondary schools. Each morning they gather outside for a pre-class prayer. Muslim students may say their midday prayers in the library or empty classrooms. Jewish clubs conduct activities in public schools. Students often initiate prayers at school events. These activities are permissible provided that they are student-run and voluntary.[98]

Conservative Christians have learned to drop their demands for official school prayer. They recognize that America has too many religious persuasions to accept centralized control by a single doctrine. Ralph Reed, spokesman for Christian Coalition, told a Jewish audience in 1995 that his organization supported a nation "where no child of any faith is forced by government to recite a prayer with which they disagree."[99]

97. Id. at 1083–85 (emphasis in original).
98. "At Public Schools, Religion Thrives," Washington Post, May 7, 1998, at A1.
99. Kenneth D. Wald, Religion and Politics in the United States 237 (1997); also available at http://cc.org April 3, 1995.

Continued Challenges

Nothing the Supreme Court decides and nothing that Congress passes ever "settles" an issue that deeply divides the nation. Secretary of State George Shultz identified a central principle of government in 1987 when he testified on the Iran-Contra affair. A staff attorney asked whether he thought there had been a change in a particular policy he had established. He replied: "It wasn't that nothing had changed, but as you well know, or perhaps you don't—you are not a Washingtonian—nothing ever gets settled in this town. You have to keep fighting, every inch of the way."[100] In one form or another, the prayer issue will reemerge and make its presence felt, prompting new judicial rulings, legislative activity, and changes in community practice.

The constitutionality of graduation prayers split the Court 5–4 in 1992. The case involved the practice in Rhode Island middle and high schools of inviting members of the clergy to give invocations and benedictions at school graduate ceremonies. School officials advised speakers that the addresses should be nonsectarian. Ironically, because of that guidance, the Court concluded that state officials were directing the performance of a formal religious exercise, resulting in state-sponsored and state-directed activity. The school principal selected the religious participant and provided guidelines on the content of the prayer. Such activities were proscribed by *Engel* and earlier decisions. The fact that the graduation exercises were "voluntary" did not permit school officials to use indirect coercion against students and parents who wanted to attend a very significant event but objected to religious exercises. The Court distinguished between the school prayers at issue in this case (involving young people subject to indoctrination and peer pressure) and the use of chaplains earlier allowed in adult institutions such as the Nebraska legislature and the U.S. Congress.[101]

States continue to use other methods to bring prayers into graduation exercises. A Texas school district permitted public high school seniors to choose student volunteers to deliver nonsectarian, nonproselytizing invocations at their graduation ceremonies. Unlike the Rhode Island case,

---

100. "Iran-Contra Investigation" (Vol. 100–9), joint hearings before the Senate Select Committee on Secret Military Assistance to Iran and the Nicaraguan Opposition and the House Select Committee to Investigate Covert Arms Transactions with Iran, 100th Cong., 1st Sess. 48 (1987).

101. Lee v. Weisman, 505 U.S. 577 (1992).

outside clergy were not invited, nor did school officials become involved in directing or monitoring the content of these prayers. The Fifth Circuit upheld the Texas practice in 1992; a year later the Supreme Court let this decision stand without comment.[102]

The issue of school prayer returned to the Court in 2000 when it ruled, 6 to 3, that prayers led by students at high school football games are unconstitutional when they are officially sanctioned. Rejecting arguments that the prayers were voluntary and private, the Court regarded the prayers as "authorized by a government policy and take place on government property at government-sponsored school-related events."[103] During the course of the litigation, the school tried to remove some of its fingerprints from the system of prayer, but its presence remained obvious to the Court. Although school authorities cannot organize student-led prayers to be given over a public address system, nothing can stop students from standing up to give prayers at the start of a football game, or other sporting event, if the prayers seem spontaneous and undirected by school officials.

Alabama has been the most persistent state in advocating school prayer. In 1978, the state legislature passed a statute authorizing a one-minute period of silence in public elementary schools, the time to be set aside "for meditation." In 1981, when Governor Fob James began his first term, the legislature passed another statute authorizing a one-minute period of silence in public schools "for meditation or voluntary prayer." A third statute the following year authorized teachers to lead "willing students" in a prayer composed by the teacher or one specified by law. The Supreme Court struck down the last two statutes in 1984 and 1985 on the ground that their purpose was to advance religion.[104]

Alabama responded with another statute in 1993, this time authorizing public school prayers that were nonsectarian, nonproselytizing, student-initiated, and voluntary. In 1997, a federal district court held the statute to be unconstitutional. First, it held that the statute unconstitutionally restricted the private speech and religious freedom rights of students by limiting them to the prescribed prayer. It also held that the statute was (1) not enacted for a secular purpose and thus violated the Establishment Clause (2) had the primary effect of endorsing religion, and (3) created

---

102. Jones v. Clear Creek Independent School Dist., 977 F.2d 963 (5th Cir. 1992), cert. denied, 508 U.S. 967 (1993).

103. Santa Fe Independent School Dist. v. Doe, 120 S.Ct. 2266 (2000).

104. Wallace v. Jaffree, 466 U.S. 924 (1984); Wallace v. Jaffree, 472 U.S. 38 (1985).

excessive entanglement between religion and the state.[105] The court pointed out that schoolchildren, who are particularly susceptible to peer pressure, have few options when prayer is introduced at school. If they find the prayer offensive, they cannot express their dissent by "walking away" or verbally objecting.[106] Even when the prayer is "student-initiated" and "voluntary," the use of school facilities sends a message that the state is associated with the speaker's religion and endorses it.[107] Although the court struck down this statute, it emphasized the many forms of student religious expression that are permitted in public schools:

(1) individual or group prayer or religious discussion outside of organized classes or school-sponsored events;

(2) reports, homework and artwork which reflect students' religious beliefs;

(3) distribution of religious literature (provided that the school generally permits students to distribute other literature not related to the school curriculum and that the religious literature is distributed in accordance with all applicable time, place and manner restrictions);

(4) display of religious symbols, articles and medals (e.g., Crosses, Stars of David, St. Christopher and other religious medals, even replicas of the Ten Commandments) and/or clothing bearing religious messages (provided that the school allows students to display non-religious expressive symbols and apparel and such display is in accordance with all applicable time, place and manner restrictions); and

(5) religious activity permitted by the Equal Access Act. Additionally, students may pray silently at any time so long as it does not interfere with their school work.[108]

This decision created a bit of a judicial slugfest. On June 23, 1997, Governor James sent the district judge a thirty-four-page letter stating that the religion clauses of the First Amendment do not apply to the states, and that the case should be dismissed "for lack of a federal question." On October 29, the judge responded with a permanent injunction that barred state and school officials from enforcing the statute. The injunction, spelling out in detail what the state could and could not do, directed the

105. Chandler v. James, 958 F.Supp. 1550 (M.D. Ala. 1997).
106. Id. at 1556.
107. Id. at 1557.
108. Id. at 1562.

state to conduct a mandatory in-service training session for school officials to familiarize them with the provisions of the injunction.[109] The judge followed with an opinion of November 12, holding that prayer conducted over the school public address system violated the First Amendment—regardless of whether it was student-initiated—and that the practice of asking students to volunteer to lead prayer was also unconstitutional.[110] A separate opinion issued the same day ruled that student-led prayers at high school football games violated the First Amendment.[111]

On May 1, 1998, Governor James filed a petition to the Supreme Court, asking for a writ of mandamus. He wanted the Court to direct the district court to dismiss the case for lack of federal subject matter jurisdiction and to vacate the injunction. On June 22, the Court rejected his petition.[112]

The following year, the Eleventh Circuit rejected the Governor's contention that the First Amendment's prohibition against the establishment of a religion does not apply to the states by virtue of the Fourteenth Amendment. The district court had dismissed that argument, and so now did the Eleventh Circuit. Except for the Governor, other state officials did not contest the district court's holding that the statute was facially unconstitutional, and that the school had engaged in unconstitutional, officially organized or sponsored religious activities. Therefore, the Eleventh Circuit did not review the district court's determinations of those issues. Alabama school officials now conceded that they may not prescribe prayer or allow state employees to lead, participate in, or otherwise endorse prayer of any type during curricular or extracurricular events.[113]

The Eleventh Circuit also decided that the permanent injunction issued by the district court was too broad because it appeared to prohibit all student-initiated prayer, even when unrelated to school efforts to promote prayer. Such a restriction would interfere with the private religious speech available to all students. The plaintiffs bringing the case against Alabama agreed that the Establishment Clause bans *state* prayer, not prayer.[114] The Eleventh Circuit directed the district court to rewrite the permanent injunction to permit genuinely student-initiated religious speech, subject to the time, place, and manner restrictions that would be

109. Chandler v. James, 985 F.Supp. 1062 (M.D. Ala. 1997).
110. Chandler v. James, 985 F.Supp. 1068 (M.D. Ala. 1997).
111. Chandler v. James, 985 F.Supp. 1094 (M.D. Ala. 1997).
112. In re James, 525 U.S. 936 (1998).
113. Chandler v. James, 180 F.3d 1254,1257 (11th Cir. 1999).
114. Id. at 1258.

appropriate for secular speech by students.[115] Thus, students can proselytize in the lunchroom or during breaks, but not in the middle of a class.

When this case came before the Supreme Court, it remanded it to the Eleventh Circuit for further consideration in light of the decision regarding prayers at Texas football games, *Santa Fe Independent School District* v. *Doe*.[116] On October 19, 2000, the Eleventh Circuit held that its decision was not in conflict with *Santa Fe*. It therefore reinstated its opinion by holding that the district court's injunction had been overbroad and that the school district may not prohibit genuinely student-initiated religious speech, nor apply restrictions on the time, place, and manner of that speech that would exceed those placed on students' secular speech.[117] Whereas *Sante Fe* had condemned school *sponsorship*, the Eleventh Circuit had condemned school censorship of student prayer. The two cases were thus "complementary rather than inconsistent."[118] On June 18, 2001, the Supreme Court refused to review the Eleventh Circuit's decision.[119]

Is this the "final word"? Probably not. While this litigation was proceeding, the Alabama legislature on April 27, 1998, adopted a statute requiring teachers to conduct, at the beginning of each school day, "a brief period of quiet reflection for not more than 60 seconds with the participation of every pupil in the classroom." On August 11, 1999, the Alabama Attorney General and the general counsel of the state department of education issued guidelines, based on the Eleventh Circuit's rulings, regarding religious activities that are allowable in public schools. With a governor less confrontational to the federal courts, Alabama might have worked out an acceptable accommodation. This is all part of the broad public debate that occurs on constitutional disputes.

After the terrorist attacks of September 11, 2001, some communities promoted prayer before football games, making use of the schools' loudspeakers. The prayers included references "in the name of Jesus." Most of these challenges to judicial rulings on prayer have been limited and located primarily in the South.[120]

---

115. Id. at 1265–66.
116. Chandler v. Siegelman, 120 S.Ct. 2714 (2000).
117. Chandler v. Siegelman, 230 F.3d 1313 (11th Cir. 2000).
118. Id. at 1315.
119. Chandler v. Siegelman, 121 S.Ct. 2521 (2001).
120. "After a Surge, Limits Return to School Prayer," New York Times, October 23, 2001, at A16.

7

INDIAN RELIGIOUS FREEDOM

For most of U.S. history, little was done at the national or state level to protect the religious practices of Indians. Initially they were to be "civilized," assimilated, and acculturated into American society. Later stages led to exclusion of most Indians from the East Coast, the creation of additional reservations, and termination of federal responsibility for some tribes. There were few efforts by governmental institutions or private societies to safeguard and preserve the unique religious beliefs of Indian tribes. To the extent that religion played a part, it was to provide funds and assistance to convert Indians to Christianity. Only in recent decades has the national government taken steps to secure the religious heritage of Indians, and that initiative has come largely from the political branches, not the courts. An expansion of Indian religious rights depends primarily on statutes, presidential leadership, agency regulations, and the political process.

Propagating the Gospel

By the time of the American Revolution, religious missions to the Indians had been operating in America for more than a century.[1] The first Virginia charter of 1606 directed colonists to be active in "propagating of *Christian* Religion to such People . . . and may in time bring the Infidels and Savages, living in those parts, to human Civility."[2] The Charter of Massachusetts Bay in 1629 expressed the intention that the natives learn of "the Knowledg and Obedience of the onlie true God and Sauior of Mankinde, and the Christian Fayth."[3]

1. R. Pierce Beaver, Introduction to Native American Church History (1983); R. Pierce Beaver, "Church, State, and the Indians: Indian Missions to the New Nation," 4 J. Church & State 11 (1962).
2. 7 Thorpe 3784 (emphasis in original).
3. 3 Thorpe 1857.

On February 5, 1776, the Continental Congress resolved that "a friendly commerce between the people of the United Colonies and the Indians, and the propagation of the gospel . . . may produce many and inestimable advantages to both." Congress directed the commissioners of Indian affairs to select individuals who would live among the Indians "and instruct them in the Christian religion."[4] Other entries in the journals of the Continental Congress refer to efforts by Christian missionaries to spread their faith among the Indians. A resolution of December 3, 1784, noted the satisfaction of Congress "with the readiness expressed by the Indians to receive a Missionary among them and being desirous to embrace every opportunity of diffusing the benign precepts of Christianity among those nations."[5] In 1785, a special committee received a petition requesting the assistance of Congress to instruct Indians "in reading, writing and the principles of the Christian religion."[6] The committee endorsed that policy.[7] In 1787 and 1788, the Continental Congress set aside land for the Moravian Brethren or the Society of the United Brethren, for the purpose of "civilizing the Indians and promoting Christianity."[8]

Those values carried over to the administration of George Washington. His Secretary of War, Henry Knox, proposed on July 7, 1789, that missionaries "of excellent moral character" be appointed to live among the Indians. Their duties ranged far beyond religious instruction. They would supply the implements of husbandry, the necessary stock for a farm, and serve as "their friends and fathers."[9] A 1790 treaty signed with the Creeks prepared them to become "herdsmen and cultivators, instead of remaining in a state of hunters," and toward that end the United States would contribute domestic animals and tools of agriculture.[10]

In 1796, Congress passed legislation that set aside three tracts of land for the Society of United Brethren "for propagating the gospel among the heathen."[11] The legislative debate merely describes the bill as introduced, referred to committee, and acted upon on the floor, without offering greater details on the policy of spreading Christianity among the

4. 4 Journals of the Continental Congress 111 (1906) (hereafter "Journals").
5. 27 Journals 660 (1928).
6. 28 Journals 374 (1933).
7. Id. at 399–400.
8. 28 Journals 429–430 (1936); 34 Journals 485–87 (1937).
9. 1 American State Papers: Indian Affairs 54 (1834).
10. Id. at 82.
11. 1 Stat. 491, § 5 (1796).

Indians.[12] However, debate on another bill in 1796, concerning trade with the Indians, reveals an understanding among some legislators about the natural rights of Indians and the obligation of Congress to secure those rights.[13] Upon hearing a colleague remark that Indians had no right to their land, Theodore Sedgwick of Massachusetts said he "believed that wherever the natives of a country had possession, there they had a right, and not because they did not dress like us, were not equally religious, or did not understand the arts of civilized life, they were to be deprived of their possessions, but that their rights or their possessions were as sacred as the rights of civilized life. . . . Indians will never submit to be told they have no rights."[14]

In 1803, William Henry Harrison, as governor of the Indiana Territory, signed a treaty at Vincennes recognizing that the Kaskaskia tribe had been baptized and received into the Catholic Church. The treaty promised that the United States would provide $100 for the next seven years to support a Catholic priest. Another sum of $300 would help the tribe erect a church.[15]

The national government encouraged Indians to make a transition from a nomadic, hunter state to a settled agricultural existence. A message by President Thomas Jefferson to Congress on January 18, 1803, spoke of various measures needed for Indian tribes. The first: "To encourage them to abandon hunting, to apply to the raising of stock, to agriculture, and domestic manufacture, and thereby prove to themselves that less land and labor will maintain them in this better than in their former mode of living."[16] Jefferson found much among the Indians to admire, describing them as brave, moral, responsible, caring of family and friends, and "in body and mind equal to the white man."[17] He gave serious and respectful study to their culture, character, and language, anticipating that Indians "will mix with us by marriage. Your blood will run in our veins, and will spread with us over this great land."[18] Yet it was Jefferson's initiative with the Louisiana Purchase, opening up a vast territory to the west,

12. 5 Annals of Cong. 96, 108, 111–12, 113, 116, 297, 1349 (1796).
13. Id. at 897–98 (Representatives Cooper and Hillhouse).
14. Id. at 901.
15. 1 American State Papers: Indian Affairs 687 (1834).
16. 1 Richardson 340.
17. Anthony F. C. Wallace, Jefferson and the Indians: The Tragic Fate of the First Americans 77 (1999).
18. Id. at 317.

that set the stage for the forced removal policy of the 1830s and 1840s.[19] The theme of Indians tilling soil reappears in other presidential messages. In his first annual message to Congress on December 2, 1817, President James Monroe spoke about the "duty to make new efforts for the preservation, improvement, and civilization of the native inhabitants." The hunter state, capable of existing only "in the vast uncultivated desert," would necessarily yield to denser populations. The earth was given to mankind "to support the greatest number of which it is capable, and no tribe or people have a right to withhold from the wants of others more than is necessary for their own support and comfort." He was pleased that reservations of land to the tribes on Lake Erie had been made "with a view to individual ownership among them and to the cultivation of the soil by all."[20]

Monroe elaborated on that philosophy a year later in an address to Congress. Experience had demonstrated that "independent savage communities can no longer exist within the limits of a civilized population," and that the progress of the latter "almost invariably terminated in the extinction of the former." To civilize the Indian tribes and prevent their extinction, "it seems to be indispensable that their independence as communities should cease, and that the control of the United States over them should be complete and undisputed." With cultivation of land substituting for the hunter state, the Indian communities would be replaced by "a new character to every individual."[21]

In 1819, Congress enacted legislation "for the purpose of providing against the further decline and final extinction of the Indian tribes." In an effort to introduce among the tribes "the habits and arts of civilization," the statute authorized the President to employ individuals to instruct Indians "in the mode of agriculture suited to their situation," and to teach their children in reading, writing, and arithmetic.[22] Congress pledged $10,000 annually for this purpose. There was little legislative debate on what has come to be known as the "civilization fund."[23] Although the statute and the legislative history make no mention of instructing Indians in the tenets of Christianity, that became a key objective. Monroe and his

---

19. Id. at 257, 273–75.
20. 2 Richardson 585.
21. Id. at 615.
22. 3 Stat. 516 (1819).
23. Annals of Cong., 15th Cong., 2d Sess. 546, 1426, 1427, 1431, 1435 (1819).

Secretary of War, John C. Calhoun, used the money to support the effort of missionaries and religious societies brought in to establish schools for Indian children.[24]

President John Quincy Adams told Congress in 1828 that "it was our policy and our duty to use our influence in converting to Christianity and in bringing within the pale of civilization." The national government tried to "bring them to the knowledge of religion and of letters." By appropriating their hunting grounds, government had an obligation to teach them "the arts of civilization and the doctrines of Christianity."[25] Thomas L. McKenney, who served as superintendent of Indian trade and head of the Office of Indian Affairs, helped implement this policy from 1812 to 1830. Of Quaker background, he believed in the equality of the races and cited the Bible for support. It was his responsibility to manage missionary efforts for the Indians.[26] The civilization fund lasted until 1873.

Religious missions demonstrated little interest or respect for Indian religious beliefs. Their attack on Indian religions "and their relegating of all his beliefs and ritual practices to the realm of superstition deprived the missionaries of use of the Indian spiritual values and ideas as bridges to the gospel and to acceptance of the Christian faith in terms meaningful to Indians."[27] Although some missionaries understood this potential link, it would not be until the 1930s that steps began to be taken to safeguard Indian religious beliefs and practices.

Indian Removal

Indians on the East Coast gradually lost their lands. The Treaty of Hopewell in 1785 guaranteed the Cherokees their tribal lands, but persistent encroachments by white settlers led to new agreements from 1791 to 1806, each time compensating the Cherokees for land that they

24. Margaret Connell Szasz and Carmelita Ryan, "American Indian Education," in 4 Handbook of North American Indians 284–300 (William C. Sturtevant ed. 1988).
25. 3 Richardson 981–82.
26. Francis Paul Prucha, The Great Father 141–42, 148–51 (1995).
27. R. Pierce Beaver, "Protestant Churches and the Indians," in 4 Handbook of North American Indians 439 (Sturtevant ed. 1988). See also Robert F. Berkhofer, Jr., Salvation and the Savage: An Analysis of Protestant Missions and American Indian Response, 1787–1862 (1965).

had ceded to Georgia, Tennessee, and Kentucky. In 1816, the Cherokees ceded all their lands in South Carolina.[28] Beginning in 1816, the governor of Tennessee recommended that the Cherokees be relocated west of the Mississippi; those that remained would be given 640 to 1,000 acres to develop.[29]

In 1821, the Creeks in Georgia agreed to cede some land, and pressure was applied to the Cherokees to do the same. Other states and territories asked that Indians be removed from their lands.[30] A Monroe message to Congress in 1824 expressed the hope that "by the establishment of these tribes beyond the Mississippi, their improvement in civilization, their security, and happiness, would be promoted."[31] By 1825, it appeared that whether Indians "liked it or not, or whether they had become civilized or not," they were to be moved.[32] Monroe told the Senate in 1825 that the basis for the removal of the tribes within Georgia seemed "peculiarly strong."[33]

Georgia precipitated a legal crisis by withdrawing rights from Cherokees and seizing their land. The Cherokees and church groups appealed to Congress to reverse Georgia, but no such remedial legislation emerged.[34] The American Board of Commissioners for Foreign Nations, which had sponsored missions to the Cherokees and the Choctaws, prepared a legal suit for the Cherokee Nation.[35] While this case was being heard, President Jackson persuaded Congress to pass the Removal Act of 1830, which called for Indians to be moved west of the Mississippi River.[36] After Georgia and its judiciary put two American Board missionaries in prison, the Board took the case to the U.S. Supreme Court. William Wirt, who had served Presidents Monroe and Adams as Attorney General, argued the case for the Cherokees.

In 1831, the Court acknowledged that the Cherokee Nation was a state with which the United States had dealt successively by treaty. However, it

28. Donald Grinde, "Cherokee Removal and American Politics," 8 Indian Historian 33, 33–34 (1975).

29. Reginald Horsman, The Origins of Indian Removal, 1815–1824, at 6 (1970).

30. Id. at 12–15.

31. Annals of Cong., 18th Cong., 1st Sess. 462–63 (1824).

32. Horsman, The Origins of Indian Removal, at 17.

33. 2 American State Papers: Indian Affairs 541 (1834).

34. Joseph C. Burke, "The Cherokee Cases: A Study in Law, Politics, and Morality," 21 Stan. L. Rev. 500, 505–6 (1969).

35. Beaver, Introduction to Native American Church History, at 69.

36. 4 Stat. 411 (1830).

ruled that the Cherokees were not a "foreign state" and were not entitled to present the case as one of original jurisdiction. Whatever rights the Indians possessed regarding their lands, they were not legally positioned to ask the Court to prevent Georgia from exercising its legislative power.[37]

The dispute returned a year later, with the plaintiff this time being Samuel A. Worcester, one of the missionaries imprisoned by Georgia. In 1830, Georgia had passed legislation prohibiting white persons without a state license from residing in lands occupied by the Cherokees. Worcester, one of seven whites who defied the statute, was imprisoned along with Elizur Butler for four years at hard labor. He argued that he entered the Cherokee Nation in the capacity of a missionary authorized by the American Board and the U.S. President, and that his prosecution by Georgia violated several U.S.-Cherokee treaties. Those treaty rights, he said, could not be interfered with by any state.

Speaking for the Court, Chief Justice John Marshall first determined that congressional statutes gave the Court jurisdiction to hear and decide the case. Furthermore, he said that the Indian nations "had always been considered as distinct, independent political communities, retaining their original natural rights, and the undisputed possessors of the soil, from time immemorial."[38] The single exception to that status was their exclusion from intercourse with other nations. The laws of Georgia could therefore have no force on the Cherokee Nation unless with the consent of the Cherokees and in conformity with treaties and congressional statutes. The law of Georgia under which Worcester was prosecuted "is consequently void, and the judgment a nullity." The acts of Georgia "are repugnant to the constitution, laws, and treaties of the United States."[39]

Marshall was well aware that political institutions might not comply with his ruling. The Georgia legislature had passed a resolution warning that any attempt by the U.S. Supreme Court to reverse the Georgia Superior Court "will be held by this State as an unconstitutional and arbitrary interference in the administration of her criminal laws and will be treated as such."[40] After Marshall issued his decision, Georgia indeed ignored it and Jackson refused to use federal troops to enforce the court order. It is unlikely that Jackson said what is often attributed to him: "Well, John Marshall has made his decision, now let him enforce

37. Cherokee Nation v. Georgia, 30 U.S. 1 (1832).
38. Worcester v. Georgia, 31 U.S. 515, 559 (1832).
39. Id. at 561.
40. 1 Charles Warren, The Supreme Court in United States History 754 (1937).

it."[41] The judicial process never reached the point where it mandated Jackson to do anything.[42] Wirt tried to get Congress to pass legislation that would force Jackson's hand, but was unsuccessful.[43]

On the crucial issue of preserving national power over the states, Jackson looked to the Supreme Court as an ally. If Georgia could thumb its nose at the national government, so could other states. That is what South Carolina did on November 24, 1832, when its legislature passed the Nullification Ordinance, part of which attacked the jurisdiction of the U.S. Supreme Court and promised to treat any interference by the Court in state matters as a nullity. Jackson's proclamation of December 10 strongly repudiated South Carolina's position.[44] In a message to Congress on January 16, 1833, Jackson urged legislation giving federal courts additional authority to deal with the threat from South Carolina.[45] If South Carolina's challenge to federal judicial authority was unacceptable, so was Georgia's. In response to Jackson's stand, the governor of Georgia issued a pardon to the missionaries and released them from prison.[46]

The removal of Indians was carried out at different times, with different tribes, and in different places over the next decade. Some Cherokees left early. The main move in 1838 involved about seventeen thousand who were forced into temporary stockades and then marched eight hundred miles west. Deaths from illness, inadequate food, exposure, and trauma might have reached as high as eight thousand.[47] Many of the deaths occurred after they arrived in Indian Territory.[48] The Choctaws, Chickasaws, Creeks, and Seminoles also suffered huge losses during the removal. In 1843, the Secretary of War reported that 89,000 Indians had been moved west and 22,846 remained east of the Mississippi River.[49]

41. Id. at 759–64.

42. Id. at 764–65; Burke, "The Cherokee Cases," 21 Stan. L. Rev. at 525–27; William F. Swindler, "Politics as Law: The Cherokee Cases," 3 Am. Ind. L. Rev. 7, 16 (1975).

43. Jill Norgren, The Cherokee Cases: The Confrontation of Law and Politics 123–24 (1996).

44. 3 Richardson 1203.

45. Id. at 1192–93.

46. Warren, The Supreme Court in United States History, at 776.

47. Norgren, The Cherokee Cases, at 143. See Grant Foreman, Indian Removal: The Emigration of the Five Civilized Tribes of Indians (1932).

48. Russell Thornton, "The Demography of the Trail of Tears Period: A New Estimate of Cherokee Population Losses," in William L. Anderson, ed., Cherokee Removal: Before and After (1991).

49. John K. Mahon, "Indian–United States Military Situation, 1775–1848," in 4 Handbook of North American Indians 160 (Sturtevant ed. 1988).

Grant's Peace Policy

The forced removal of Indians disrupted the work of Protestant missionaries. American Indian missions "dwindled to dormancy."[50] However, chronic corruption within the Bureau of Indian Affairs prompted President Ulysses S. Grant to act. He appointed Ely S. Parker, a Seneca Indian, to serve as Commissioner of Indian Affairs and removed all but two of the former superintendents of Indian schools. He relied on Quakers, who had developed a strong trust among the Indians, to nominate superintendents and agents.[51] In his first annual message on December 6, 1869, he reminded Congress that the management of Indian affairs had long been "a subject of embarrassment and expense." On the other hand, the Society of Friends was "well known as having succeeded in living in peace with the Indians in the early settlement of Pennsylvania," and had a reputation for "strict integrity and fair dealings." With that record in mind he asked them to manage some Indian reservations, and "the result has proven most satisfactory."[52]

In 1869, Congress appropriated $2 million to enable the President "to maintain the peace among and with the various tribes, bands, and parties of Indians." The statute authorized the President to create a board of commissioners, consisting of no more than ten persons, to exercise joint control with the Secretary of the Interior over the funds appropriated by the statute.[53] The Board of Indian Commissioners became known as the "church board" because its members were active laymen in the Presbyterian, Methodist, Congregational, Episcopal, Baptist, and Friends churches.[54] Board members soon discovered how little power they had. By 1880, the Orthodox Friends and the Reformed Church had withdrawn from the system.[55]

The federal government entered into contracts with mission schools and paid them an annual amount for each student enrolled. Beginning in 1881, Roman Catholics became involved in administering Indian schools and within a short time expanded its number of contract schools. By 1888, the Catholic Indian schools had become the principal

---

50. Robert Keller, "Christian Indian Missions and the American Frontier," 5 Am. Indian J. 19, 21 (1979).

51. Beaver, "Protestant Churches and the Indians," at 443.

52. 9 Richardson 3992–93.

53. 16 Stat. 40, § 4 (1869).

54. Beaver, "Protestant Churches and the Indians," at 443.

55. Id. at 449.

beneficiaries of federal funds. Tension between Protestants and Catholics grew worse in 1888 after Benjamin Harrison defeated Grover Cleveland for President. One of Harrison's appointments in 1889 was Thomas J. Morgan, a Baptist minister, to the position of Commissioner of Indian Affairs. For Superintendent of Indian Schools he picked the Reverend Daniel Dorchester, a Methodist clergyman. Catholics, concerned about having two Protestant ministers in these positions, attacked both appointees. Dorchester in 1888 had published a book called *Romanism versus the Public School System,* which called the Catholic school system "not only un-American but anti-American." Morgan had also made anti-Catholic statements. In 1888 he accused the Catholics of wanting to substitute their religious schools for the public school system.[56]

Although Protestants had pressed their religious tenets on Indians for years, Congress now received complaints about the scope of Catholic instruction in Indian schools. By 1888, several of the Protestant churches decided it would be better to run the Indian schools without federal funds.[57] The Indian appropriations act in 1897 stated it to be "the settled policy of the Government to hereafter make no appropriation whatever for education in any sectarian school." Two years later, the Indian appropriations act included what Congress called "the final appropriation for sectarian schools."[58] After the elimination of congressional appropriations, churches continued to operate Indian schools, sometimes relying on tribal trust funds and treaty funds.[59]

For almost a century, Indian tribes had been treated as foreign nations subject to the treaty-making power of the President and the Senate. However, the Constitution also empowers Congress to "regulate Commerce with foreign Nations, and among the several States, and with the Indian

56. Francis Paul Prucha, The Churches and the Indian Schools, 1888–1912, at 10–13 (1979).

57. 2 Stokes 289.

58. 30 Stat. 79 (1897); 40 Stat. 942 (1899). See also Peter J. Rahill, The Catholic Indian Missions and Grant's Peace Policy, 1870–1884 (1953).

59. R. Pierce Butler, "The Churches and President Grant's Peace Policy," 4 J. Church & State 174, 189–90 (1962). In Quick Bear v. Leupp, 210 U.S. 50 (1908), the Supreme Court held that tribal and trust funds, used to compensate Indians for lands they had ceded to the United States, could be used to educate Indians in sectarian schools without violating the Establishment Clause. See also Elsie Mitchell Rushmore, The Indian Policy during Grant's Administration (1914).

Tribes." Partly because of corruption and mismanagement in the Office of Indian Affairs, the House of Representatives began to object to the Senate's prerogative in Indian affairs. In 1869, the Senate added funds to an appropriations bill to fulfill Indian treaties it had approved, but the House refused to grant the funds.[60] The House completed its reassertion two years later by enacting this language: "*Provided,* That hereafter no Indian nation or tribe within the territory of the United States shall be acknowledged or recognized as an independent nation, tribe, or power with whom the United States may contract by treaty."[61] The House now had coequal power with the Senate over Indian affairs.

Toward the end of the nineteenth century, a number of Indian religious practices were curbed. Indian children were taken from their families and placed in boarding schools for up to eight years, where they learned English, wore Western-style clothing, and had their hair cut Western-style. Anything Indian, including dress, language, and religious practices, was systematically eliminated.[62] Administrative officials declared Indian funeral ceremonies illegal and banned the Sun Dance (requiring the individual to thrust a sharpened stick through his skin) in 1881. Some government officials and Army officers thought that every Indian dance was a war dance. Misapprehension about the "ghost dance," which promised Indians that they could meet their dead relatives, led to tragedy. With Indians wearing ghost shirts painted with magic symbols and moving in a hypnotic state, whites feared a major Indian uprising. The massacre at Wounded Knee in 1890 killed two hundred or more Indians and twenty-nine whites.[63]

Circulars issued by the Office of Indian Affairs from 1921 to 1923 expressed satisfaction that Indian dances were growing less frequent and had fewer "barbaric features," but noted that on a number of reservations, "the native dance still has enough evil tendencies to furnish a retarding influence." The Sun Dance and similar dances were considered "Indian Offenses" under departmental regulations, with "corrective penalties" provided. One of the circulars offered a number of recommendations,

60. Felix Cohen, Handbook of Federal Indian Law 66 (1971).

61. 16 Stat. 566 (1871).

62. Peter Farb, Man's Rise to Civilization as Shown by the Indian of North America from Primeval Times to the Coming of the Industrial State 257 (1968).

63. David E. Witheridge, "No Freedom of Religion for American Indians," 18 J. Church & State 5, 14–15 (1976); Dee Brown, Bury My Heart at Wounded Knee (1971).

including that "none take part in the dances or be present who are under 50 years of age."[64] Dances of supposed sexual excess, such as the Hopi Snake Dance, were singled out for criticism.

The Stirrings of Reform

Congressional legislation in 1919 granted citizenship to Indians who had served in the military services during World War I and had received, or would receive, an honorable discharge.[65] Five years later, Congress passed legislation giving citizenship to the remaining Indians. The statute reads: "All non-citizen Indians born within the territorial limits of the United States be, and they are hereby, declared to be citizens of the United States: *Provided,* That the granting of such citizenship shall not in any manner impair or otherwise affect the right of any Indian to tribal or other property."[66] Few could miss the irony of granting U.S. citizenship to original Americans after it had been granted to American blacks and to women.

John Collier, Executive Secretary of the American Indian Defense Association, testified at House hearings in February 1923 in defense of Indian dances. In later writings he described the dances as religious in nature and entitled to protection along with other religions in America.[67] When Representative Scott Leavitt of Montana drafted legislation in 1926 to empower Indian superintendents to jail reservation Indians for six months without trial or review, under regulations drawn up by the Interior Department, Collier successfully fought against the bill and prevented it from being reported out of committee.[68]

In 1928, the Institute for Government Research published a comprehensive work entitled *The Problem of Indian Administration.* Referred to as "The Meriam Report" because of its technical director, Lewis Meriam, the study was highly critical of U.S. policy toward the Indians. With straightforward language, it noted the "common failure to study sympa-

64. "The Denial of Indian Civil and Religious Rights," 8 Indian Historian 43, 44 (1975); see also Prucha, The Great Father, at 800–06.
65. 41 Stat. 350 (1919).
66. 43 Stat. 253 (1924). The Dawes Allotment Act of 1887 had granted citizenship to Indians who accepted an allotment of land and "adopted the habits of civilized life." 24 Stat. 390, § 6 (1887).
67. Kenneth Philp, "John Collier and the Crusade to Protect Indian Religious Freedom, 1920–26," 1 J. Ethnic Studies 22, 26–27 (1973).
68. Id. at 33–34.

thetically and understandingly the Indians' own religions and ethics and to use what is good in them as the foundation upon which to build. . . . The attempt blindly to destroy the whole Indian religion may in effect be an attack on some of the very elements of religious belief which the missionary himself espouses and which he hopes the Indian will adopt."[69] The report criticized the boarding schools for dietary deficiencies, health conditions, overcrowded dormitories, overly strict discipline, and a weakening of family life.[70]

Collier became Commissioner of Indian Affairs in 1934 and remained in that position until 1945. He helped persuade Congress to repeal a number of obsolete laws that covered Indians.[71] Those statutes dated back to the period from 1830 to 1850, when many Indians were considered hostile. For example, the statutes prohibited the sending or carrying of seditious messages and any correspondence with foreign nations to excite Indians to war.[72] The repeal statute passed without debate.[73]

The major piece of legislation was the Indian Reorganization Act of 1934, which ended the land allotment provisions of the Dawes Severalty Act of 1887.[74] During its forty-seven years, the Dawes Act permitted the breaking up of tribal or reservation lands into individual allotments. The objective, expressed piecemeal in earlier treaties, was to give Indians the incentive to work an individual piece of property that they owned. This philosophy took its most comprehensive form with the Dawes Act.[75] After property had been allotted from a reservation, the Secretary of the Interior could negotiate with the tribe and purchase the remaining (or "surplus") land. As the process of allotment continued, the surplus lands were transferred to the whites. Thus, in 1881 the Indians held in trust 155,632,312 acres. That amount declined to 104,314,349 by 1890 and to 77,865,373 by 1900. Of the remaining acres in 1900, only 5,409,530 had been allotted.[76] The 1934 statute provided for the return of some surplus lands to tribal ownership.

69. The Problem of Indian Administration 845–46 (1928).
70. Id. at 11–14, 574–77.
71. 48 Stat. 487 (1934).
72. S. Rept. No. 634, 73d Cong., 2d Sess. (1934).
73. 78 Cong. Rec. 7271, 8222, 8351, 8361, 8447–48, 8607 (1934).
74. 48 Stat. 984 (1934).
75. Francis Paul Prucha, American Indian Policy in Crisis: Christian Reformers and the Indian, 1865–1900, at 227–55 (1976).
76. Id. at 257.

Collier's draft bill contained a title on Indian education, stating the purpose and policy of Congress "to promote the study of Indian civilization, including Indian arts, crafts, skills, and traditions." That title, promising a step toward the protection of Indian religious liberty, was deleted from the bill.[77] In seeking funds for the sections of the bill that survived, Collier ran into resistance from the appropriations subcommittees and the Bureau of the Budget.[78] What he could not obtain in legislative authority or appropriations he tried to achieve by administrative action.[79] In 1934 he issued an order expressing the policy of the Indian Office regarding religion:

> No interference with Indian religious life or ceremonial expression will hereafter be tolerated. . . . Violations of law or of the proprieties, if committed under the cloak of any religion, Indian or other, or any cultural tradition, Indian or other, are to be dealt with as such, but in no case shall punishment for statutory violations or for improprieties be so administered as to constitute an interference with, or to imply censorship over, the religious or cultural life, Indian or other.
>
> The fullest constitutional liberty, in all matters affecting religion, conscience and culture, is insisted on for all Indians.[80]

With a number of legislators opposed to Collier and his policies, federal interest in Indian affairs suffered a reverse in the late 1940s and 1950s. House hearings in 1947 focused on bills to "emancipate" Indians from the Bureau of Indian Affairs (BIA). In that same year Acting Commissioner William Zimmerman testified before Congress concerning the elimination of BIA services.[81] In March 1949, the Hoover Commission recommended that the BIA be transferred from the Interior Department to a proposed new department—the Federal Security Agency—which would handle social security and educational functions. Federal policy for Indians should look to "their complete integration into the mass of the

77. Lawrence C. Kelly, "The Indian Reorganization Act: The Dream and the Reality," in John R. Wunder, ed., Constitutionalism and Native Americans, 1903–1968, at 134, 139 (1996).

78. Id. at 306–7, 308.

79. Id. at 298–299.

80. 2 Stokes 452. See Kenneth R. Philp, John Collier's Crusade for Indian Reform, 1920–1954 (1977).

81. Charles F. Wilkinson & Eric R. Biggs, "The Evolution of the Termination Policy," 5 Am. Ind. L. Rev. 139, 146 (1977).

population as full, tax-paying citizens." Pending the achievement of complete integration, "the administration of social programs for the Indians should be progressively transferred to State government."[82] Other recommendations included transfer of responsibility for medical services to local governments or to quasi-public bodies, and termination of tax exemption for Indian lands.[83] With these reforms implemented, "special Federal aid to State and local governments for Indian programs should end."[84] In a dissent, Vice Chairman Dean Acheson objected that the recommendations exceeded the commission's charter, especially the proposal "to assimilate the Indian and to turn him, his culture, and his means of livelihood over to State control."[85] Other dissents were written by commissioners James H. Rowe, Jr. and James Forrestal.[86]

In 1952, the House adopted a resolution calling for a full and complete investigation of the BIA, with the goal of preparing legislation "designed to promote the earliest practicable termination of all Federal supervision and control over Indians."[87] At the end of the year, the House Committee on Interior and Insular Affairs issued a sixteen-hundred-page report in response to the resolution, including discussion of some of the considerations needed to be taken into account before terminating federal supervision and control over the Indians. For example, legislation would be needed to shift federal civil and criminal jurisdiction over Indians to state and local government authorities.[88]

The Eisenhower administration agreed to shift some federal responsibilities to the states. Legislation enacted in 1953 (Public Law 280) conferred jurisdiction on California, Minnesota, Nebraska, Oregon, and Wisconsin with respect to criminal offenses and civil actions committed or arising on Indian reservations within those states.[89] Considering the importance of this legislation, one would expect vigorous debate and dissent, but the legislative history is almost barren. The measure went through the

82. The Commission on Organization of the Executive Branch of the Government, Social Security and Education, Indian Affairs 65 (March 1949).
83. Id. at 66.
84. Id. at 75.
85. Id. at 78.
86. Id. at 79–80.
87. 98 Cong. Rec. 8788 (1952).
88. H. Rept. No. 1503, 82d Cong., 2d Sess. 30 (1952).
89. 67 Stat. 588 (1953).

two chambers with minimal discussion.[90] Although Eisenhower said he had "grave doubts as to the wisdom of certain provisions" in the bill, he signed it. He stated that in the five states at issue, "the Indians have enthusiastically endorsed this bill." His objection concerned two sections of the bill that permitted other states to impose criminal and civil jurisdiction over Indian tribes within their borders, without requiring full consultation with the Indians or final approval by the federal government.[91]

Consistent with this legislation, in 1953 Congress passed House Concurrent Resolution 108, stating the policy of Congress, "as rapidly as possible, to make the Indians within the territorial limits of the United States subject to the same laws and entitled to the same privileges and responsibilities as are applicable to other citizens of the United States, to end their status as wards of the United States, and to grant them all of the rights and prerogatives pertaining to American citizenship."[92] Similar to Public Law 280, the legislative history of committee reports and floor debate is remarkably brief.[93] The combined effect of the concurrent resolution, Public Law 280, and tribal termination bills is referred to as the policy of "termination."

The attempt by the federal government to disengage from Indian affairs and transfer responsibility to the states was never tenable. Through a combination of treaties, statutes, and formal and informal agreements, the federal commitments had made commitments—legal and moral—to the Indians. It could not, at some later date, wash its hands. Presidents John F. Kennedy and Lyndon B. Johnson attacked the termination policy and appointed executive officials sympathetic to greater federal assistance, with the eventual goal of Indian self-sufficiency.[94] President Nixon told Congress on July 8, 1970, that the "removal of Federal trusteeship responsibility has produced considerable disorientation among the affected Indians and has left them unable to relate to a myriad of Federal, State and local assistance efforts. Their economic and social condition has often been worse after termination than it was before."[95]

90. H. Rept. No. 848, 83d Cong., 1st Sess. (1953); S. Rept. No. 699, 83d Cong., 1st Sess. (1953); 99 Cong. Rec. 9962–63, 10782–84, 10928 (1953).

91. Public Papers of the Presidents, 1953, at 564–66.

92. 67 Stat. B132 (1953).

93. H. Rept. No. 841, 83d Cong., 1st Sess. (1953); S. Rept. No. 794, 83d Cong., 1st Sess. (1953); 99 Cong. Rec. 9968, 10815 (1953).

94. Prucha, The Great Father, at 1087–1100.

95. Public Papers of the Presidents, 1970, at 566.

Protective Legislation

Beginning in 1962, Congress passed a number of bills to protect Indian religious freedom, covering such areas as eagle feathers, Indian civil rights, Taos religious shrines, an Indian religious freedom statute, the Klamath Indians, and the protection of Indian graves and funereal objects. Although these statutes gave greater recognition to Indian religions, they sometimes lacked enforcement provisions. During litigation on these statutory provisions, courts regularly advise plaintiffs to seek remedies not from judicial activism but from more explicit legislation enacted by Congress.

EAGLE FEATHERS

One of the first Indian religious issues addressed by Congress concerned legislation to protect eagles. In 1940, Congress passed a law to protect the bald eagle, which the Continental Congress had adopted in 1782 as the national symbol. The bald eagle, representing the American ideal of freedom, was threatened with extinction in the twentieth century. The 1940 statute prohibited the taking, possession, sale, purchase, export, or import of any bald eagle. It authorized the Secretary of the Interior to lift those prohibitions by issuing permits for certain purposes, but did not specify the religious use of eagle feathers by Indians.[96] Nothing in the sparse legislative record referred to the need to protect Indian religious practices.[97]

The issue returned in 1962. Congress learned that immature bald eagles, similar in appearance to golden eagles, were sometimes killed by persons who confused the two. Only in the fourth year does the bald eagle grow its characteristic white feathers on the head and neck. To protect the bald eagle, Congress extended similar protections to the golden eagle. The legislative history explains the importance of the eagle for many Indian tribes, particularly in the Southwest, that performed ceremonies of religious significance. The eagle, "by reason of its majestic, solitary, and mysterious nature, became an especial object of worship." Every tribe believed in eagle beings, such as the man-eagle who "lays aside his plumage" after flights in which he spreads devastation, and the

---

96. 54 Stat. 250 (1940).

97. H. Rept. No. 2104, 76th Cong., 3d Sess. (1940); 86 Cong. Rec. 6446–47, 7006–7 (1940).

hero who slays him is "carried to the house in the sky by eagles of several species, each one in turn bearing him higher."[98]

The legislation authorized the Secretary of the Interior to issue regulations allowing exceptions for various reasons, including "the religious purposes of Indian tribes."[99] In defining the possession and use of eagles for religious purposes, a regulation issued in 1963 restricted permits to Indians "who are authentic, bona fide practitioners of such religion."[100] Current regulations require an applicant to be "an Indian who is authorized to participate in *bona fide* tribal religious ceremonies."[101]

Litigation has clarified some issues. The Bald Eagle Protection Act does not allow Indians to make commercial sales of eagles or eagle parts. Not only is the sale of eagle parts incompatible with Indian religious beliefs, Indians deplore the sale of eagle parts as a matter of tribal custom and religion.[102] The prosecution of Indians for selling eagle parts imposes no burden on an Indian's free exercise of religion.[103] These cases did not involve an exchange among Indians of eagle parts for religious use. The people who bought the eagle feathers were non-Indians who made it clear that they had only a commercial interest in the items.[104]

Indians prosecuted for shooting bald eagles sometimes cite treaties to justify their actions. If a treaty recognized the right of Indians to hunt and fish within a tract of land, that right continues unless Congress abrogates or modifies it in a subsequent statute. In 1974, the Eighth Circuit held that nothing in the statutes or legislative histories extending protection to bald eagles and golden eagles affected Indian hunting rights on a reservation.[105] In 1980 the Ninth Circuit, guided in part by the Supreme Court's broad reading of the Eagle Protection Act,[106] ruled that the bald eagle statute *did* modify Indian treaty rights.[107] The conflict between these two circuits led to a Supreme Court ruling in 1986 that treaty rights were abrogated by the Eagle Protection Act.[108] This litigation involved the

98. H. Rept. No. 1450, 87th Cong., 2d Sess. 4 (1962).
99. 76 Stat. 1246 (1962).
100. 28 Fed. Reg. 976, § 11.5 (1963).
101. 50 C.F.R. § 22.22 (c)(2) (10-1-00 edition) (emphasis in original).
102. United States v. Top Sky, 547 F.2d 486, 487 (9th Cir. 1976).
103. Id. at 488.
104. United States v. Top Sky, 547 F.2d at 485.
105. United States v. White, 508 F.2d 454 (8th Cir. 1974).
106. Andrus v. Allard, 444 U.S. 51 (1979).
107. United States v. Fryberg, 622 F.2d 1010 (9th Cir. 1980).
108. United States v. Dion, 476 U.S. 734 (1986), rev'g United States v. Dion, 752 F.2d 1261 (8th Cir. 1985).

taking and selling of eagles for commercial purposes, not the religious use of eagle feathers. Other cases have explored the use of eagle feathers and parts for Indian religious ceremonies.[109]

On April 29, 1994, President Clinton issued a memorandum concerning the distribution of eagle feathers for Indian religious purposes. He said that eagle feathers "hold a sacred place in Native American culture and religious practices," and that the administration had changed policy and procedures to "facilitate the collection and distribution of scarce eagle bodies and parts for this purpose." He directed executive departments and agencies to work cooperatively with tribal governments to accommodate Native American religious practices "to the fullest extent under the law."[110]

THE INDIAN CIVIL RIGHTS ACT

In 1968, as part of an omnibus bill providing penalties for certain acts of violence or intimidation, Congress passed what is called the Indian Civil Rights Act. Actually, it reads more like a bill of rights. Federal courts had decided that in cases of religious liberty, neither the First Amendment nor the Fourteenth Amendment applied to Indian tribal governments, and that Congress had not passed legislation making those constitutional provisions applicable to Indians.[111] Senator Sam Ervin (D-N.C.) took the lead in extending constitutional rights to Indians.[112]

As with any bill of rights, the statute extends protections to individuals and imposes restrictions on government, in this case the tribal governments. Thus, no Indian tribe exercising powers of self-government shall "make or enforce any law prohibiting the free exercise of religion." Because some tribes have a theocratic foundation, an establishment of religion clause was not included. An Establishment Clause might have worked "to the disadvantage of tribal religion."[113] Other First Amendment rights are listed, prohibiting the tribal governments from abridging the freedom of speech or of the press, or the right of people peaceably to

109. United States v. Abeyta, 632 F.Supp. 1301 (D. N.M. 1986): United States v. Dion, 762 F.2d 674 (8th Cir. 1985). See John Geb, "Native American Culture: The Use of Feathers as a Protected Right," 2 Am. Ind. L. Rev. 105 (1974).

110. 59 Fed. Reg. 22953 (1994).

111. Native American Church v. Navajo Tribal Council, 272 F.2d 131 (10th Cir. 1959).

112. Prucha, The Great Father, at 1106–7.

113. Milner S. Ball, "Constitution, Court, Indian Tribes," 1987 Am. Bar Foundation Research J. 1, 132 (1987).

assemble and to petition for a redress of grievances. Indian tribes may not conduct unreasonable search and seizures, subject persons for the same offense to be twice put in jeopardy, compel persons in a criminal case to be a witness against themselves, take private property for a public use without just compensation, or take other actions injurious to individual rights.

Much of the statute is directed toward safeguards of criminal proceedings, such as the right to a speedy and public trial, to be informed of the nature and cause of the accusation, to be confronted with witnesses against you, to have compulsory process for obtaining witnesses in your favor, and to have the assistance of counsel. Other provisions prohibit excessive bail, excessive fines, cruel and unusual punishments, the denial of equal protection, deprivation of liberty or property without due process of law, bills of attainder, ex post facto laws, or the denial of a trial by jury of not less than six persons.[114] The statute directed the Secretary of the Interior to draft a model code to govern the administration of justice by courts of Indian offenses on Indian reservations. In drafting the code, the Secretary "shall consult with the Indians, Indian tribes, and interested agencies of the United States."

A bill establishing rights for individuals in their relations with Indian tribes passed the Senate on December 7, 1967, by voice vote.[115] The House took no action on that legislation, but on March 6, 1968, in a special message to Congress on the problems of the American Indian, President Lyndon B. Johnson urged Congress to enact a bill of rights for Indians.[116] Two days later the Senate passed the legislation by a vote of 81 to zero.[117] The House accepted the Senate language and it became law on April 11, 1968. Some members of the Indian community did not support the legislation. They worried that it would pit an individual "against his or her society, in the traditional judicial system they favored, which was highly religious and required a fine sense of Indian customs."[118] Also, the statute gave Indians an opportunity to appeal to federal courts the decisions reached by tribal courts, undercutting to some extent the principle of Indian self-government.[119]

114. 82 Stat. 77–78, § 202 (1968).
115. 113 Stat. 35471–77 (1967).
116. Public Papers of the Presidents, 1968–69, I, at 342.
117. 114 Cong. Rec. 5835–38 (1968).
118. Vine Deloria, Jr. & Clifford M. Lytle, American Indians, American Justice 128 (1983).
119. Id. at 131–36; John R. Wunder, ed., The Indian Bill of Rights, 1968 (1996).

TAOS RELIGIOUS SHRINES

In 1969, the House Committee on Interior and Insular Affairs reported legislation to grant to the Pueblo de Taos Indians in New Mexico trust title to approximately forty-eight thousand acres of federally owned land that had been taken from the Indians in 1906, by presidential order, without payment of any compensation. Congress had passed legislation in 1933 to give the Pueblo a fifty-year special use permit to the area,[120] but the Taos Indians wanted a more permanent arrangement. Placing great significance on the land, they urged the government to return the title to the land rather than compensate them with money. The Indians argued that preservation of the area and placing limits on non-Indian use were essential in protecting religious interests and the sacredness of the land. The integrity of their religion required complete privacy.[121] The most sacred shrine in the area is the Blue Lake.

To explain the successful enactment of legislation in 1970, one study emphasized that "nothing was more important than the persistent determination of the Taos people themselves."[122] Taos delegations traveled throughout the United States to promote their cause, enlisted the support of many individuals and organizations, and allowed a television documentary to be filmed of the Pueblo and at Blue Lake.[123]

On the choice between payment and conveying land, the House Committee on Interior and Insular Affairs concluded that "the equities are on the side of the Indians" and that the land should be restored to the Pueblo.[124] The bill passed the House in 1969 by voice vote, with little opposition.[125] On July 8, 1970, President Nixon "wholeheartedly" endorsed the legislation "as an important symbol of this government's responsiveness to the just grievances of the American Indians."[126] Senator George McGovern put the emphasis more on religious liberty:

Mr. President, what is involved here is far more than simply a legal claim, important as that is. What really is involved here is a deeply

120. 48 Stat. 109, § 4 (1933).
121. H. Rept. No. 91-326, 91st Cong., 1st Sess. 2 (1969).
122. John J. Bodine, "Blue Lake: A Struggle for Indian Rights," 1 Am. Ind. L. Rev. 23, 24 (1973).
123. Id. at 28.
124. H. Rept. No. 91-326, at 3.
125. 115 Cong. Rec. 24871, 24878– 86 (1969).
126. Public Papers of the Presidents, 1970, at 569.

spiritual and religious matter, which goes right to the heart of freedom of religion and freedom of conscience in our country, because
the Blue Lake area which is in dispute, and which has been in dispute for so many years, is regarded as the most sacred of all places by
the Indian people, and particularly the Taos Pueblo Indians.[127]

After two days of debate, the Senate passed the bill by a vote of 70 to
12, and it became law.[128]

Other legislation by Congress during this period strengthened Indian
autonomy. In 1975, Congress granted Indians greater participation in
federal programs and increased educational assistance. The Indian Self-
Determination Act recognized that prolonged federal domination of Indian service programs "has served to retard rather than enhance the progress of Indian people."[129]

AMERICAN INDIAN RELIGIOUS FREEDOM ACT

In 1978, Congress passed a joint resolution expressing the principles of
religious freedom for Indians. The resolution, called the American Indian Religious Freedom Act (AIRFA), begins by recognizing that freedom of religion is an "inherent right" for all people and "fundamental to
the democratic structure of the United States." Moreover, the individual
right to practice religion has produced "a rich variety of religious heri-
tages in this country." Included within this culture are the religious practices of the American Indian, "such practices forming the basis of Indian
identity and value systems." After citing the instances in which federal
laws and practices had abridged and infringed on the religious freedom
of American Indians, the legislation resolves that "henceforth it shall be
the policy of the United States to protect and preserve for American Indians their inherent right of freedom to believe, express, and exercise the
traditional religions of the American Indian, Eskimo, Aleut, and Native
Hawaiians, including but not limited to access to sites, use and possession of sacred objects, and the freedom to worship through ceremonials
and traditional rites."[130]

127. 116 Cong. Rec. 39331 (1970).
128. See S. Rept. No. 91-1345, 91st Cong., 2d Sess. (1970); 116 Cong. Rec. 39327–
38, 39586–610 (1970).
129. 88 Stat. 2203 (1975).
130. 92 Stat. 469 (1978).

Section 2 of the resolution states that the President "shall direct" the various federal departments, agencies, and other instrumentalities to evaluate their policies and procedures, in consultation with native traditional religious leaders, in order to determine appropriate changes necessary to "preserve and protect Native American religious cultural rights and practices." The resolution expresses only a general policy and lacks enforcement mechanisms. As the floor manager in the House said: "It has no teeth in it."[131] Still, it demonstrates an awareness and a sensitivity to Indian religious freedom that would not have been expressed by Congress (or any other branch of government) in previous years. The legislative history is quite brief. The resolution passed the Senate by voice vote and by a margin of 337 to 81 in the House.[132]

Two years later, the Tenth Circuit decided a case originally brought in 1974 but one that also cited the resolution. The complaint claimed that in impounding water to form Lake Powell on the Colorado River, the government had put some of the Navajo gods underwater, denied the Navajo access to a prayer spot sacred to them, and by allowing tourists to visit the Rainbow Bridge permitted desecration of the site. Balancing the government's interest in assuring public access to natural attractions, the court denied that the free exercise of Indian religions had been infringed.[133]

Similarly, in 1980 the Sixth Circuit ruled that the Cherokee Indians failed to show that their free exercise of religion would be infringed by a proposed dam that would flood a site sacred to the Cherokee religion. The plaintiffs cited AIRFA. The court noted that Congress, in an appropriations bill enacted in 1979, had directed the construction of the dam notwithstanding the Endangered Species Act "or any other law."[134] The record convinced the court that the dam affected not religious interests but rather cultural heritage and tradition, which are not protected by the Free Exercise Clause.

In a 1983 case, Navajo and Hopi tribes challenged a permit that would allow private interests to expand and develop a government-owned ski

131. 124 Cong. Rec. 21445 (Representative Udall).
132. S. Rept. No. 95–709, 95th Cong., 2d Sess. (1978); H. Rept. No. 95-1308, 95th Cong., 2d Sess. (1978); 124 Cong. Rec. 8365–66, 21443–46, 21450–52 (1978).
133. Badoni v. Higginson, 638 F.2d 172 (10th Cir. 1980), cert. denied, 452 U.S. 954 (1981).
134. Sequoyah v. Tennessee Valley Authority, 620 F.2d 1159, 1161 (6th Cir. 1980), cert. denied, 449 U.S. 953 (1980).

area in Arizona, claiming that it impaired their ability to gather sacred objects and to conduct religious ceremonies. The D.C. Circuit held that development of the area did not violate AIRFA or the National Historic Preservation Act. In reviewing the statutory language and legislative history of AIRFA, the court concluded that they do not indicate "the extent to which Congress intended that policy to override other land use considerations."[135] The court cited this statement by one of the bill's principal sponsors, Representative Morris Udall: "It is not the intent of my bill to wipe out laws passed for the benefit of the general public or to confer special religious rights on Indians."[136] Prior to issuing the permit, the government held meetings with Indian religious practitioners and conducted public hearings on the Hopi and Navajo reservations, at which the practitioners testified.[137] Also in 1983, the Eighth Circuit reviewed a case brought by Indian spiritual leaders and religious practitioners, claiming that South Dakota, by restricting access to a site of traditional religious ceremonial grounds, had violated the Free Exercise Clause, AIRFA, and other statutes. The district court held that Indian interests had been outweighed by compelling state interests, and the Eighth Circuit agreed.[138]

In 1988, the Supreme Court decided that the federal government did not violate the Free Exercise Clause by permitting timber harvesting and construction of a road through a portion of a national forest that has traditionally been used for Indian religious purposes. After a study commissioned by the Forest Service concluded that construction of the road would cause "serious and irreparable damage to the sacred areas which are an integral and necessary part of the belief systems and lifeway of Northwest California Indian peoples," the government selected a route that was removed as far as possible from the sites used by Indians for spiritual activities.[139] Indian organizations claimed that the Forest Service's decision violated the Free Exercise Clause and several statutes, including AIRFA. Although the Court recognized that the logging and road building "could have devastating effects on traditional Indian religious practices," it denied the Indians' claim because "government simply could not operate if it were

135. Wilson v. Block, 708 F.2d 735, 746 (D.C. Cir. 1983).
136. Id.
137. Id. at 747.
138. Crow v. Gullet, 706 F.2d 856 (8th Cir. 1983).
139. Lyng v. Northwest Indian Cemetery Prot. Assn., 485 U.S. 439, 442–43 (1988).

required to satisfy every citizen's religious needs and desires."[140] Writing for the majority, Justice O'Connor emphasized that remedies would have to be found outside the Court. She noted that the Constitution

> does not, and courts cannot, offer to reconcile the various competing demands on government, many of them rooted in sincere religious belief, that inevitably arise in so diverse a society as ours. That task, to the extent that it is feasible, is for the legislature and other institutions. Cf. The Federalist No. 10 (suggesting that the effects of religious factionalism are best restrained through competition among a multiplicity of religious sects).[141]

O'Connor said that the dissenting Justices wanted the Court to referee disputes between the government and religious groups by deciding which public lands are "central" or "indispensable" to certain religions, and to weigh the value of religious beliefs that are threatened by a government program. Such an approach "would cast the Judiciary in a role that we were never intended to play."[142]

KLAMATH INDIANS

Twice in the 1980s Congress passed legislation to recognize the rights of Klamath Indians in Oregon. In 1980, a private law set aside in special trust status certain lands in the Winema National Forest for Edison Chiloquin. As part of the "termination" policy in the 1950s, federal supervision over Klamath Indian property came to an end. Adult members of the tribe were given the option of holding their interests in common under Oregon law or converting the interests to cash. In a 1958 election, approximately 77 percent of the tribal members voted to sell their property. Edison Chiloquin wanted to retain his interests in the land. As a result of the election, 631,000 acres were sold to a private corporation (91,000 acres), the Department of the Interior (15,000), and the Department of Agriculture (525,000).[143] The government used the land to create the Winema National Forest.

140. Id. at 451, 452.
141. Id. at 452.
142. Id. at 458.
143. Background on the Edison Chiloquin bill comes from H. Rept. No. 1406, 96th Cong., 2d Sess. (1980). See also Garrett Epps, To an Unknown God: Religious Freedom

In 1969, a majority of the remaining members of the tribe elected to terminate the trust. Legislation in 1973 directed the Secretary of Agriculture to acquire 135,000 acres of land to be added to the Winema National Forest. Purchase of the land resulted in the disbursement of $270,000 to each Indian beneficiary. Chiloquin, who had helped create the "Committee to Save the Remaining Klamath Indian Lands," refused to accept the money. Instead, he wanted land to establish a village founded on traditional values and the preservation of Indian culture, ways, and spiritual beliefs. To underscore his determination, he built a tipi in the forest, became a squatter, and kept a sacred council fire lit.

The purpose of the private bill for Chiloquin was to avoid, as Senator Mark Hatfield said, "confrontation and all other kinds of unpleasantries of trying to expel this man from the lands that are his ancestral home."[144] The bill specifies that the land set aside for Chiloquin "shall not be inconsistent with its cultural, historical, and archeological character." If the land were used by Chiloquin or his heirs for other than "traditional Indian purposes," it would revert to the United States to protect archaeological, cultural, and traditional values associated with the property.[145]

There remained some unfinished business with the Klamaths, long recognized by the federal government as an Indian tribe. However, in 1954, as part of the termination policy, Congress passed legislation terminating federal supervision over the tribe and putting an end to federal services to tribal members. The Termination Act gave members a choice of either withdrawing from the tribe and taking their share of the sale of land in cash, or remaining with the tribe and keeping their share in trust.[146] In reporting legislation in 1986, the House Committee on Interior and Insular Affairs said that the government had never properly asked tribal members whether they were in favor of the 1954 bill. In fact, the tribe had voted to send a slate of delegates to Congress to state their opposition to the bill.[147] Legislation in 1986 restored federal recognition of the Klamath Indian tribe. Rights and privileges that may have been lost because of the 1954 statute were restored.

---

on Trial 49–52 (2001), and Theodore Stern, The Klamath Tribe: A People and Their Reservation 249–52 (1965).

144. 126 Cong. Rec. 30379 (1980).
145. 94 Stat. 3613 (1980).
146. 68 Stat. 719 (1954).
147. H. Rept. No. 99-630, 99th Cong., 2d Sess. 3 (1986).

Any federal services and benefits given to Indian tribes recognized by the federal government are also to be given to the Klamath Indians.[148]

INDIAN GRAVES AND FUNEREAL OBJECTS

Native Americans, believing that they have a spiritual connection with ancestral remains, have had little success in litigating disputes about development of Indian burial grounds, removal of gravestones by developers, or malicious disturbance of Indian tombs or graves.[149] While it can be said that "only recently" have Native Americans "felt they were in a position to bring a white government to court,"[150] the more effective avenue has been to bring a white government to Congress.

In 1989, Congress passed legislation to establish the National Museum of the American Indian within the Smithsonian Institution. Part of the statute required the Secretary of the Smithsonian Institution, in consultation and cooperation with traditional Indian religious leaders and government officials of Indian tribes, to inventory the Indian human remains and Indian funerary objects in the possession or control of the Smithsonian Institution, and to return to the descendants or tribes the human remains and associated funerary objects that can be associated with the descendants and tribes.[151]

The following year, Congress passed the Native American Graves Protection and Repatriation Act. In reporting the bill, the House Committee on Interior and Insular Affairs explained its purpose: "To protect Native American burial sites and the removal of human remains, funerary objects, sacred objects, and objects of cultural patrimony on Federal, Indian and Native Hawaiian lands."[152] Persons who excavate or do archaeological work on federal lands would have to receive a permit. If any human remains or funerary objects were discovered, and it is known which tribe is closely related to them, that tribe is given the opportunity to reclaim

148. 100 Stat. 849 (1986). For floor debate, see 132 Cong. Rec. 13753–55, 21775–76 (1986).

149. Wana the Bear v. Community Const., Inc., 180 Cal. Rptr. 423 (Ct. App. 1982); State v. Glass, 273 N.E.2d 893 (Ohio 1971); Newman v. State, 174 So.2d 479 (Fla. 1965); Carter v. City of Zanesville, 52 N.E. 126 (Ohio 1898).

150. June Camille Bush Raines, "One Is Missing: Native American Graves Protection and Repatriation Act: An Overview and Analysis," 17 Am. Ind. L. Rev. 636, 646 (1992).

151. 103 Stat. 1343, § 11 (1989).

152. H. Rept. No. 101–877, 101st Cong., 2d Sess. 8 (1990).

the remains or objects. If they decide not to take possession, the Secretary of the Interior will determine the disposition after consulting with Native American, scientific, and museum groups. In previous years, Indian tribes had tried to have the human remains and funerary objects of their ancestors returned to them. During consideration of the legislation, some Indian representatives testified that the spirits of their ancestors would not rest until they had been returned to their homeland.[153]

The bill passed the House under suspension of the rules, a procedure usually adopted for uncontroversial legislation with strong bipartisan support.[154] It requires a two-thirds majority. Representative Ben Nighthorse Campbell, whose father was Northern Cheyenne, discussed an order by the Surgeon General in 1868 to have Army field officers send him Indian skeletons. The purpose of the study was to determine whether the Indian was inferior to the white man, because of a smaller cranium, and to show that the Indian was not capable of being a landowner.[155] Indian tribes wanted to recover these and other remains. The bill passed the Senate by voice vote, with little debate.[156] Differences between the two chambers were resolved with little difficulty.[157] As enacted, the bill provides for criminal penalties for those engaged in illegal trafficking in Indian human remains and cultural items.[158]

These are some of the pieces of legislation passed by Congress to protect Indian religious freedom. The judiciary has sometimes played a significant role, but most of the initiative and momentum comes from Indian groups and other organizations that apply pressure to political institutions: Congress, the President, federal agencies, and the states. Religious liberty for Indians has been secured primarily through the regular political process, not by judicial rulings. The same conclusion applies to protecting the religious use of peyote, the subject of the next chapter.

153. Id. at 13.
154. 136 Cong. Rec. 31941 (1990).
155. Id. at 31937.
156. Id. at 34061–62.
157. Id. at 35677–81, 36814–15.
158. 104 Stat. 3052, § 4 (1990).

8

RELIGIOUS USE OF PEYOTE

What began as a denial by Oregon of unemployment benefits to an American Indian and a white man, because they had ingested peyote during a religious ceremony, led in time to a highly disputed ruling by the Supreme Court in 1990. In sustaining the denial of benefits, the Court announced standards that many considered a disturbing setback for religious liberty. Public opposition to the decision prompted hearings by Congress and legislative action. Both Oregon in 1991 and Congress in 1994 passed legislation authorizing the use of peyote as part of a religious ceremony. The Religious Freedom Restoration Act (RFRA) of 1993 restored religious freedom to its position before the Court's ruling, but four years later the Court declared the statute unconstitutional. Thus closed (temporarily) one more round of this public dialogue about the meaning of religious freedom. With congressional enactment of new legislation ("Son of RFRA") in 2000, the public debate continues.

Peyotism

The peyote religion among Indian tribes in the United States begins at the end of the nineteenth century, although its use by Indians in other territories dates back much earlier.[1] Peyote grows in small buttons at the top of a spineless cactus and contains a number of alkaloids, including the psychotropic mescaline. With its hallucinogenic properties, peyote offers a supernatural alternative to other religions by establishing an intermediate spirit (peyote, Jesus, or both) and a Supreme Being (the Great Spirit or God).[2] As used by the Native American Church (NAC), the drug is considered a sacrament (like bread and wine) and an object of worship.

1. Omer C. Stewart, Peyote Religion: A History 16–30 (1987).
2. George de Verges, "Peyote and the Native American Church," 2 Am. Ind. L. Rev. 71 (1974); H. Rept. No. 103-675, 103d Cong., 2d Sess. 3 (1994).

Prayers are devoted to it just as prayers are devoted to the Holy Ghost. By ingesting peyote, members of the NAC say they enter into direct contact with God. Peyote is not injurious to the Indian religious user, is not addictive or habit-forming, and is often helpful in controlling alcoholism and alcohol abuse among Indian people.[3]

Initially, the states responded to peyote by forbidding its use. In 1899, Oklahoma prohibited use of the mescal bean but repealed the law in 1908.[4] Other states enacted legislation to prohibit the use of peyote: Colorado, Nevada, and Utah in 1917; Kansas in 1920; Arizona, Montana, North Dakota, and South Dakota in 1923; Iowa in 1924; New Mexico and Wyoming in 1929; and Texas in 1937.[5] This legislation had little application for peyote used on Indian reservations, where states had no jurisdiction. Enforcement could come on state property or state highways. In 1926, the Supreme Court of Montana held that under some circumstances the state could enforce the state law prohibiting peyote against an Indian who uses it within a reservation.[6]

Congress had prohibited the sale of intoxicating drinks to Indians in 1897.[7] Lawmakers made an effort in 1913 to provide funds to suppress the use of peyote, but conferees deleted the money, explaining that "the Indians claim this peyote is used in their religious worship and would cause a great deal of confusion."[8] The enacted bill did not contain money to suppress peyote.[9]

In 1918, the House Committee on Indian Affairs reported legislation to prohibit the sale of peyote to Indians. The committee, accepting the recommendation of the Indian Bureau and relying on published articles, described peyote as "poison" and referred to "night orgies in a close [*sic*] tent polluted with foul air."[10] The bureau recognized that peyote was used by Indians "as a substitute for intoxicating liquors," but instead of using that evidence to support the use of peyote, the committee argued that substitution was a ground to prohibit it.[11] The reason behind this position

3. H. Rept. No. 103-675, 103d Cong., 2d Sess. 3 (1994).

4. Omer C. Stewart, "Peyote and the Law," in Christopher Vecsey, ed., Handbook of American Indian Religious Freedom 60 (1991).

5. de Verges, "Peyote and the Native American Church," at 77 n.14.

6. State v. Big Sheep, 242 P. 1067 (Mont. 1926).

7. 29 Stat. 506 (1897).

8. H. Rept. No. 28, 63d Cong., 1st Sess. 6 (1913).

9. 38 Stat. 78 (1913).

10. H. Rept. No. 560, 65th Cong., 2d Sess. 26 (1918).

11. Id. at 2.

is that action on the peyote bill was caught up in the national campaign for prohibition in general, eventually leading to ratification of the Eighteenth Amendment in 1919. Curiously, the committee report includes an encyclopedia article that accurately describes peyote as "producing a pleasant dreaminess without, however, overmastering the will power," and states that peyote "effectively checks tendencies toward alcoholism."[12]

The House passed the committee-reported bill to prohibit the sale of intoxicating liquor, Indian hemp, or peyote to any Indian. An amendment to permit the sale of peyote when used for religious purposes was rejected, and the bill as a whole passed.[13] The Senate took no action on this House bill. Instead, it debated an amendment to prohibit the introduction of peyote into Indian territories. The amendment was rejected on a point of order because it constituted general legislation on an appropriations bill.[14] Although this bill did not pass, Interior Department appropriations acts from 1923 to 1934 contained funds to suppress "the traffic in intoxicating liquors and deleterious drugs, including peyote, among Indians."[15]

The religious use of peyote was opposed by some tribal leaders, who considered it a threat to their authority.[16] In 1962, the D.C. Circuit affirmed the action of the Secretary of the Interior in approving a resolution adopted by the Navajo Tribal Council, banning the sale, use, or possession of peyote. The NAC had challenged the resolution, considering peyote as indispensable for their religious ceremonies, but the Navajo Tribal Council regarded peyote as not connected with "any Navajo religious practice" and harmful and foreign to the Navajo traditional way of life.[17]

REFORM MOVEMENT

Montana in 1957 and New Mexico in 1959 amended their narcotic laws to provide that the prohibition against narcotics "shall not apply to the possession, sale or gift of peyote for religious sacramental purposes

12. Id. at 11.
13. 56 Cong. Rec. 11113–15 (1918).
14. Id. at 4129–33.
15. 42 Stat. 1182 (1923); 43 Stat. 396 (1924); 43 Stat. 1147 (1925); 44 Stat. 458 (1926); 44 Stat. 939 (1927); 45 Stat. 204 (1928); 45 Stat. 1566 (1929); 46 Stat. 1119 (1931); 47 Stat. 94 (1932); 47 Stat. 824 (1933); 48 Stat. 366 (1934). Funds for peyote suppression were not included in the 1935 Interior appropriations bill; 49 Stat. 182 (1935).
16. de Verges, "Peyote and the Native American Church," 2 Am. Ind. L. Rev. at 72.
17. Oliver v. Udall, 306 F.2d 819, 821 (D.C. Cir. 1962).

by a bona fide religious organization incorporated under the laws of the state."[18] In 1959, the Tenth Circuit decided a case brought by the NAC, which sought an injunction against an ordinance adopted by the Navajo Tribal Council making it an offense to introduce peyote into Navajo country. The Navajos entered the house of an NAC member while he conducted religious ceremonies, and without a search warrant searched the premises and arrested several people. The NAC claimed that the ordinance was void because it violated the church's rights and the rights of its members under the First, Fourth, and Fifth Amendments of the U.S. Constitution. The court held that in the absence of a constitutional provision or a congressional statute making the Bill of Rights applicable to Indian nations, federal courts lacked jurisdiction over tribal laws or regulations.[19]

In 1960, an Arizona trial court ruled against the state in a case involving a Navajo woman arrested for illegal possession of peyote. The court held that her religious interests outweighed whatever governmental interest the state could present. The judge wrote that the use of peyote was "essential to the existence of the peyote religion. Without it, the practice of the religion would be effectively prevented."[20] The state appealed, but the Arizona Supreme Court affirmed the holding of the trial judge.[21]

Several years later, in 1964, the California Supreme Court reached a similar result in *People* v. *Woody*. State police arrested a group of Navajos who used peyote during a religious ceremony. They were convicted under a state statute that prohibited the unauthorized possession of peyote. The court ruled that since the defendants used peyote "in a bona fide pursuit of a religious faith," and since there was no compelling state interest to override that use, application of the statute in this instance violated the First Amendment. Although the First Amendment was not applicable to Indian nations (and would not be until 1968), it applied to the states.[22] The court explained that peyote serves a sacramental purpose similar to bread and wine in certain Christian churches, but "it is more than a sacrament. Peyote constitutes in itself an object of

18. People v. Woody, 394 P.2d 813, 819 (Cal. 1964).
19. Native American Church v. Navajo Tribal Council, 272 F.2d 131 (10th Cir. 1959).
20. Carolyn N. Long, Religious Freedom and Indian Rights 18 (2000).
21. Neither decision in this case, *Arizona* v. *Attakai*, Criminal No. 4098, Coconino County, was reported, but it is cited in People v. Woody, 394 P.2d at 813 n. 5.
22. People v. Woody, 394 P.2d at 815.

worship; prayers are directed to it much as prayers are devoted to the Holy Ghost. On the other hand, to use peyote for nonreligious purposes is sacrilegious."[23]

After the California Supreme Court accepted the religious use of peyote in *Woody*, two years later a California trial court rejected an individual's argument that he had a religious right to plant, cultivate, and smoke marijuana. He was not a member of any organized religion. What he called religion was his "own personal philosophy and way of life," unlike the religious practices of the Native American Church and the established use of peyote as a sacrament.[24] In 1969, a California appellate court upheld the conviction of someone who said he used marijuana "for meditative communication with the Supreme Being." The court found no similarity between the use of marijuana in this case and the NAC's use of peyote as an object of worship.[25]

In 1966, the North Carolina Supreme Court decided another kind of peyote case. Someone who called himself a "Peyotist with Buddhist leanings" and a member of the Neo-American Church (unrelated to the Native American Church) claimed that his use of peyote and marijuana was protected by the First Amendment. The Neo-American Church was incorporated in California in 1965, its head is Chief Boo Hoo, and the members (Boo Hoos) join the organization to take psychedelic drugs as sacramental foods and "manifestations of the Grace of God."[26] Although there was some doubt that this member of the Neo-American Church used drugs solely for religious purposes, the court held that the First Amendment did not protect even sincere users. Religious beliefs are protected, but not religious acts that "constitute threats to the public safety, morals, peace and order."[27]

Other cases decided during this period also went against the use of drugs for supposedly religious reasons. In 1968, a federal court rejected the argument of a Neo-American Church member who claimed that her ingestion of marijuana and LSD was required for a religious experience. The court held that the statutes under which she was indicted were rational, constitutional, and served a substantial government interest. Her

23. Id. at 817. See also In re Grady, 394 P.2d 728 (Cal. 1964), in which the California Supreme Court again insisted that the religious use of peyote must be honest and bona fide.
24. People v. Mitchell, 52 Cal.Rptr. 884, 887–88 (1966).
25. People v. Collins, 78 Cal.Rptr. 151 (1969).
26. United States v. Kuch, 288 F.Supp. 439, 443 (D.D.C. 1968).
27. State v. Bullard, 148 S.E.2d 565, 569 (N.C. 1966).

case involved more than the personal use of drugs; she was also indicted for unlawful sale and delivery.[28]

These cases in the 1960s were decided either by state courts or by lower federal courts. The case that went to the Supreme Court and received nationwide attention concerned Timothy Leary, who championed the use of drugs as a psychedelic, mystical, and religious experience. The Fifth Circuit affirmed his conviction against his claim of a First Amendment right to free exercise of religion. Like some of the cases already discussed, Leary was not charged with merely using marijuana. He was convicted of transporting and concealing the drug. His daughter Susan, age eighteen, was also convicted under the transportation and concealment charges. He testified that he was aware that his failure to pay a transfer tax for the marijuana violated federal law.[29] The court rejected any similarity between his actions and the use of peyote upheld in *Woody*.[30] Unlike the California law that prohibited the religious use of peyote, the court ruled that Congress had a compelling governmental interest in passing laws against marijuana.

Leary's conviction was reversed by the Supreme Court because of issues concerning self-incrimination under the Fifth Amendment and questions of due process. His religious freedom argument was not at issue, nor was there any question about the compelling need of the national government to control marijuana. The Court closed with this observation: "Nothing in what we hold today implies any constitutional disability in Congress to deal with the marihuana traffic by other means."[31]

None of these cases challenged *Woody*'s support for using peyote in a religious ceremony conducted by the NAC. In 1972, when that identical issue was before an appellate court in Arizona, the court upheld the use of peyote in a religious ceremony (a wedding) convened by the Native American Church. Peyotism, said the court, "is not a twentieth century cult nor a fad subject to extinction at a whim."[32] Like the California court in *Woody*, the court held that Arizona had failed to show a compelling state interest in prohibiting the use of peyote as part of a religious ceremony. The trial record showed that peyote is not a narcotic and is not a habit-forming substance.[33] The appellate court remarked:

28. United States v. Kuch, 288 F.Supp. 439 (D.D.C. 1968).
29. Leary v. United States, 383 F.2d 851, 856 n. 7 (5th Cir. 1967).
30. Id. at 861.
31. Leary v. United States, 395 U.S. 6, 54 (1969).
32. State v. Whittingham, 504 P.2d 950, 952 (Ariz. 1972).
33. Id. at 953.

"The fact that the use of peyote will not result in addiction is crucial because the State would have a great interest in protecting its citizens from drug abuse."[34] In deciding a peyote case in 1974, the Ninth Circuit agreed with much in *Woody* without actually embracing it as federal law.[35]

Going against these cases was an Oregon decision in 1975. The state police, after arresting an individual for failure to have a driver's license, discovered peyote during a search. Convicted of unlawfully possessing mescaline, or peyote, he was not given an opportunity to present evidence of his religious beliefs or his membership in the Native American Church. The Court of Appeals of Oregon affirmed his conviction.[36]

In 1977, an Oklahoma appellate court reviewed an Indian's conviction for possessing peyote. When arrested, he had a string of peyote buttons around his neck and other peyote buttons wrapped and tied in a handkerchief inside his pocket. At trial, he testified that he was a member of the Otoe tribe, the Ponca tribe, and the NAC. He admitted to possessing peyote, but said it was used for religious ceremonies and not for illicit drug purposes. The past president of the NAC of Oklahoma testified that it was permissible for members to carry peyote as a religious symbol. Several people told the trial court that the defendant was a member of the NAC. The appellate court ruled (1) that the defendant was a member of the church (2) his possession of peyote "was and is protected," and (3) the state had failed to show a compelling interest in preventing NAC members from possessing and transporting peyote within the state.[37]

FEDERAL CONTROLS

Federal actions during this period also seemed to secure the religious use of peyote by NAC members. Congress passed a drug abuse act in 1965, leaving to the administration broad discretion in making exemptions for depressant or stimulant drugs. The House bill had provided the NAC with a specific exemption for peyote, but the Senate—and the enacted

34. Id.
35. Golden Eagle v. Johnson, 493 F.2d 1179, 1183 (9th Cir. 1974).
36. State v. Soto, 537 P.2d 142 (Ore. 1975), cert. denied, 424 U.S. 955 (1976).
37. Whitehorn v. State, 561 P.2d 539, 547 (Okla. 1977). See Robert Johnston, "Whitehorn v. State: Peyote and Religious Freedom in Oklahoma," 5 Am. Ind. L. Rev. 229 (1977).

bill—left that issue to administrative regulation.[38] The following year, the Commissioner of Food and Drugs listed a number of drugs that had a depressant effect on the central nervous system, including mescaline and its salts and peyote. The notice in the *Federal Register* explains that the listing of peyote "does not apply to non-drug use in bona fide religious ceremonies of the Native American Church; however, persons supplying the product to the Church are required to register and maintain appropriate records of receipts and disbursements of the article."[39]

In 1978, the Drug Enforcement Administration (DEA) of the Justice Department issued a notice to discuss implementation of a federal regulation that specifically exempted NAC members from the registration requirement—under the Controlled Substances Act—for the use of peyote in bona fide religious ceremonies.[40] The purpose of the notice was not to rescind or reduce the exemption, but rather to discuss the difficulty of identifying bona fide church members and to search for ways of preventing unauthorized persons from taking advantage of the exemption. In 1981, the Office of Legal Counsel (OLC) of the Justice Department released an opinion expressing its view that the DEA regulation exempting peyote use in connection with NAC religious ceremonies accurately reflected congressional intent.[41]

The special exemption for NAC members has been challenged by other churches that want to use peyote in their religious ceremonies. The Church of the Awakening, a non-Indian religious body, asked a federal court to add its name in the *Code of Federal Regulations* along with the NAC. In 1972, the Ninth Circuit acknowledged that the federal regulation was arbitrary in classifying the NAC one way and other churches another way, but said it would be equally arbitrary to place the NAC and the Church of the Awakening in one category and all other churches in another.[42] In 1984, the Fifth Circuit received another challenge to the special exemption, this time from the Peyote Way Church of God. The court remanded the case to the district court to determine whether the federal regulation denied religious freedom to the Peyote

38. 111 Cong. Rec. 14608 (1965); 79 Stat. 226 (1965).
39. 31 Fed. Reg. 4679 (1966); the peyote exception for the NAC currently appears in 21 C.F.R. § 1307.31 (4-1-01 ed.).
40. 43 Fed. Reg. 56106 (1978).
41. 5 Op. Off. Legal Counsel 403 (1981).
42. Kennedy v. Bureau of Narcotics and Dangerous Drugs, 459 F.2d 415 (9th Cir. 1972).

Way Church.[43] When the case returned, the Fifth Circuit upheld the special exemption for the NAC on the grounds that Congress had been given extraordinary authority over Indian matters and the special exemption was rationally related to the legitimate governmental objective of preserving Indian culture.[44]

In 1979, a federal district court in New York read the peyote exception differently. In addition to the NAC, it ruled that the exception covered the Native American Church of New York, which is not affiliated with the NAC, and only a few of its roughly one thousand members are Indians. Also, the Native American Church of New York expresses a belief that all psychedelic drugs, including LSD and marijuana, are deities.[45] The district court concluded that the exemption for peyote is available to any bona fide religious organization that uses peyote for sacramental purposes and regards peyote as a deity.[46]

The Case of Al Smith and Galen Black

Alfred Smith, a Klamath Indian and member of the NAC, served as a counselor for alcoholics since 1971. He worked for ADAPT (Alcohol and Drug Abuse Prevention and Treatment) from August 25, 1982, until his discharge on March 5, 1984. ADAPT required counselors to abstain from alcohol and mind-altering drugs and warned Smith that he could be discharged for using peyote, even if part of a religious ceremony. After ingesting peyote during a weekend service conducted by the NAC, Smith was fired and subsequently denied unemployment benefits because of the drug use.[47]

In 1986, the Supreme Court of Oregon held that the denial of benefits did not violate state constitutional provisions regarding freedom of worship and religious opinion, but it did violate the Free Exercise Clause of the First Amendment of the U.S. Constitution.[48] It relied on the standards announced in 1963 by the U.S. Supreme Court in *Sherbert v. Verner:*

43. Peyote Way Church of God, Inc. v. Smith, 742 F.2d 193 (5th Cir. 1984).

44. Peyote Way Church of God, Inc. v. Thornburgh, 922 F.2d 1210, 1216 (5th Cir. 1991).

45. Native American Church of New York v. United States, 468 F.Supp. 1247, 1248 (S.D.N.Y. 1979), aff'd 633 F.2d 205 (2d Cir. 1980).

46. Id. at 1251.

47. Smith v. Employment Div., 721 P.2d 445, 445–46 (Ore. 1986).

48. Id. at 446–49.

the person claiming the free exercise right must show that the application of law "significantly burdens" the free exercise of religion, and the state must show that the constraint on religious activity is the "least restrictive" means of achieving a "compelling" state interest.[49] A companion case involved Galen Black, a non-Indian who belonged to the NAC. He was also denied unemployment benefits after being fired for ingesting peyote during a religious ceremony.

Under Oregon law, the possession of peyote was a crime. Unemployment benefits could be denied when an employee was discharged for misconduct, in this case by ingesting peyote. Although the state defended the law as part of its general policy against drug use, the Oregon Supreme Court held that the state had not shown that the financial stability of the unemployment insurance fund would be "imperiled by claimants applying for religious exemptions if this claimant receives benefits."[50]

Dave Frohnmayer, Attorney General of Oregon, took the case to the U.S. Supreme Court. In 1988, the Court vacated the Oregon ruling and returned the case with the request that the Oregon Supreme Court decide whether the religious use of peyote was legal in that state. The U.S. Supreme Court pointed out that the results reached in *Sherbert* and other unemployment benefits cases "might well have been different if the employees had been discharged for engaging in criminal conduct."[51] Passages in the decision seemed to send a green light to Oregon that it would be permissible to deny unemployment benefits to Smith and Black:

> If a bigamist may be sent to jail despite the religious motivation for his misconduct, surely a State may refuse to pay unemployment compensation to a marriage counselor who was discharged because he or she entered into a bigamous relationship. The protection that the First Amendment provides to "*legitimate* claims to the free exercise of religion," . . . does not extend to conduct that a State has validly proscribed.[52]

A dissent by Brennan, joined by Marshall and Blackmun, criticized the Court for deciding the case and misconstruing the words of the Oregon Supreme Court. Brennan predicted that the state court "is most likely to

49. Id. at 449.
50. Id. at 451.
51. Employment Div. v. Smith, 485 U.S. 660, 671 (1988).
52. Id. (emphasis in original).

respond to our efforts by merely reiterating what it has already stated with unmistakeable clarity."[53] That is precisely what happened. The Oregon Supreme Court reaffirmed its earlier ruling by holding that the First Amendment entitled Smith and Black to their unemployment benefits. The state court pointed out that when Congress passed the Drug Abuse Control Amendments of 1965, for the purpose of bringing peyote under federal control, it expected the implementing regulation to exempt the religious use of peyote. In 1970 and 1978, Congress passed additional legislation offering support for the peyote religion.[54] As anticipated by Congress, the implementing regulation issued in 1971 stated that the listing of peyote as a controlled substance "does not apply to the nondrug use of peyote in bona fide religious ceremonies of the Native American Church."[55]

The Oregon Supreme Court therefore sought guidance from a range of judicial and nonjudicial sources: its own state constitutional heritage, rulings from the U.S. Supreme Court, constitutional judgments from Congress, and legislation from other states that provided some type of exemption for the sacramental use of peyote.[56] With public participation on the issue so broad and deep, it was unlikely that anything the U.S. Supreme Court announced would be received with any degree of finality.

Frohnmayer urged the U.S. Supreme Court to review this latest decision of the Oregon Supreme Court. The case presented this question: Does the Free Exercise Clause of the First Amendment "protect a person's religiously motivated use of peyote from the reach of a state's general criminal law prohibition?" Frohnmayer objected strongly to the reliance by the state supreme court on congressional interpretations of the Constitution:

> The Oregon Supreme Court's holding is not a product of the court's independent assessment of what the first amendment requires. At most, it represents a choice to defer to congressional assumptions about the requirements of the federal constitution. . . . This process of canvassing congressional understanding to resolve an important first amendment question would be troubling under any circumstance.[57]

53. Id. at 679.
54. Smith v. Employment Division, 763 P.2d 146, 149 (Ore. 1988).
55. 21 C.F.R. § 1307.31.
56. Smith v. Employment Division, 763 P.2d at 148, n. 2.
57. Petition for Writ of Certiorari to the Supreme Court of the State of Oregon, Employment Division v. Smith; 196 Landmark Briefs 425.

Frohnmayer defended the state's interest in controlling drugs. Few regulatory areas, he said, invoke governmental interests in public health and safety "with force equal to that of drug use." Few drugs trigger that interest "with strength equal to that of hallucinogens, such as peyote."⁵⁸ Although some state courts had held that the federal Free Exercise Clause protects the use of peyote by NAC members, Frohnmayer pointed to contrary rulings by the Oregon courts.⁵⁹

By the time the case returned to the U.S. Supreme Court, some of the original conditions had changed substantially to raise the question whether the dispute was still a live controversy. For example, as part of a federal consent decree, ADAPT agreed that religious use of peyote by NAC members would no longer be considered work-related misconduct. The conditions that led to the denial of benefits to Smith and Black could not arise again in Oregon.⁶⁰ Smith and Black won back pay.⁶¹ Other factors pointed to mootness. Smith and Black exhausted the unemployment benefits they received as a result of the first decision by the Oregon Supreme Court; under Oregon law they could not be forced to repay the benefits even if the second decision of the state court was reversed by the U.S. Supreme Court; and the time period for charging Smith and Black with violating Oregon's drug laws had passed.⁶² Frohnmayer disputed some of these points, claiming that there was still time for the state to collect the benefits from Smith and Black.⁶³

THE COURT DECIDES IN 1990

Despite efforts within Oregon to resolve the issue, the state's supreme court and the Attorney General were clearly at loggerheads. In 1990, the U.S. Supreme Court attempted to settle the matter by holding that the Free Exercise Clause permits a state to prohibit sacramental peyote use

58. Id. at 426.
59. Brief for Petitioners, 196 Landmark Briefs 478 n. 26, citing State v. Soto, 537 P.2d 142 (Ore. 1975), cert. denied, 424 U.S. 955 (1976), upholding the prohibition of mescaline even for religious purposes.
60. Brief in Opposition to Petition for Writ of Certiorari, Employment Division v. Smith; 196 Landmark Briefs 2.
61. Garrett Epps, "To an Unknown God: The Hidden History of *Employment Division v. Smith*," 30 Ariz. St. L. J. 953, 989 (1998).
62. Brief for Respondents, Employment Division v. Smith; 196 Landmark Briefs 542.
63. Reply Brief for Petitioners, Employment Division v. Smith; 196 Landmark Briefs 552.

and to deny unemployment benefits to persons discharged for such use. In *Employment Division* v. *Smith,* delivered by Justice Scalia, the Court ruled that state law may prohibit the possession and use of a drug even if it incidentally prohibits a religious practice, provided that the state law is neutral and generally applicable to all individuals.[64]

Under this test, there was no need for the state to show a compelling interest or to use the least restrictive means. The issue of abandoning the compelling interest test was not before the Court. It was neither argued nor briefed. Remarkably, Scalia twice cited *Minersville School District* v. *Gobitis* (1940), a decision bitterly attacked when it appeared and one that survived only three years before the Court overturned it.[65] Scalia acknowledged that his test would place religious minorities at the mercy of the political process, but discriminatory treatment was an "unavoidable consequence of democratic government."[66] One might add that discriminatory treatment is often the consequence of judicial rulings, with remedies coming from democratic institutions.

Although Scalia wrote for a 6–3 majority, with dissents from Blackmun, Brennan, and Marshall, the division within the Court was much sharper. O'Connor's concurrence wrote bitingly that the Court's holding "dramatically departs from well-settled First Amendment jurisprudence, appears unnecessary to resolve the question presented, and is incompatible with our Nation's fundamental commitment to individual religious liberty."[67] Elsewhere she said that Scalia had given "a strained reading of the First Amendment" and accused him of presenting a "parade of horribles."[68] Further, she noted that there "is nothing talismanic about neutral laws of general applicability or general criminal prohibitions, for laws neutral toward religion can coerce a person to violate his religious conscience or intrude upon his religious duties just as effectively as laws aimed at religion."[69]

Immediately following the Court's decision, a broad coalition of religious groups sought a rehearing in the case. They argued that the new standard developed by Scalia would require a "massive reordering of the delicate relationship between individuals and religious organizations and

64. Employment Division v. Smith, 494 U.S. 872 (1990).
65. Id. at 879.
66. Id. at 890.
67. Id. at 891.
68. Id. at 892, 902.
69. Id. at 901.

the power of the state," and would encourage states to enact restrictions that would affect religious practices ranging from Jewish and Muslim ritual slaughter of animals, to circumcision, and to the use of communion wine by Christians. Among the groups represented in this effort: American Friends Service Committee, American Jewish Committee, American Jewish Congress, Americans United for Separation of Church and State, Baptist Committee on Public Affairs, Christian Legal Society, Lutheran Church Missouri Synod, National Council of Churches, National Association of Evangelicals, and the Presbyterian Church USA. The litigation director for Concerned Women for America expressed dismay. The conservatives on the Court that "all the Christians were shouting 'hurray' about" when President Reagan placed them on the Supreme Court, except for O'Connor, "were all the people who stabbed us in the back on this thing. Scalia wrote the opinion, and Rehnquist and Kennedy joined it."[70] As expected, the Court denied the motion for a rehearing.[71]

LEGISLATIVE REMEDIES

With the judiciary offering no relief, interest groups turned to legislative remedies in Congress and Oregon. A bill introduced in Congress in 1990, the Religious Freedom Restoration Act (RFRA), was drafted to reinstate the *Sherbert* standard for protecting religious liberties. Congressman Stephen Solarz took the lead in crafting the bill, working in concert with the National Council of Churches and other religious groups. It was agreed that the objective should be to restore *Sherbert* and there should be no focus on the sacramental use of peyote. Otherwise, the legislation would become known as "a drug bill."[72]

The effect of Scalia's decision in *Smith* was already being felt in the lower courts. When a Laotian immigrant died and a medical examiner insisted on performing an autopsy, the individual's parents protested on religious grounds (animism) that autopsies were abhorrent mutilations of the body that prevented the spirit from being set free. In January 1990, before Scalia's ruling, a district judge sustained their position. After Scalia's decision the judge announced with "deep regret" that the Supreme

70. "High Court Urged to Reconsider," Washington Post, May 12, 1990, at C11. See "Hail Mary Pass," Legal Times, May 14, 1990, at 11.
71. Employment Division v. Smith, 496 U.S. 913 (1990).
72. Long, Religious Freedom and Indian Rights, at 213.

Court's opinion forced him to deny their claim.[73] Other restrictions on religious liberty flowed from Scalia's decision.[74]

Although the Religious Freedom Restoration Act enjoyed strong support in Congress, from liberals as well as from conservatives, the National Right to Life Committee argued that the bill would create a loophole enabling women to seek abortions on religious grounds. There was also concern that RFRA would make it easier for prison inmates to challenge security policies and for soldiers to resist military dress codes.[75]

While Congress considered this proposal, the Oregon legislature repaired some of the damage of the U.S. Supreme Court's decision by enacting a bill that protects the sacramental use of peyote by the Native American Church. The state bill was sponsored by Representative Jim Edmunson and assigned to the judiciary committee, on which he served.[76] Al Smith testified in favor of the bill, advising the committee that the "drug we have to worry about is alcohol."[77] Frohnmayer's office took no position on the bill.[78] As enacted in 1991, the bill states that in any prosecution for the manufacture, possession, or delivery of peyote, it is an affirmative defense that the peyote is being used or is intended for use (1) in connection with the good faith practice of a religious belief (2) as directly associated with a religious practice, and (3) in a manner that is not dangerous to the health of the user or others who are in the proximity of the user.[79]

The Religious Freedom Restoration Act (RFRA)

After the introduction of RFRA in 1990, a broad coalition of religious and civil liberties groups worked closely to overturn *Smith*. Congressional

73. Yang v. Sturner, 750 F.Supp. 558 (D.R.I. 1990); You Vang Yang v. Sturner, 728 F.Supp. 845 (D.R.I. 1990).

74. "Reins on Religious Freedom?" Washington Post, March 9, 1991, at A1.

75. "Abortion Dispute Entangles Religious Freedom Bill," CQ Weekly Report, April 13, 1991, at 913–918. The House Judiciary Committee held hearings on September 27, 1990; "Religious Freedom Restoration Act of 1990," hearing before the House Committee on the Judiciary, 101st Cong., 2d Sess. (1990).

76. "Legislator Will Introduce Bill to Protect Peyote's Sacred Use," Eugene Register Guard, April 20, 1990, at 5B.

77. "Panel Listens to Peyote Testimony," Salem, Oregon, Statesman Journal, April 6, 1991, at D1.

78. Garrett Epps, To An Unknown God: Religious Freedom on Trial 235 (2001).

79. Oregon Laws, Chap. 329, § 1 (June 24, 1991); reprinted in 1995 Oregon Revised Statutes 475.992, § 5 (v. 9, p. 80).

hearings in 1992 explored the authority of Congress to enact legislation to overturn the Supreme Court on constitutional issues. Congressman Henry Hyde, a senior member of the House Judiciary Committee, argued that Congress had no authority to enact RFRA: "Congress is institutionally unable to restore a prior interpretation of the first amendment once the Supreme Court has rejected that interpretation. We are a legislature, not the Court."[80]

Yet throughout its history, Congress has often countermanded the Court on constitutional issues. Scholars and lobbyists at the hearings testified strongly that Congress had a right and a duty to act when the Court endangers fundamental freedoms. Robert Dugan, Jr., representing the National Association of Evangelicals, said that the Supreme Court, intended to be a guardian of constitutional freedoms, has "deprived us of our birthright as Americans" and emptied the Free Exercise Clause of its meaning. The system of checks and balances, he said, empowered Congress "to overrule the Court by restoring the compelling interest test."[81] Dallin H. Oaks, from the Mormon Church, regarded the statutory restoration of the compelling interest standard as "both a legitimate and a necessary response by the legislative branch to the degradation of religious freedom resulting from the *Smith* case."[82] Nadine Strossen of the ACLU appealed to Congress to act:

> The Supreme Court has cast us back into the good graces of this legislature, and it does depend on you, our elected representatives, to restore to all of us the religious freedom that should be protected by the Constitution but that the U.S. Supreme Court has refused to protect that way. Please restore our religious liberty through legislation.[83]

At Senate hearings, one witness called *Smith* "the Dred Scott of first amendment law."[84] Stalled for two years, RFRA began to move in 1993 when the House Judiciary Committee, voting 35 to zero, ordered the measure reported. The bill was designed to create a "statutory right" to

80. "Religious Freedom Restoration Act of 1991," hearings before the House Committee on the Judiciary, 102d Cong., 2d Sess. 7 (1992).
81. Id. at 10, 14.
82. Id. at 25.
83. Id. at 64–65.
84. "The Religious Freedom Restoration Act," hearing before the Senate Committee on the Judiciary, 102d Cong., 2d Sess. 42 (1992). Oliver S. Thomas, general counsel, Baptist Joint Committee on Public Affairs.

require the compelling governmental interest test in cases in which the free exercise of religion has been burdened by a law of general applicability.[85] For constitutional authority to pass the bill, the committee pointed to Section 5 of the Fourteenth Amendment and the Necessary and Proper Clause embodied in Article I, Section 8. Congress could provide "statutory protection for a constitutional value when the Supreme Court has been unwilling to assert its authority."[86]

The House bill did not mandate that all states permit the ceremonial use of peyote; it merely subjected any prohibition to the compelling interest test.[87] The committee recognized that religious liberty claims in the context of prisons and the military posed "far different problems" than in civilian settings.[88] Turning to the issue of abortion, the committee did not believe that the bill would either expand, contract, or alter that right.[89] The bill passed the House under suspension of the rules, which requires a two-thirds majority.[90]

The Senate Judiciary Committee, by a vote of 15 to 1, reported RFRA for floor consideration.[91] By the time the bill headed for final passage, sixty-eight religious and civil liberties groups were lined up behind it.[92] The Senate considered and rejected an amendment to exempt prisoners from the bill's application. The vote was 41 to 58.[93] On final passage, the bill passed 97 to 3.[94] Under a motion of unanimous consent, the House passed the bill.[95] As enacted, RFRA provided that governments may substantially burden a person's religious exercise only if they demonstrate a compelling interest and use the least restrictive means of furthering that interest. The term "government" applied to any branch, department, agency, instrumentality, or official at the federal, state, and local level.[96]

85. H. Rept. No. 103-88, 103d Cong., 1st Sess. 1–2 (1993).
86. Id. at 9.
87. Id. at 7.
88. Id. at 8.
89. Id.
90. 139 Cong. Rec. 9680–87 (1993).
91. S. Rept. No. 103-11, 103d Cong., 1st Sess. 2 (1993).
92. "Disparate Groups Unite Behind Civil Rights Bill on Religious Freedom," Washington Post, October 16, 1993, at A7.
93. 139 Cong. Rec. 26178–97, 26407–14 (1993).
94. Id. at 26416.
95. Id. at 27239–41 (1993).
96. 107 Stat. 1488 (1993).

CONGRESSIONAL LEGISLATION IN 1994

A year after enacting RFRA, Congress passed legislation to permit the use of peyote by Native Americans during religious ceremonies.[97] As Senator Paul Wellstone remarked, leaving the definition of standards for religious freedom "up to the judiciary has not proven very effective for native American religions."[98] Patrick H. Lefthand, a member of the Kootenai tribe, told the Senate Committee on Indian Affairs that the Supreme Court decided that "our religion did not deserve the same protection afforded to all Americans who practice Judeo-Christian religions," and urged Congress to pass legislation "to ensure the continuation and vitality of Indian communities."[99]

There were precedents to support a statutory exemption for peyote. In 1978, Congress had passed the American Indian Religious Freedom Act to "protect and preserve" religious beliefs of American Indians, including their freedom "to worship through ceremonials and traditional rites."[100] The legislative history explained that although previous congressional statutes "prohibit the use of peyote as a hallucinogen, it is established Federal law that peyote is constitutionally protected when used by a bona fide religion as a sacrament."[101] The Drug Enforcement Agency (DEA) then issued an interpretative rule, stating that the listing of peyote "as a controlled substance in Schedule I does not apply to the nondrug use of peyote in bona fide religious ceremonies of the Native American Church, and members of the Native American Church so using peyote are exempt from registration."[102] A memo from the Office of Legal Counsel (OLC) concluded that DEA had accurately reflected congressional intent.[103] Despite the 1978 statute, its clear legislative history, the interpretation by the DEA, and the subsequent blessing by the OLC, the religious use of peyote by members of the Native American Church still lacked full legal protection.

The bill that became law in 1994 originally attempted to redress a

97. 108 Stat. 3125 (1994).

98. 139 Cong. Rec. 10971 (1993).

99. "Native American Free Exercise of Religious Freedom Act," hearing before the Senate Committee on Indian Affairs, 103d Cong., 2d Sess. 98–99 (1993).

100. 92 Stat. 469 (1978).

101. S. Rept. No. 95-709, 95th Cong., 2d Sess. 3 (1978). The same sentence appears in H. Rept. No. 95-1308, 95th Cong., 2d Sess. 2 (1978).

102. 21 C.F.R. § 1307.31 (1978), referred to as a notice in 43 Fed. Reg. 56106 (1978).

103. 5 Ops. O.L.C. 403 (1981).

number of Supreme Court decisions that gave short shrift to Indian religious rights. In addition to *Smith,* the bill responded to the Court's decision in 1988 that denied protection of an Indian religious site on public land.[104] Senate hearings disclosed that RFRA "fails to clearly address the fundamental issue of native access to sacred sites."[105] Senator Daniel Inouye, sponsor of the legislation, explained that the bill would provide "protection of native American sacred sites and puts into place a mechanism for resolving disputes."[106] Senator Mark Hatfield said it was important that the 1988 decision "not be allowed to continue to deny native American input into Government actions that might affect historically sacred sites."[107] This part of the legislation was never enacted. However, President Clinton issued an executive order in 1996 to direct executive branch agencies to (1) accommodate access to and ceremonial use of Indian sacred sites by Indian religious practitioners and (2) avoid adversely affecting the physical integrity of such sacred sites.[108]

DEA officials testified that the religious use of peyote by Indians has nothing to do with the vast and violent traffic in illegal narcotics in the United States. The DEA was also unaware of the diversion of peyote to any illicit market.[109] The bill enacted in 1994 specifically recognizes that "for many Indian people, the traditional ceremonial use of the peyote cactus as a religious sacrament has for centuries been integral to a way of life, and significant in perpetuating Indian tribes and cultures."[110] The statute also notes that the Supreme Court's decision in *Smith* did not protect Indian practitioners who used peyote in Indian religious ceremonies.[111]

CONSTITUTIONAL REVIEW OF RFRA

Early in 1995, a district court in Texas held RFRA to be unconstitutional. Relying on dicta from *Baker* v. *Carr* (1962) and *United States* v. *Nixon* (1974) that the Court regards itself as the ultimate interpreter of the

---

104. Lyng v. Northwest Indian Cemetery Prot. Assn., 485 U.S. 439 (1988).
105. 139 Cong. Rec. 10971 (statement by Senator Wellstone).
106. Id. at 10963.
107. Id. at 10970.
108. Executive Order 13007, 61 Fed. Reg. 26771 (1996).
109. H. Rept. No. 103-675, 103d Cong., 2d Sess. 4 (1994).
110. 108 Stat. 3125, § 2 (amending the American Indian Religious Freedom Act of 1978 by adding section 3(a)(1)).
111. Id., § 3(a)(4).

Constitution, the district court concluded that Congress cannot enact legislation that has the effect of overturning a Supreme Court decision, and that RFRA violated the doctrine of separation of powers by "intruding on the power and duty of the judiciary."[112] That decision was overturned a year later by the Fifth Circuit. The executive and legislative branches, said the appellate court, "also have both the right and duty to interpret the constitution."[113] Although the Justice Department described RFRA as "simply a statute over and above that provided by the Constitution," the Fifth Circuit dismissed that as "facile and ultimately incomplete" and refused to "pretend that RFRA is anything but a direct response to the Supreme Court's decision in *Smith*."[114]

The Fifth Circuit found nothing unusual about Congress protecting constitutional rights to a greater degree than the Supreme Court. In 1959, the Supreme Court upheld literacy tests in voting elections; the Voting Rights Act of 1965 prohibited the tests.[115] While it is the judiciary's duty to say what the law is, "that duty is not exclusive."[116] Other branches may participate in the debate over constitutional values. The Fifth Circuit referred to a section from *Smith* where Justice Scalia seemed to invite other branches to protect rights left unguarded by the courts.[117] In that sense, RFRA was consistent with Scalia's appeal to nonjudicial bodies to enhance rights and liberties beyond the minimum levels established by courts.

Other courts also upheld the constitutionality of RFRA.[118] In some cases, plaintiffs lost their case against the state because courts did not find

112. Flores v. City of Boerne, 877 F.Supp. 355, 357 (W.D. Tex. 1995).

113. Flores v. City of Boerne, Tex., 73 F.3d 1352, 1356 (5th Cir. 1996).

114. Id. at 1361.

115. Id. at 1363 (citing Lassiter v. Northhampton County Bd. of Elections, 360 U.S. 45 (1959)).

116. Id. at 1363.

117. Id. at 1362 ("Values that are protected against government interference through enshrinement in the Bill of Rights are not thereby banished from the political process. Just as a society that believes in the negative protection accorded to the press by the First Amendment is likely to enact laws that affirmatively foster the dissemination of the printed word, so also a society that believes in the negative protection accorded to religious belief can be expected to be solicitous of that value in its legislation as well." Employment Division v. Smith, 494 U.S. at 890).

118. E.E.O.C. v. Catholic University of America, 83 F.3d 455, 470 (D.C. Cir. 1996); Abordo v. Hawaii, 902 F.Supp. 1220 (D. Hawaii 1995); Sasnett v. Department of Corrections, 891 F.Supp. 1305 (W.D. Wis. 1995), aff'd, Sasnett v. Sullivan, 91 F.3d 1018 (7th Cir. 1996); Belgard v. Hawaii, 883 F.Supp. 510 (D. Hawaii 1995). In 1996, a district court

a "substantial" burden on their free exercise of religion.[119] Contrary to the
fears of some Senators, prison inmates did not use the statute successfully
to argue for religious liberties that interfere with the security needs of
prison administrators. In those cases, prisons were able to satisfy the
higher standards required by RFRA.[120]

Whatever the Court decided to do with RFRA, it would acknowledge
the role of nonjudicial bodies in protecting religious rights. If it upheld
the statute, it would recognize that religious groups, in concert with Congress, could define religious freedom more generously than the Court. If
it struck it down, it would merely reaffirm the 1990 *Smith* holding, which
itself depended on the political process to protect religion. As the Court
noted in *Smith:* "It may fairly be said that leaving accommodation to the
political process will place at a relative disadvantage those religious practices that are not widely engaged in; but that unavoidable consequence of
democratic government must be preferred to a system in which each conscience is a law unto itself or in which judges weigh the social importance
of all laws against the centrality of all religious beliefs."[121]

RFRA STRUCK DOWN

In 1997, the Supreme Court ruled that Congress exceeded the scope of
its enforcement power under Section 5 of the Fourteenth Amendment in
enacting RFRA.[122] In many ways, Congress had asked for a black eye by

---

in Maryland held that RFRA usurped the Supreme Court's authority to determine the
scope and meaning of the First Amendment and violated the separation of powers. Keeler
v. Mayor & City Council of Cumberland, 928 F.Supp. 591 (D. Md. 1996).

119. Goodall by Goodall v. Stafford County School Bd., 60 F.3d 168 (4th Cir. 1995),
cert. denied, 516 U.S. 1046 (1996).

120. Mack v. O'Leary, 80 F.3d 1175 (7th Cir. 1996); Hamilton v. Schriro, 74 F.3d
1545 (8th Cir. 1996), reversing Hamilton v. Schriro, 863 F.Supp. 1019 (W.D. Mo. 1994);
Werner v. McCotter, 49 F.3d 1476 (10th Cir. 1995), cert. denied, 515 U.S. 1166 (1995);
Bryant v. Gomez, 46 F.3d 948 (9th Cir. 1995); Brown-El v. Harris, 26 F.3d 68 (8th Cir.
1994); Abordo v. Hawaii, 902 F.Supp. 1220 (D. Hawaii 1995); May v. Baldwin, 895
F.Supp. 1398 (D. Ore. 1995); Belgard v. Hawaii, 883 F.Supp. 510 (D. Hawaii 1995);
Phipps v. Parker, 879 F.Supp. 734 (W.D. Ky. 1995); Diaz v. Collins, 872 F.Supp. 353
(E.D. Tex. 1994). But see Sasnett v. Sullivan, 908 F.Supp. 1429 (W.D. Wis. 1995) and
Lawson v. Dugger, 844 F.Supp. 1538 (S.D. Fla. 1994) (holding that prison officials did
not meet the least restrictive standard of RFRA).

121. Employment Division v. Smith, 494 U.S. 872, 890 (1990).

122. Boerne v. Flores, 521 U.S. 507 (1997).

attempting to reimpose a constitutional standard *(Sherbert v. Verner)* that the Court had specifically rejected in *Smith*.[123] The Court could not sit still and have Congress ram *Sherbert* down its throat. But the reasoning and premises in the decision are superficial, unpersuasive, and internally inconsistent. They invite continued challenges and legislative activity. Although the Court strongly hinted that it has the last and final word in deciding the meaning of the Constitution, it in fact left the door wide open for future congressional action.

The Court announced that "Under our Constitution, the Federal Government is one of enumerated powers."[124] Of course that is not true. The federal government is not limited to enumerated powers. The Court itself has recognized a number of implied powers. Congress has the power to investigate, issue subpoenas, and hold executive officials in contempt.[125] The President has the right to remove certain executive officials.[126] If the federal government is one of enumerated powers, where does the Court get the power of judicial review to hold RFRA unconstitutional? Curiously, after the Court makes its statement about enumerated powers, it supplies this citation for support: *McCulloch* v. *Maryland* (1819), which recognized *an implied right* for Congress to create a U.S. Bank.[127]

In deciding that Congress exceeded its power under Section 5 of the Fourteenth Amendment, the Court reasoned that Section 5 is limited to "enforcement" and "remedial" actions.[128] It then charges: "Legislation which alters the meaning of the Free Exercise Clause cannot be said to be enforcing the Clause. Congress does not enforce a constitutional right by changing what the right is." In enacting RFRA, Congress did not alter the meaning of the Free Exercise Clause, any more than the Court alters the meaning of the Free Exercise Clause with its rulings. It could be equally said that the Court does not enforce a constitutional right by changing what the right is, even though the Court changes rights whenever it rules or reverses itself.

123. See Neal Devins, "How Not to Challenge the Court," 39 Wm & Mary L. Rev. 645 (1998).

124. 521 U.S. at 516.

125. McGrain v. Daugherty, 272 U.S. 135, 175 (1927) (the right to investigate); Eastland v. United States Servicemen's Fund, 421 U.S. 491, 505 (1975) (the right to issue subpoenas); Anderson v. Dunn, 6 Wheat. 204 (1821) (the right to hold executive officials in contempt).

126. Myers v. United States, 272 U.S. 52 (1926).

127. 521 U.S. at 516.

128. Id. at 519.

The Court acknowledged, as it had to, that the "line between measures that remedy or prevent unconstitutional actions and measures that make a substantive change in the governing law is not easy to discern."[129] An understatement, to be sure, and nothing in the decision adds any clarity to that line. Although "Congress must have wide latitude in determining where it lies, the distinction exists and must be observed."[130] If the distinction did not exist before and does not exist as a result of this decision, how can Congress or anyone else observe it?

The Court invited future congressional action by noting that there "must be a congruence and proportionality between the injury to be prevented or remedied and the means adopted to that end."[131] Does that mean that RFRA was merely incongruent and disproportional and that adjustments in a redrafted bill might pass muster? That is the clear implication. Other remarks in the decision seemed to encourage a redrafting of RFRA: "While preventive rules are sometimes appropriate remedial measures, there must be a congruence between the means used and the ends to be achieved. The appropriateness of remedial measures must be considered in light of the evil presented."[132] In comparing RFRA to the Voting Rights Act, the Court says that RFRA's "legislative record lacks examples of modern instances of generally applicable laws passed because of religious bigotry. The history of persecution in this country detailed in the hearings mentions no episodes occurring in the past 40 years."[133] Is that the problem? If Congress, with findings, could identify recent examples of religious persecution, would that justify RFRA? The Court merely remarks: "This lack of support in the legislative record, however, is not RFRA's most serious shortcoming."[134] Then why bring it up?

The Court continued to suggest that the defect of RFRA could be cured with additional legislation: "RFRA is so out of proportion to a supposed remedial or preventive object that it cannot be understood as responsive to, or designed to prevent, unconstitutional behavior."[135] That again suggests that the statute was poorly drafted, rather than

129. Id.
130. Id. at 520.
131. Id.
132. Id. at 530.
133. Id.
134. Id. at 531.
135. Id. at 532.

being intrinsically at odds with Section 5. The "sweeping coverage" of RFRA "ensures its intrusion at every level of government, displacing laws and prohibiting official actions of almost every description and regardless of subject matter."[136] Would a rewritten, less intrusive, RFRA be acceptable to the Court? RFRA "has no termination date or termination mechanism."[137] That seems a trivial point. If Congress acts within its power, it does not need to include termination dates, any more than that is required for judicial rulings. As the Court later concedes: "When Congress acts within its sphere of power and responsibilities, it has not just the right but the duty to make its own informed judgment on the meaning and force of the Constitution."[138]

In reviewing the legislative history of the Fourteenth Amendment, the Court recognizes that Section 5 was unusual in giving Congress enforcement powers. As a leading study concluded: "Congress, and not the courts, was to judge whether or not any of the privileges or immunities were not secured to citizens in the several States."[139] No doubt Congress shares with the Court the power to interpret and apply the Fourteenth Amendment, but the Court could not bring itself to admit such an obvious point. Instead, it squirted black ink with this bromide: "The power to interpret the Constitution in a case or controversy remains in the Judiciary."[140] No one denies that. That is what the Constitution plainly provides. But the power of the judiciary to interpret the Constitution in a case or controversy does not mean that the Court is the exclusive or final voice. Such platitudes seemed designed to obscure the scope of congressional power and falsely exalt the Court's power.

The Court warned about the risks of congressional action. "If Congress could define its own powers by altering the Fourteenth Amendment's meaning, no longer would the Constitution be 'superior paramount law, unchangeable by ordinary means.'"[141] There is no intelligible distinction between what Congress does by statute and what the Court does by case law in changing the meaning of the Fourteenth Amendment. Both are done outside the amendment process. The Court inserted some unin-

136. Id.
137. Id.
138. Id. at 535.
139. Id. at 524 (citing H. Flack, The Adoption of the Fourteenth Amendment).
140. Id.
141. Id. at 529.

tended humor with this grave admonition: "Shifting legislative majorities could change the Constitution and effectively circumvent the difficult and detailed amendment process contained in Article V."[142] The same result flows from Court decisions that reflect shifting judicial majorities or changes in the way that a Justice analyzes an issue. As Professor Michael McConnell has written, "'Shifting legislative majorities' have no greater and no less capacity than shifting *judicial* majorities to 'circumvent' the amendment process of Article V."[143] Two days before the Court invalidated RFRA, it overruled a decision from 1985 that had limited federal assistance to parochial schools.[144]

The Court concluded with the suggestion that constitutional interpretation is a judicial monopoly. "Our national experience teaches that the Constitution is preserved best when each part of the Government respects both the Constitution and the proper actions and determinations of the other branches. When the Court has interpreted the Constitution, it has acted within the province of the Judicial Branch, which embraces the duty to say what the law is."[145] Nothing in two hundred years of constitutional practice and construction supports such a static formulation. The Court closes its eyes to what is plainly conspicuous in American history: the reality and capacity of all three branches and the general public to participate in shaping constitutional values, either before or after judicial rulings.

A separate question concerned the constitutionality of RFRA as applied not to the states but to the federal government. In 1998, the Eighth Circuit held that RFRA was constitutional as applied to federal law, it did not violate the separation of powers doctrine, and it did not violate the Establishment Clause.[146] In 2001, the Tenth Circuit ruled that RFRA was a legitimate congressional action under Article I to govern the conduct of federal prison officials.[147]

142. Id.
143. Michael W. McConnell, "Institutions and Interpretation: A Critique of City of Boerne v. Flores," 111 Harv. L. Rev. 153, 174 (1997) (emphasis in original).
144. Agostini v. Felton, 521 U.S. 203 1997 (1997), reversing Aguilar v. Felton, 473 U.S. 402 (1985).
145. Boerne v. Flores, 521 U.S. at 535–36.
146. In re Young, 141 F.3d 854 (8th Cir. 1998), cert. denied, sub nom. Christians, Trustee v. Crystal Evangelical Free Church, 525 U.S. 811 (1998).
147. Kikumura v. Hurley, 242 F.3d 950 (10th Cir. 2001).

"SON OF RFRA"

Following *Boerne*, the House Judiciary Committee held hearings to consider alternative legislation. Representative Robert Scott said that RFRA could be reconfigured by relying on the Interstate Commerce Clause or the Spending Clause.[148] Representative Jerrold Nadler offered some conventional views about the relative competence of Congress and the courts in protecting minority rights. He said that RFRA was "based on the recognition that legislatures, which are responsive to the popular will, are inherently less suited to granting such exemptions than is the independent judiciary."[149] He claimed that judicial independence "was established to protect the rights of minorities from the majority. RFRA was premised on the belief that the courts, and not the legislatures, should continue in that role."[150] If courts were that competent in protecting minority rights, there would have been no need for Congress to pass any legislation in response to *Smith*. Evidently Congress and the religious lobbies were not so enchanted with the Court's competence in deciding constitutional questions. Legislation—congressional action—was necessary to give added protection to religious liberty.

The Senate Judiciary Committee held hearings in 1997 to explore the legislative options available to Congress.[151] The following year, Senator Orrin Hatch introduced the Religious Liberty Protection Act (RLPA) to respond to *Boerne*. He relied primarily on the commerce and spending powers.[152] A similar bill, which passed the House the following year, was supported by ninety-two religious and civil liberties groups, including Protestant, Catholic, Jewish, Muslim, and Native American organizations.[153] The bill stated that a government shall not "substantially burden" a person's religious exercise (1) in a program or activity, operated by a government, that receives federal financial assistance, or (2) in any case in which the substantial burden on religious exercise affects commerce with foreign nations, among the states, or with Indian tribes.[154] With *Smith* in

148. "Protecting Religious Freedom After Boerne v. Flores," hearing before the House Committee on the Judiciary, 105th Cong., 1st Sess 2 (1997).

149. Id. at 10.

150. Id.

151. "Congress' Constitutional Role in Protecting Religious Liberty," hearings before the Senate Committee on the Judiciary, 105th Cong., 1st Sess. (1997).

152. 144 Cong. Rec. S5791 (daily ed. June 9, 1998).

153. 145 Cong. Rec. H5583 (daily ed. July 15, 1999).

154. Id. at H5584.

mind, the bill provided that this principle applies "even if the burden results from a rule of general applicability."[155] Finally, the bill permitted
government to substantially burden a person's religious exercise if the
government can demonstrate that the burden furthers a compelling governmental interest and is the least restrictive means to further that interest.[156] The bill passed the House by a vote of 306 to 118.[157]

By the time the bill cleared both chambers in 2000, it had been restricted to provide two kinds of protections. First, it offers religious
groups protection in land-use disputes, such as zoning issues (the kind
that triggered *Boerne*). Second, the statute makes it easier for prisoners
and other persons confined in state-run institutions to practice their
faith. The statute applies to any organization that receives federal money,
including state and local prisons that get federal construction and maintenance funds. Finally, the statute relies on congressional power over
interstate commerce, because construction materials are shipped between
states for the renovation of buildings owned by religious organizations.[158]

The national debate over the religious use of peyote contains many lessons. The public's broad involvement in basic constitutional questions of
religious liberty underscores why it is impracticable and misleading, on
both political and legal grounds, to look automatically (and optimisti-
cally) to the courts for the protection of minority rights. The Indians
found victory not in courtrooms but in legislative chambers. They prevailed because they were effective in working with many other interest
groups in safeguarding rights that were unobtainable from the courts.
They prevailed because their case was sound and they persisted in the face
of many setbacks. The statutory rights they won, both from Congress
and from state legislatures, are far more secure than any favorable judicial
ruling they might have received.

155. Id.
156. Id.
157. Id. at H5608.
158. 114 Stat. 803 (2000).

9

STATUTORY EXEMPTIONS

Earlier chapters described statutory exemptions for religious purposes in such areas as chaplains, conscientious objectors, religious apparel in the military, and Indian religious freedoms. Other important exemptions exist, including religious exemptions for property and income taxes. In passing legislation in 1919 to prohibit intoxicating liquors, Congress made exceptions for the drinking of sacramental wine. It decided that the Amish should not be compelled to pay social security taxes. Congressional statutes prohibit discrimination on the basis of religion in employment and housing decisions, but exceptions exist for religious organizations. In regulating the slaughter of poultry, Congress recognizes a separate status for slaughter when performed under religious dietary laws. Each of these decisions requires Congress to evaluate the religious values of different organizations and devise accommodations consistent with the Free Exercise and Establishment Clauses.

Tax Exemptions

From early colonial times, churches received tax exemptions for their property. Favorable tax treatment for religious groups has even been traced to biblical times.[1] Critics of this assistance regard it as an indirect state subsidy in violation of the Establishment Clause. However, efforts to tax church property would trigger another objection: interference with the free exercise of religion. Courts recognize that legislatures may adjust their system of taxation to provide exemptions for property owned by religious organizations.[2] To the extent that programs operated by religious

1. Arvo Van Alstyne, "Tax Exemption of Church Property," 20 Ohio State L. J. 461, 462 n. 6 (1959).
2. Bell's Gap R.R. v. Pennsylvania, 134 U.S. 232, 237 (1890); Washington Ethical Society v. District of Columbia, 249 F.2d 127, 129 (D.C. Cir. 1957).

institutions promote social benefits, they relieve the public of burdens that would have to be met by general taxation.[3] Although Madison and Jefferson were able to defeat the assessments bill for the Anglican Church in Virginia, and states after that gradually disestablished their churches, tax exemption for church property continued with broad acceptance.[4]

PROPERTY TAXES

Exemption from property taxes is primarily a matter of state law. Nevertheless, in his seventh annual message to Congress in 1875, President Grant called attention to "an evil" that threatened to cause great trouble: "the accumulation of vast amounts of untaxed church property." He suggested that all property be taxed equally, whether church or corporation, "exempting only the last resting place of the dead and possibly, with proper restrictions, church edifices."[5] What ended up in the last resting place was Grant's proposal.

For religious organizations, the exemption for property taxes can cover places of religious worship (both church buildings and adjacent land), clergymen's living quarters (parsonages), cemeteries, church-affiliated schools and colleges, and such charitable properties as hospitals, orphanages, homes for the aged, asylums, poorhouses, and missionary societies.[6] To qualify for an exemption, a religious organization need not be theistic. The Fellowship of Humanity, a nonprofit corporation organized under the laws of California, was entitled to exemption from property taxes despite the corporation's lack of belief in a Supreme Being. In 1957, a California court ruled that language in the state constitution regarding property used "solely and exclusively for religious worship" must be interpreted without discriminating between the types of religious belief: those that believe in a Supreme Being and those that do not. Such efforts would offend both the federal and the state constitutions. The only inquiry "is the objective one of whether or not the belief occupies the same place in the lives of its holders that the orthodox beliefs occupy in the lives of believing majorities."[7]

3. 3 Stokes 419.
4. John Witte, Jr., "Tax Exemption of Church Property: Historical Anomaly or Valid Constitutional Practice?," 64 S. Cal. L. Rev. 363, 380–81 (1991).
5. 9 Richardson 4288–89.
6. Van Alstyne, "Tax Exemption of Church Property," at 463–64, 470, 479, 484, 490, 496–97.
7. Fellowship of Humanity v. County of Alameda, 315 P.2d 394, 406 (Cal. 1957).

Courts often have to determine whether a religious organization is qualified to receive property tax exemption. Otherwise, ordinary citizens could escape taxation by claiming some religious purpose. In 1986, the Supreme Court of Oregon reviewed a case from the state tax court, which had denied a tax exemption for real property to a group called Golden Writ of God. The group sought exemption for 230 acres of farmland, which they called a "tabernacle" and necessary to accomplish its religious objectives. They claimed to see God everyplace on the land and in every piece of vegetation. Under Oregon law, only property "actually and exclusively occupied or used in . . . charitable work" is entitled to be exempt from taxation. The state supreme court, finding nothing in the record to demonstrate that the entire parcel of land was used "actually and exclusively" for religious or charitable purposes, affirmed the decision of the tax court.[8]

The U.S. Supreme Court has examined congressional statutes to determine the extent to which church lands are exempt from taxation.[9] In 1970, the Court decided the constitutionality of property tax exemptions for religious organizations. A plaintiff argued that the tax exemption for religious purposes, included in the New York Constitution, constituted an establishment of religion prohibited by the First Amendment. The Court, pointing out that all fifty states provided for tax exemption of places of worship and that a number of federal statutes granted tax exemptions for churches, denied that these state and federal practices either "established" religion or reasonably threatened to do so.[10] Justice Douglas was the sole dissenter.

FEDERAL INCOME TAX

Exemption from federal income taxes is a more recent development. The Tariff Act of 1894, which included an income tax, provided that it did not apply to corporations "conducted solely for charitable, religious, or educational purposes."[11] After the Supreme Court in *Pollock* v. *Farmer's Loan and Trust Co.* (1895) struck down the federal income tax, Congress responded with the Sixteenth Amendment. As ratified in 1913, it

8. Golden Writ of God v. Dept. of Rev., 713 P.2d 605 (Ore. 1986).
9. Gibbons v. District of Columbia, 116 U.S. 404 (1886).
10. Walz v. Tax Commission, 397 U.S. 664, 676– 68 (1970).
11. 28 Stat. 556 (1894).

empowered Congress to lay and collect taxes on incomes without apportionment among the states and without regard to any census or enumeration. When legislation in 1913 included a federal income tax, it stipulated that it did not apply to any corporation or association "organized and operated exclusively for religious, charitable, scientific, or educational purposes."[12] Income taxes in the War Revenue Act of 1917 and a revenue statute enacted in 1919 also exempted corporations organized and operated exclusively for religious purposes.[13]

This exemption today appears in Section 501(c)(3) of the Internal Revenue Code. Once an organization qualifies for exempt status, it may also qualify for exemption from state and local income taxes, property taxes, use or other taxes, preferred postal rates, exemption from taxes imposed under the Federal Insurance Contribution Act and the Federal Unemployment Tax Act, and may be eligible for special preferential tax provisions regarding retirement annuities.[14]

Tax exemptions for religious purposes requires close scrutiny by the IRS. Resourceful individuals may try to use legitimate exemptions for tax-avoidance schemes. For example, the IRS does not tax the income of an employee in a religious order who has taken a vow of poverty. When a nurse's salary goes entirely to the order, it is not taxed. This relationship between the employee and employer was manipulated in the 1970s and 1980s by people who received ordination to the ministry from the Universal Life Church. These "mail-order ministers" then declared their homes to be churches and proceeded to receive car, shelter, food, entertainment, insurance, and other benefits without any of it taxed. IRS rulings put a halt to that practice.[15]

Tax benefits are available for the rental value of parsonages. In the case of "a minister of the gospel," gross income does not include the rental value of a home furnished to the minister as part of his compensation, or the rental allowance paid to the minister as part of his compensation.[16] The housing allowance includes down payment, mortgage payments,

12. 38 Stat. 172 (1913).
13. 40 Stat. 330 (1917); 40 Stat. 1076, § 231(6) (1919).
14. Terry L. Slye, "Rendering Unto Caesar: Defining 'Religion' for Purposes of Administering Religion-based Tax Exemptions," 6 Harv. J. L. & Pub. Pol. 219, 220 (1983).
15. Ronald B. Flowers, "Tax Exemption and the Clergy: On Vows of Poverty and Parsonage Allowances," in James E. Wood, Jr., ed., Religion and the State 359 (1985).
16. 26 U.S.C. § 107 (1994).

interest, taxes, repairs, furniture payments, garage costs, and utilities. The estimated revenue loss to the federal government for this provision is about $400 million a year.[17]

Federal law offers other benefits for religious groups. Taxpayers take deductions for their contributions to charities, including to "a church or a convention or association of churches."[18] Charitable donations extend to other institutions, such as educational organizations, hospitals, medical research organizations, and private foundations.[19]

In a number of cases, individuals have cited religious grounds for seeking an exemption from federal income taxes. Because their religious beliefs are opposed to killing, they argue that they should be excused from paying the federal income tax or at least the portion used to fund military activities. In deciding against taxpayers in these cases, courts regard it as unworkable to allow individuals to withhold a portion of their taxes because they have moral or religious objections to various governmental programs.[20]

BOB JONES UNIVERSITY CASE

After *Brown* v. *Board of Education,* tax exemption became a way to avoid racial integration in the schools. With thousands of white students transferring from public schools to private schools, the IRS allowed private schools tax exemptions regardless of their racial policy. This policy continued until January 12, 1970, when a three-judge federal court issued a preliminary injunction prohibiting the IRS from according tax-exempt status to private schools in Mississippi that practiced racial discrimination in their admission policy.[21] In July, the IRS announced that it could no longer legally justify a tax-exempt status for private schools that practiced racial discrimination. Moreover, it would no longer treat gifts to such schools as charitable contributions for income tax purposes. On November 30, the IRS formally notified private schools of this change in policy. On June 30,

17. "Exclusion of Rental Allowances for Ministers' Homes," in Senate Committee on the Budget, Tax Expenditures: Compendium of Background Material on Individual Provisions 363 (December 1998).

18. 26 U.S.C. § 170(b)(1)(A)(i) (1994).

19. Id. at § 170(b)(1)(A).

20. Browne v. United States, 22 F.Supp.2d 309 (D. Vt. 1998); Packard v. United States, 7 F.Supp.2d 143 (D. Conn. 1998); Adams v. Commissioner, 110 T.C. 137 (1998).

21. Green v. Kennedy, 309 F.Supp. 1127 (D.D.C. 1970).

1971, the three-judge court issued another opinion on the Mississippi case and approved the IRS's amendment to the tax code.[22]

During the Carter administration, the IRS proposed a broader tax-exemption policy. It would now deny tax-exempt status to private schools that had an insignificant number of minority students and had been formed or expanded at the time of public school desegregation. Christian fundamentalists protested the policy change, as did many members of Congress. In 1979, Congress passed legislation to deny funds to implement the proposed IRS plan.[23] The Republican Party platform in 1980 stated that "we will halt the unconstitutional regulatory vendetta launched by Mr. Carter's IRS Commissioner against independent schools."[24]

On January 8, 1982, the Justice Department in the Reagan administration announced that the IRS lacked statutory authority for its 1970 policy denying tax exemption to discriminatory institutions. It asked Congress to enact that policy into law rather than leave it to agency interpretation.[25] A case challenging the IRS policy was before the Supreme Court, involving two religious schools that practiced racial discrimination and wanted tax exemption: Bob Jones University and Goldsboro Christian Schools. Bob Jones University cited biblical grounds to support its policy against interracial dating. The American Jewish Committee and the United Church of Christ filed briefs in support of the IRS. Briefs written in support of continued tax exemption for the two religious schools were filed by the American Baptist Church, United Presbyterian Church, the Center for Law and Religious Freedom, and the National Association of Evangelicals.[26]

In 1983, an 8 to 1 Court sustained the IRS. The Court explained that tax exemption is not a constitutional right. It is a privilege granted by Congress to organizations that provide a public benefit. As to the claim that the IRS violated the Free Exercise Clause by denying tax exemption to schools that cite religious grounds for racial discrimination, the Court held that the governmental interest in this case prevailed. The two schools could continue to operate and observe their religious

22. Green v. Connally, 330 F.Supp. 1150 (D.D.C. 1971), summarily aff'd sub nom. Coit v. Green, 404 U.S. 997 (1971).
23. 93 Stat. 562, § 103 (1979).
24. 1980 CQ Almanac 63-B.
25. Public Papers of the President, 1982, I, at 38.
26. Volume 136 of Landmark Briefs.

tenets, including racial discrimination, but not with the benefit of tax exemption.[27]

SALES TAXES

Tax exemptions are acceptable when they apply to a broad array of religious and secular institutions, such as "religious, educational or charitable purposes." In 1989, the Court examined a Texas statute that exempted sales and use taxes solely for religious periodicals. Justice Brennan, writing for a plurality, held that the exemption lacked sufficient breadth to pass scrutiny under the Establishment Clause. The Court said that Texas was free to widen the exemption—to include nonreligious publications—or withdraw the exemption.[28] Only Marshall and Stevens joined Brennan's decision. The rest of the Justices were scattered among White's concurrence, Blackmun's concurrence (joined by O'Connor), and a dissent by Scalia (joined by Rehnquist and Kennedy). However, on the key point that a tax exemption limited to the sale of religious literature by a religious organization violates the Establishment Clause, five Justices agreed: Brennan, Marshall, Stevens, Blackmun, and O'Connor.

States may impose sales taxes on religious materials if the tax is generally applicable to both religious and nonreligious materials. These taxes can be applied to in-state sales as well as mail-order sales. The Supreme Court treats this type of tax as a neutral tax on retail purchases. Bibles sold by a religious organization are taxed just as Bibles sold in a secular bookstore. The Constitution does not *require* states to grant religious organizations a tax exemption.[29] While it is permissible to apply a general sales tax to religious materials, states may not resort to a flat license tax or fee that would operate as a prior restraint on the exercise of religious liberty. For example, they may not require religious organizations that canvass or solicit within a city to pay a flat fee for a license.[30] Nor may states require all booksellers, religious or secular, to procure a license to sell books.[31]

27. Bob Jones University v. United States, 461 U.S. 574, 602–4 (1983).
28. Texas Monthly, Inc. v. Bullock, 489 U.S. 1 (1989).
29. Swaggart Ministries v. Cal. Bd. of Equalization, 493 U.S. 378 (1990).
30. Murdock v. Pennsylvania, 319 U.S. 105 (1943).
31. Follett v. McCormick, 321 U.S. 573 (1944).

Prohibition Statutes

From 1912 to 1919, Congress passed a number of statutes and constitutional amendments to prohibit the manufacture and selling of intoxicating beverages. Each time it made exception for the use of sacramental wines for religious ceremonies. Legislation in 1912, designed to suppress the traffic of intoxicating liquors among Indians, made it lawful to introduce and use wines "solely for sacramental purposes, under church authority."[32] A constitutional amendment in 1913 prohibited intoxicating beverages but gave Congress the power to provide for the manufacture and sale of intoxicating liquors for certain exceptions, including sacramental purposes.[33] The proposal, attracting committee and floor interest, failed to pass either chamber.[34] The Webb-Kenyon Act of 1913 flatly prohibited the shipment of intoxicating liquors into a state in violation of its laws.[35] Although the statute made no mention of sacramental wine, legislators understood that virtually every state allowed wines to be used for sacramental purposes.[36]

Federal legislation enacted on February 14, 1917, prohibited the manufacture or sale of alcoholic liquors in the Territory of Alaska. The Alaskan legislature had passed a bill on April 13, 1915, putting before the people the proposition as to whether they wanted prohibition. By a vote of 7,958 to 4,431 on November 7, 1916, a majority favored prohibition.[37] Although the bill debated by Congress to implement this referendum was described as "a bone-dry bill,"[38] designed to totally prohibit the consumption of alcohol, the bill as introduced made an exception for sacramental wine. The bill's language seemed confined to the use of communion wine by Christians:

SEC. 8. That any common carrier or any person operating a boat or vehicle for the transportation of goods, wares, or merchandise may

---

32. 37 Stat. 519 (1912). The provision for sacramental wine was added in conference committee: H. Rept. No. 1185, 62d Cong., 2d Sess. 15 (1912); H. Rept. No. 1238, 62d Cong., 2d Sess. 14 (1912).

33. 51 Cong. Rec. 615 (1913).

34. Richard F. Hamm, Shaping the Eighteenth Amendment: Temperance Reform, Legal Culture, and the Polity, 1880–1920, at 228–29 (1995).

35. 37 Stat. 699 (1913).

36. 54 Cong. Rec. 3396 (1917) (exchange between Senators Vardaman, Kenyon, and Reed).

37. Id. at 2303, 2524.

38. Id. at 2530.

accept for transportation and may transport to any place within the Territory of Alaska shipments of wine for sacramental purposes when there is attached to such shipment a certificate in substantially the following form:

"I (or we) certify that this package contains only _____ (amount) of _____ (wine), which has been ordered by _____ _____, who represents himself to be a duly authorized and officiating priest or minister of the _____ church at _____, and that said wine is desired for sacramental purposes only.

_____ _____."39

No one during Senate debate discussed the exemption for sacramental wine.40 In the House, Representative William Houston (D-Tenn.) said that Alaskans would be able to possess alcoholic beverages only "for medical purposes and for scientific and sacramental purposes."41 Representative Jacob Meeker (R-Mo.) objected to the stringency of the legislation, remarking that "we are come to a time when the wine served at the Lord's table is marked as practically outlawed."42 The bill, including the exception for sacramental wine, was enacted.43

Also in 1917, Congress prohibited the mailing of any letter, postal card, circular, newspaper, pamphlet, or publication from containing any advertisement of "spirituous, vinous, malted, fermented, or other intoxicating liquors of any kind." Individuals would be punished for ordering, purchasing, or transporting intoxicating liquors, but an exception was carved out "for scientific, sacramental, medicinal, and mechanical purposes."44 The general term "sacramental" was broad enough to cover not only communion wine used by Christians but also wine consumed at dinner during a Jewish seder. Later in the year, Congress amended the prohibition on the mailing of ads promoting intoxicating liquors. It would now not apply to "the use of the mails by regularly ordained ministers of religion, or by officers of regularly established churches, for ordering wines for sacramental uses, or by manufacturers and dealers for quoting and billing such wines for such purposes

39. S. 7963, 64th Cong., 2d Sess. 6 (1917).
40. 54 Cong. Rec. 2303–8 (1917).
41. Id. at 2521.
42. Id.
43. 39 Stat. 905, § 8 (1917).
44. 39 Stat. 1069, § 5 (1917).

only."[45] This language was not in the bill as introduced,[46] but was agreed to in conference committee.[47]

World War I placed great strains on the national economy. In an effort to help in the prosecution of the war, Congress passed legislation in 1918 to prohibit the use of any grains, cereals, fruit, or other food products for the manufacture of beer, wine, "or other intoxicating malt or vinous liquor for beverage purposes." No beer, wine, or other intoxicating malt or vinous liquor could be sold for beverage purposes except for export.[48] The government was authorized to prescribe rules and regulations regarding the manufacture and sale of distilled spirits and for the manufacture, sale, and distribution of wine for "sacramental, medicinal, or other than beverage use."[49] As introduced, the bill said nothing about intoxicating beverages.[50] However, Representative Charles Randall was successful in having this language accepted as a floor amendment: "That in order to further eliminate waste and to promote conservation of food, it shall be unlawful during the existence of the war with Germany to use any food or food materials in the manufacture or preparation of alcoholic beverages."[51] The accommodation for sacramental wines was added later in the Senate.[52]

Finally, the National Prohibition Act of 1919 (the Volstead Act) prohibited intoxicating beverages and regulated the manufacture, production, use, and sale of high-proof spirits intended for other than beverage purposes. The statute pledged to ensure an ample supply of alcohol and to promote its use in scientific research and in the development of fuel, dye, and other lawful industries. It prohibited any person after the Eighteenth Amendment took effect (January 16, 1919) from manufacturing, selling, bartering, transporting, importing, exporting, delivering, furnishing, or possessing any intoxicating liquor. However, an exception was made for liquor in the form of "wine for sacramental purposes," subject to government regulation.[53] That language appeared in the bill as introduced.[54]

---

45. 40 Stat. 329, § 1110 (1917).
46. H.R. 4280, 65th Cong., 1st Sess. (1917).
47. H. Rept. No. 172, 65th Cong., 1st Sess. 52 (1917).
48. 40 Stat. 1046 (1918).
49. Id. at 1047.
50. H.R. 11945, 65th Cong., 2d Sess. (1918).
51. 56 Cong. Rec. 6866–72 (1918).
52. Id. at 8854, 8892–93, 9625–51.
53. 41 Stat. 308, § 3 (1919).
54. H.R. 6810, 66th Cong., 1st Sess. 9 (1919).

Representative Richard McKiniry (D-N.Y.) objected to any governmental role in policing sacramental wine:

> One of the most dangerous and subtle provisions of this act is its interference with the exercise of his religious duties by a minister or priest of those great religions which have existed for centuries and which have been the bulwark of civilization. It places in the hands of a governmental official the control of the sacramental use of wine, and a violation of any technical provision of this act or of any State act, no matter how slight or no matter how lacking in criminal intent, can prevent a priest or minister for the period of one year from exercising his right to celebrate the divine services required by his conscience and by his church.[55]

A floor amendment, adopted in the House, provided that nothing in the act would apply to the manufacture, sale, importation, possession, or distribution of wine for sacramental purposes, with some exceptions. The amendment, adopted 98 to zero, referred not only to ministers and priests but to rabbis as well.[56] The same language was adopted by the Senate and accepted by the conferees.[57] The statute reads:

> Nothing in this title shall be held to apply to the manufacture, sale, transportation, importation, possession, or distribution of wine for sacramental purposes, or like religious rites, except section 6 (save as the same requires a permit to purchase) and section 10 hereof, and the provisions of this act prescribing penalties for the violation of either of said sections. No person to whom a permit may be issued to manufacture, transport, import, or sell wines for sacramental purposes or like religious rites shall sell, barter, exchange, or furnish any such to any person not a rabbi, minister of the gospel, priest, or an officer duly authorized for the purpose by any church or congregation, not to any such except upon an application duly subscribed by him, which application, authenticated as regulations may prescribe, shall be filed and preserved by the seller. The head of any conference or diocese or other ecclesiastical jurisdiction may designate any rabbi, minister, or priest to supervise the manufacture of wine to be

55. 58 Cong. Rec. 2894 (1919).
56. Id. at 2968.
57. Id. at 4843; H. Rept. No. 360, 66th Cong., 1st Sess. 5 (1919). Senate and House acceptance of the conference language appears at 58 Cong. Rec. 6432, 6550, 6687 (1919).

used for the purposes and rites in this section mentioned, and the person so designated may, in the discretion of the commissioner, be granted a permit to supervise such manufacture.[58]

A federal case brought in 1929 explains how the statute operated. For example, the Bureau of Prohibition in the Treasury Department issued a regulation permitting each Jewish family five gallons of wine each year. No person would receive wine unless they were a member of the congregation, and the chief rabbi would place the seal of the congregation on the container of wine.[59]

The Eighteenth Amendment, driven by a variety of religious and secular values, gained momentum with mobilization for World War I. Offering a cure worse than the disease, it was repealed by the Twenty-first Amendment, ratified on December 5, 1933.

Exemptions from Social Security

Congress has exempted some members of religious orders from paying into the social security trust fund if their religious principles are opposed to accepting social security benefits. Any individual who is a duly ordained, commissioned, or licensed minister of a church or a minister of a religious order may qualify. The exemption also covers Christian Science practitioners. These individuals may apply for the exemption by stating that they are conscientiously opposed to, or because of religious principles opposed to, the acceptance of payments from a public insurance program.[60] Moreover, any member of a "recognized religious sect or division thereof" who believes that their tenets oppose the acceptance of payments in the event of death, disability, old age, or retirement may also file for the exemption.[61]

The Amish encounter with social security began in 1955, when the program was first extended to cover self-employed farmers. The IRS, in an effort to collect the social security payroll tax from the Amish, even seized and sold the farm animals of Amish who refused to pay into social security. Newspaper editorials condemned these actions by the government.[62]

58. 41 Stat. 311 (1919).
59. Shapiro v. Lyle, 30 F.2d 971, 972 (W.D. Wash. 1929).
60. 26 U.S.C. § 1402(e) (1994).
61. Id. at § 1402(g).
62. Peter J. Ferrara, "Social Security and Taxes," in Donald B. Kraybill, ed., The Amish and the State 132 (1993).

Neither the IRS nor the Department of Health, Education, and Welfare was sympathetic to the religious beliefs of the Amish.[63]

Congress added the social security exemption for members of a religious group in 1965. The House Ways and Means Committee explained that the exemption should be one of individual choice rather than applied to an entire group. To exclude all members "would not take account of the variances in individual beliefs within any religious group, and would deny social security protection to those individuals who want it."[64] That policy was enacted into law.[65]

The scope of that exemption reached the Supreme Court in 1982. The plaintiff, a member of the Old Order Amish, employed several other Amish to work on his farm and in his carpentry shop. He failed to file social security tax returns required of employers, did not withhold social security taxes from his employees, and did not pay the employer's share of social security taxes. He believed that the Amish religion makes the community responsible for its members, including those dependent on assistance. He followed the biblical injunction: "But if any provide not . . . for those of his own house, he hath denied the faith, and is worse than an infidel" (1 Timothy 5:6).[66] Members of the Old Amish Order "consider it a sin against God to pay money into the Social Security System, either directly through their employer or by themselves."[67]

A district court held that any law requiring him to pay social security and unemployment insurance taxes was unconstitutional because it would violate the religious belief of the Amish that they are morally obligated to provide for their own elderly and needy. The district court concluded that the loss of revenue from this grant of exemption "would be negligible" because the Old Order Amish was clearly defined and small in number.[68]

Handling the matter as one of statutory interpretation, the Supreme Court held that the exemption provided by Congress applied only to self-

63. Id. at 132–37.

64. H. Rept. No. 213, 89th Cong., 1st Sess. 102 (1965); the same language appears in S. Rept. No. 404 (Part 1), 89th Cong., 1st Sess. 116 (1965).

65. 79 Stat. 390, § 319 (1965). For floor statements supporting this provision, see 111 Cong. Rec. 2665–66 (Rep. Gross) and 15903 (Senator Scott) (1965).

66. Joint Appendix, United States v. Lee, No. 80-767, U.S. Supreme Court, October Term, 1980, at 22.

67. Id. at 23.

68. Lee v. United States Government, 497 F.Supp. 180, 182–83 (W.D. Pa. 1980).

employed individuals, not to all employers and employees who are Amish.[69] The Court argued that the nationwide social security system depended on mandatory participation to make it financially viable, and that it would be a "contradiction in terms" to manage this program and allow for voluntary participation.[70] At issue, however, was not a nationwide social security system supported by volunteers but an exception for the Amish. The Court created a "chamber of horrors" by asking what would happen to the federal income tax if religious adherents, believing that war is a sin, could withhold a portion of their taxes devoted to war-related activities.[71] In his concurrence, Justice Stevens charged that the Court "overstates the magnitude of this risk because the Amish claim applies only to a small religious community with an established welfare system of its own."[72]

The Court exaggerated the problem in several ways. Congressional testimony in 1987 put the Amish population at about ninety thousand. With about 50 percent of that number representing children under sixteen and with 99 percent of Amish women not seeking employment outside the home, the male workforce is approximately twelve thousand.[73] Had the Court recognized a broader exemption, it was likely that more money would go into the social security fund than would be taken out. If an Amish employee worked for an Amish employer, neither would contribute to the fund and neither would accept anything from it. However, if an Amish employee worked for a non-Amish employer, the employer would be required to withhold social security but the Amish employee would never withdraw any funds from social security.[74]

As for the Court's warning that taxpayers might refuse to pay for government activities they deplore, such as war, that was never an issue in the litigation. Amish follow the biblical admonition to pay taxes and accept the division between God and Caesar. What tax money "is used for is not our concern but the Government's."[75] Amish object to social security not

69. United States v. Lee, 455 U.S. 252, 256 (1982).
70. Id. at 258.
71. Id. at 260.
72. Id. at 262.
73. "Social Security Coverage of Amish Workers," hearing before the House Committee on Ways and Means, 100th Cong., 1st Sess. 11–12 (1987).
74. Id. at 14.
75. Id. (statement of Andrew S. Kinsinger, Chairman, Old Order Amish Steering Committee).

because it is a tax but because it is an old-age insurance program that conflicts with their religious beliefs.[76]

Finding the Court's interpretation too narrow, Congress enacted legislation that broadened the exemption for the Amish. As part of the Tax Reform Act of 1988, Congress exempted employers and employees from paying social security taxes when they are members of religious faiths opposed to participation in Social Security Act programs. To qualify for this exemption, employers and employees file applications with the Department of Health and Human Services.[77] The broadened exemption was added by the House Committee on Ways and Means and accepted by the Senate.[78]

"MARK OF THE BEAST"

Some individuals present religious arguments not against the social security program but against being identified by a social security number. In 1981, the Ninth Circuit reviewed a father's refusal to obtain a social security number for his daughter. Without a number, she could not obtain benefits under the Aid to Families with Dependent Children (AFDC) program. The court held that the father's views regarding social security numbers as the "mark of the beast" were theological in nature and religious within the meaning of the First Amendment. Chapter 13 of Revelation describes the Antichrist's plan to control the world by using marks and numbers. The Ninth Circuit remanded the case to district court to determine whether the government had a compelling interest in making social security numbers a prerequisite for AFDC benefits.[79] When the case came back to the Ninth Circuit, it again remanded the case because there was no evidence that the exemption of one person from the number requirement would mandate the development of an entire nonnumerical social security system, and no evidence that more than one person would raise these religious arguments.[80]

The Ninth Circuit, in 1999, held that requiring a hospital to accom-

76. Id. See also the statement by Jesse Neuenschwander, Bishop, Eastern Pennsylvania Mennonite Church, id. at 15.
77. 102 Stat. 3781–83, § 8007 (1988); 26 U.S.C. § 3127 (1994).
78. H. Rept. No. 100-795, 100th Cong., 2d Sess. 620 (1988); 134 Cong. Rec. 20497 (1988); H. Rept. No. 100-1104, 100th Cong., 2d Sess. 258–59 (1988).
79. Callahan v. Woods, 658 F.2d 679 (9th Cir. 1981).
80. Callahan v. Woods, 736 F.2d 1269 (9th Cir. 1984).

modate an employee's religious belief in the "mark of the beast" would cause undue hardship on the employer.[81] A year later, the Eighth Circuit decided a case brought by someone who refused to provide his social security number to a prospective employer because he claimed the number represents the "mark of the beast." The court ruled that the number is required by law, not by an employer, and that there was no obligation on the part of the employer to accommodate his religious beliefs.[82]

INDIAN RELIGIOUS BELIEFS

In 1986, the Supreme Court decided a case brought by an Indian who refused to comply with the requirement that participants in the AFDC and Food Stamp programs furnish their state welfare agencies with the social security numbers of the members of their household as a condition for receiving benefits. He maintained that obtaining a social security number for his two-year-old daughter would violate his Native American religious belief that identifying her with a number would rob her spirit. His request for an exemption from the social security number requirement was denied by the Court, which held that the number requirement promoted a legitimate and important public interest.[83] The Court recognized that Congress could provide such an exemption, but Congress has not done so. On July 13, 1999, Representative John Hostettler (R-Ind.) introduced a bill to amend the tax code to provide a religious exemption from providing identifying numbers for dependents to claim certain credits and deductions on a tax return.[84] There was no committee or floor action on his bill.

Federal Discrimination Laws

The Civil Rights Act of 1964 makes it an unlawful employment practice for an employer to discriminate against individuals because of their race, color, religion, sex, or national origin. However, the statute also provides

81. Sutton v. Providence St. Joseph Medical Center, 192 F.3d 826 (9th Cir. 1999).
82. Seaworth v. Pearson, 203 F.3d 1056 (8th Cir. 2000).
83. Bowen v. Roy, 476 U.S. 693 (1986). For another case in which individual unsuccessfully offered religious objections to obtaining a social security number, but unrelated to "mark of the beast" or Indian religious beliefs, see E.E.O.C. v. Allendale Nursing Centre, 996 F.Supp. 712 (W.D. Mich. 1998).
84. H.R. 2494, 106th Cong., 1st Sess. (1999).

that it shall not be an unlawful employment practice for a religious educational institution to hire and employ individuals of a particular religion if the institution is, "in whole or in substantial part," owned by a particular religion or if the curriculum is directed toward the propagation of a particular religion.[85]

Equal Employment Opportunity Commission (EEOC) guidelines in 1967 required employers "to make reasonable accommodations to the religious needs of employees and prospective employees where such accommodations can be made without undue hardship on the conduct of the employer's business."[86] In response to decisions by the Sixth Circuit and the Supreme Court, Congress amended the Civil Rights Act in 1972 by adopting this definition of religion: "The term 'religion' includes all aspects of religious observance and practice, as well as belief, unless an employer demonstrates that he is unable to reasonably accommodate to an employee's or prospective employee's religious observance or practice without undue hardship on the conduct of the employer's business."[87] The purpose was to shield religious organizations from liability in the case of employment suits.

In 1977, the Supreme Court decided a case in which an employee's religious beliefs (Worldwide Church of God) prohibited him from working on Saturdays. The employer, TWA, made a number of accommodations to allow him to observe his Sabbath. However, transfer to a new job within TWA led to a disagreement, and he refused to report to work on Saturdays. He was later discharged for insubordination. The Court concluded that TWA had made reasonable efforts to accommodate the individual and that the alternatives proposed by the Eighth Circuit would have created an undue hardship within the meaning of the statute and as construed by the EEOC.[88] In the absence of "clear statutory language or legislative history to the contrary," the Court declined to read the statute to require TWA to discriminate against some employees (by having them work on Saturdays) "in order to enable others to observe their Sabbath."[89]

The constitutionality of the 1972 legislation—protecting religious organizations in their employment decisions—reached the Court in 1987.

85. 78 Stat. 256, § 703(e)(2) (1964).
86. 29 C.R.F. § 1605.1 (1968).
87. Now codified at 42 U.S.C. § 2000e (j) (1994); see Dewey v. Reynolds Metals Co., 402 U.S. 689 (1971); Dewey v. Reynolds Metals Co., 429 F.2d 324 (6th Cir. 1970).
88. Trans World Airlines, Inc. v. Hardison, 432 U.S. 63 (1977).
89. Id. at 85.

The Mormon Church discharged someone because he was not a member of the Church and not eligible to attend its temples. Although the employee was engaged in nonreligious activities at a nonprofit facility, the Court upheld the 1972 amendment. Any effort by government to distinguish between religious and secular activities would create too much entanglement between church and state.[90]

Open housing legislation in 1968 provided exemptions for religious organizations. Congress prohibited individuals from refusing to sell or rent because of race, color, religion, sex, familial status, or national origin.[91] However, nothing in this general policy prohibits a religious organization from limiting the sale, rental, or occupancy of dwellings that it owns or operates, other than for a commercial purpose, to persons of the same religion, or from giving preference to such persons, "unless membership in such religion is restricted on account of race, color, or national origin."[92]

BUSH'S FAITH-BASED INITIATIVE

During the presidential campaign of 2000, George W. Bush advocated an expansion of federal programs that are faith-based (also called "charitable choice"). In recent years, several federal statutes have provided funds to social services programs operated by faith-based organizations. Charitable choice was first enacted in 1996 as part of the welfare reform bill, which allows states to enter into contracts with charitable, religious, or private organizations to provide temporary assistance to needy families. Just as there is to be no discrimination against religious organizations in receiving these contracts, religious organizations are not to discriminate against an individual in regard to rendering assistance "on the basis of religion, a religious belief, or refusal to actively participate in a religious practice."[93] In return for public funds, religious groups accepted some legislative restrictions on their conduct. Charitable choice provisions were also enacted in 1998 and 2000.[94] In the 106th Congress (1999–2001), a number of charitable choice measures were adopted either by the House or the Senate but not enacted into law.

90. Corporation of Presiding Bishop v. Amos, 483 U.S. 327 (1987).
91. 82 Stat. 83, § 804 (1968); 42 U.S.C. § 3604(a) (1994).
92. 82 Stat. 84, § 807 (1968); 42 U.S.C. § 3607(a) (1994).
93. 110 Stat. 2163, § 104(g) (1996).
94. 112 Stat. 2749, § 201 (1998); 114 Stat. 1212, § 3305 (2000); 114 Stat. 2763A-619, § 144 (2000).

Responding to leadership from President Bush, the House in July 2001 passed legislation to expand government financing of the social work done by religious charities. Although the House-passed bill provides less money for tax deductions to encourage charitable giving, it offers religious organizations greater access to federal funds. One of the issues raised during legislative debate was whether religious groups receiving federal funds should retain their right to hire only people of their faith and to ignore state and local civil rights laws that protect gay men and lesbians from discrimination in hiring.

Several weeks before House passage of the bill, press reports indicated that the Bush administration had promised the Salvation Army a regulation that would allow charitable and religious groups to discriminate against gays in hiring and domestic-partner benefits without fear of lawsuits. A number of state and local governments had adopted laws to prohibit discrimination based on sexual orientation. In return for the regulation, the Salvation Army said it would budget funds to promote the administration's faith-based initiative, which contemplated directing federal funds to religious organizations that provide such social services as drug-prevention counseling and homeless shelters. The White House denied making such a commitment to the Salvation Army.[95] A day later the administration, under attack, said flatly that it would not issue the regulation.[96]

The faith-based bill bogged down in the Senate because of constitutional objections. After the terrorist attacks on September 11 shifted the focus from domestic legislation to national security concerns, President Bush met with lawmakers to encourage action on his education and faith-based bills.[97] Supporters of the bill on charitable choice recognized that the political climate after September 11 required more modest legislation and the elimination of complicated or contentious provisions.[98]

In February 2002, Bush agreed to further compromises in the Senate,

95. "Charity Cites Bush Help in Fight against Hiring Gays," Washington Post, July 10, 2001, at A1.

96. "Bush Drops Rule on Hiring of Gays," Washington Post, July 1, 2001, at A1; "Charity Is Told It Must Abide by Antidiscrimination Laws," New York Times, July 11, 2001, at A15.

97. "Bush Turns to Domestic Agenda," Washington Post, September 25, 2001, at A7.

98. "Bush Is Said to Scale Back His Religion-based Initiative," New York Times, October 14, 2001, at A14.

including the elimination of the House provision that allowed religious groups to favor members of their own faith in making employment decisions and to ignore antidiscrimination laws. If this measure passed the Senate, it was unclear how the two chambers would settle their differences and produce a bill capable of enactment.[99]

Labor Laws

Congress enacts labor laws under its constitutional authority to regulate interstate commerce. Most religious groups are not involved in commercial activities. If they are, they are governed by labor laws like any other commercial venture.[100] When activities of eleemosynary, religious, or educational organizations are performed for a business purpose, such as operating a printing plant, the Labor Department treats them as ordinary business enterprises.[101]

Federal statutes and regulations prohibit persons aged fourteen to eighteen from working in such hazardous occupations as sawmills. The Amish wanted an exemption from the law because their children complete their formal education around the age of fourteen, at the end of the eighth grade. In 1972, the Supreme Court upheld the constitutional right of the Amish to limit the education of their children to the eighth grade.[102] After that point their education depends on "learning by doing": working under the supervision of their parents or another community member. As farm jobs decline—the traditional occupation for Amish—their youth need to work in other occupations.

On September 28, 1998, the House passed legislation to amend the Fair Labor Standards Act to permit certain youth to work in sawmills. The bill, passed under suspension of the rules, applied to an individual who is at least fourteen but under the age of eighteen, and is a member "of a religious sect or division thereof whose established teachings do not permit formal education beyond the eighth grade." The legislation

99. "Accord Reached on Charity Aid Bill after Bush Gives In on Hiring," New York Times, February 8, 2002, at A19; "Bush Touts New 'Religious Charities' Plan But Critics Say It Does Not Go Far Enough," CQ Weekly Report, February 9, 2002, at 401–2.

100. Tony & Susan Alamo Foundation v. Sec'y of Labor, 471 U.S. 290 (1985); NLRB v. World Evangelism, Inc., 656 F.2d 1349 (9th Cir. 1981).

101. 29 C.F.R. § 779.214 (7-1-00 ed.). See also Richard R. Hammer, Pastor, Church & Law 466-95 (2d ed. 1991).

102. Wisconsin v. Yoder, 406 U.S. 205 (1972).

required Amish youth to be supervised by an adult. They would not be allowed to operate or assist in the operation of power-driven woodworking machines. Their work would be limited to such jobs as sweeping sawdust, stacking planks, gluing lumber, and office work.[103] Several members of the House had tried to work out an administrative solution with the Department of Labor, but the department "has been unwilling or unable to alleviate the conflict between the current regulation and the Amish community's way of life."[104]

On March 2, 1999, the House again passed this legislation under suspension of the rules, but the Senate has yet to take a vote.[105] In 1998, Senator Arlen Specter introduced legislation to accomplish the same purpose as the House-passed bill.[106] In 2001, he offered a floor amendment to allow Amish youth to work in sawmills, but agreed to withdraw the amendment to permit the Senate Committee on Health, Education, Labor, and Pensions to first hold hearings on the proposal. The Senate appropriations subcommittee on Labor-HHS had already held a hearing on the Amish bill.[107]

Animal Slaughter

In the 1880s and 1890s, Congress passed a number of statutes authorizing federal inspection of livestock to prevent importation or exportation of diseased animals. This legislation generally covered cattle, sheep, swine, and goats. Some exceptions for the inspection requirement were allowed, such as slaughtering that occurred on a farm.[108] There was no exception for slaughter done in accordance with religious ritual laws.

Over the years, states passed legislation against the inhumane treatment of animals, and many of those laws applied to slaughterhouse operations. Comparable federal legislation did not exist until 1958, when Congress passed the Humane Slaughter Act to prevent needless suffering of livestock. Although some companies had improved their procedures, most followed age-old methods: hoisting the animal by a hind leg and moving it to a "sticker," who knifed the jugular vein (not to kill the animal

103. 144 Cong. Rec. H9122-23 (daily ed. September 28, 1998).
104. Id. at H9122.
105. 145 Cong. Rec. H838 (daily ed. March 2, 1999).
106. 144 Cong. Rec. S11971 (daily ed. October 8, 1998).
107. 147 Cong. Rec. S6153-54 (daily ed. June 13, 2001).
108. 34 Stat. 679 (1906); 34 Stat. 1265 (1907).

but to cause death by loss of blood), and "knockers," who swung sledge-hammers against the animal's head (sometimes missing to knock off horns or knock out eyes).[109]

In reporting legislation in 1957, the House Committee on Agriculture decided to drop controversial criminal penalties for packers that failed to comply with federal policy. As a substitute sanction, the federal government would refuse to buy meat from any processor who used other than humane methods in slaughtering.[110] When spokesmen for Judaism "expressed concern over the implications of any humane slaughter legislation with respect to the kosher slaughtering of animals,"[111] the committee agreed to make an exception for the Jewish ritualistic method of slaughter. Many Jewish groups objected to that approach, because it seemed to imply that Congress would condemn inhumane slaughtering while tolerating Jewish slaughtering procedures so as not to offend religious freedom. Lawmakers in the House bill understood their objection and rewrote the bill to make it clear that ritualistic slaughtering is "one of the most humane methods yet devised."[112]

Even with this adjustment, the bill seemed to have little chance of enactment. The Department of Agriculture claimed there was insufficient knowledge to enable it to determine which methods were humane. They favored the creation of an advisory committee to help study the matter.[113] The powerful meatpacking industry opposed any legislation, preferring to leave the matter in the hands of private industry to devise acceptable slaughtering methods.[114] The Department of the Army, speaking on behalf of the Defense Department, opposed the provision that would prohibit federal agencies from purchasing livestock products unless in compliance with humane slaughtering procedures. The Army was worried that difficulties in satisfying the objectives of the legislative would create shortages in meat supplies.[115]

The Senate Committee on Agriculture and Forestry offered a substitute bill to call for additional research. The bill directed the Secretary of Agriculture to conduct research to develop and determine humane methods

109. 104 Cong. Rec. 1653 (1958).
110. Id. at 1654.
111. H. Rept. No. 706, 85th Cong., 1st Sess. 3 (1957).
112. 104 Cong. Rec. 1654 (1958).
113. H. Rept. No. 706, 85th Cong., 1st Sess. 3 (1957).
114. Id.
115. S. Rept. No. 1724, 85th Cong., 2d Sess. 5 (1958).

for slaughter of animals, and to submit to Congress within two years a legislative proposal.[116] In a surprise move on the floor, the committee's substitute proposal failed on a vote of 40 to 43.[117] The House bill then passed the Senate, 72 to 9, after the adoption of some amendments, and the House later agreed to those amendments.[118] The statute specifies two methods of humane slaughter:

> (a) in the case of cattle, calves, horses, mules, sheep, swine, and other livestock, all animals are rendered insensible to pain by a single blow or gunshot or an electrical, chemical or other means that is rapid and effective, before being shackled, hoisted, thrown, cast, or cut; or
> (b) by slaughtering in accordance with the ritual requirements of the Jewish faith or any other religious faith that prescribes a method of slaughter whereby the animal suffers loss of consciousness by anemia of the brain caused by the simultaneous and instantaneous severance of the carotid arteries with a sharp instrument.[119]

The legislation provided that nothing in it "shall be construed to prohibit, abridge, or in any way hinder the religious freedom of any person or group." In order to protect freedom of religion, "ritual slaughter and the handling or other preparation of livestock for ritual slaughter are exempted from the terms of this Act." The term "ritual slaughter" is defined by subsection (b) above.[120]

The bill required all federal agencies, after June 30, 1960, to purchase only livestock products that had been produced or processed in accordance with slaughtering methods designated and approved by the Secretary of Agriculture. On June 11, 1960, just as the legislation was about to take effect, the Military Subsistence Supply Agency, which purchases all meat for the armed forces, announced that it would require certification of compliance with humane slaughter regulations only for contracts exceeding $2,500. Senator Hubert H. Humphrey issued a strenuous protest, pointing out that slaughterhouses had been given two years to bring themselves into compliance with the law, and that the Defense Department was obliged with other federal agencies to follow the law. On

116. S. Rept. No. 1724, 85th Cong., 2d Sess. (1958).
117. 104 Cong. Rec. 15401 (1958).
118. Id. at 15416–17, 17427.
119. 72 Stat. 862, § 2 (1958).
120. Id. at 864, § 6.

June 14, Senator Humphrey received a statement from the Army that it would comply in full with the Humane Slaughter Act.[121]

In 1978, Congress amended the statute to toughen the sanctions. Instead of the federal government refusing to purchase livestock products that were not in compliance with the Humane Slaughter Act, the legislation covered all slaughtering conducted under federal and state inspection and all meat or meat food products imported into the United States.[122] The record of the past two decades demonstrated that approximately 90 percent of U.S. plants and foreign plants used humane methods of slaughter.[123]

Congress authorizes the Secretary of Agriculture to issue regulations governing procedures for the slaughter of poultry. Some groups are exempt from these regulations, including persons slaughtering, processing, or otherwise handling poultry "which have been or are to be processed as required by recognized religious dietary laws."[124] To qualify for the religious exemption, individuals write to the Department of Agriculture and identify the provisions of religious dietary laws that are at issue. Applications include a statement from the clerical official with jurisdiction over enforcement of the religious dietary laws, certifying that federal law and religious law are in conflict. The federal government grants exemptions to the extent necessary "to avoid conflict with the religious requirements" while still effectuating the purposes of federal law.[125]

Congress has repeatedly created statutory exemptions to take account of the religious needs of various organizations. As a political body that supposedly operates by majority vote, it has in fact recognized and given protection to the religious principles of many minority religions. These legislative judgments, balancing the needs of government against the rights of religion, are invariably upheld in the courts. Thus, the creative spark for safeguarding religious liberty depends greatly on the regular political process, driven from the outside by individuals and groups intent on preserving their religious principles. Courts play a role, but hardly a dominant one.

121. Emily Stewart Leavitt, updated and revised by Diane Halverson, "Humane Slaughter Laws," in Animals and Their Legal Rights 55 (4th ed. 1990).

122. 92 Stat. 1069 (1978); 7 U.S.C. §§ 1901–6 (1994); 21 U.S.C. §§ 603(b), 610(b) (1994).

123. 124 Cong. Rec. 24580 (1978).

124. 21 U.S.C. § 464(a) (1994).

125. 9 C.F.R. § 381.11 (1-1-01 ed.).

Conclusions

The Supreme Court has operated in the midst of political pressures for two hundred years, sometimes leading the charge for minority rights but more often pulling up the rear. Interest groups mobilize their forces to apply pressure to whatever branch is the most responsive to their needs. At times the courts satisfy interest group claims. On other occasions it is the elected branches. No single branch, including the judiciary, can lay claim to having the last word, and certainly not in the volatile world of religious politics.

A review of Supreme Court holdings reveals some victories for religious minorities and many, many defeats. First the plus side of the ledger: in 1925, the Court invalidated an Oregon law that required all children between the ages of eight and sixteen to attend public school. Were the state law to prevail, religious schools could not operate. The Court held that the law impermissibly interfered with the liberty of parents and guardians to direct the upbringing and education of their children.[1]

From 1940 to 1943, the Court handed down a number of decisions supportive of religious minorities. Jehovah's Witnesses had been convicted for "breach of the peace" in going house to house to distribute books and pamphlets about their religion. They carried a portable phonograph to help describe the books and solicit contributions. The requirement that they first obtain a certificate from a licensing officer before soliciting support amounted to a prior restraint on the exercise of their religion and a censorship of religion.[2] Similarly, the Court upheld the right of Jehovah's Witnesses to distribute handbills on the streets and to solicit orders or sell books without first obtaining a permit.[3] It struck

1. Pierce v. Society of Sisters, 268 U.S. 510 (1925).
2. Cantwell v. Connecticut, 310 U.S. 296 (1940).
3. Jamison v. Texas, 318 U.S. 413 (1943); Largent v. Texas, 318 U.S. 418 (1943).

down a license tax that had to be paid by Jehovah's Witnesses and others to solicit people to buy religious books and pamphlets.[4] Other decisions during this period also supported the right of Jehovah's Witnesses to distribute handbills by going door to door, and to solicit orders for religious literature without first obtaining a license and paying a license tax.[5]

By defining the Free Exercise Clause to mean not only freedom of religion but freedom *from* religion, the Court has granted constitutional protection to atheists and agnostics. Roy Torcaso could not be forced to declare a belief in the existence of God in order to be a notary public.[6] For conscientious objectors, the Court broadly interpreted a statutory requirement for a belief in a "Supreme Being" to include some force outside oneself, even if not a traditional deity.[7] State courts have held that religious organizations are entitled to an exemption from property taxes even if they do not believe in a Supreme Being.[8]

In a series of unemployment compensation cases, the Court supported the rights of religious minorities not to work on the day of their Sabbath. Thus, Adele Sherbert, a member of the Seventh-Day Adventist Church, was entitled to unemployment compensation after she had been discharged from her job because she would not work on Saturday, the Sabbath day of her faith.[9] This ruling was followed by other decisions sympathetic to religious minorities. In 1981, the Court held that a state could not withhold unemployment compensation from an individual who quit his job because he refused to do work (producing weapons) that would violate his religious beliefs as a Jehovah's Witness.[10] In 1987, the Court reversed a state's decision to withhold unemployment compensation benefits from a Seventh-Day Adventist who refused to work scheduled shifts on Friday evenings and Saturdays.[11] A decision in 1989 held that an individual did not have to belong to an established religious sect to constitutionally refuse to work on Sunday in violation of his personal religious beliefs.[12]

4. Murdock v. Pennsylvania, 319 U.S. 105 (1943).
5. Martin v. Struthers, 319 U.S. 141 (1943); Douglas v. Jeannette, 319 U.S. 157 (1943).
6. Torcaso v. Watkins, 367 U.S. 488 (1961).
7. United States v. Seeger, 380 U.S. 163 (1965).
8. Fellowship of Humanity v. County of Alameda, 315 P.2d 394, 406 (Cal. 1957).
9. Sherbert v. Verner, 374 U.S. 398 (1963).
10. Thomas v. Review Bd., Ind. Empl. Sec. Div., 450 U.S. 707 (1981).
11. Hobbie v. Unemployment Appeals Comm'n of Fla., 480 U.S. 136 (1987).
12. Frazee v. Illinois Employment Security Dept., 489 U.S. 829 (1989).

Ironically, another unemployment compensation case decided that states can go too far in accommodating religious beliefs. A Connecticut statute provided Sabbath observers with an absolute and unqualified right not to work on their chosen Sabbath. In 1985, the Court held that by granting unyielding weighting in favor of Sabbath observers over all other interests, the statute's primary effect was to advance religion and constituted a violation of the Establishment Clause.[13]

These unemployment compensation cases raised questions in the minds of some Justices. How could the Court repeatedly uphold the rights of Jehovah's Witnesses and Seventh-Day Adventists not to work on their Sabbath, while at the same time rejecting comparable religious claims of Orthodox Jews? If states forced all businesses to close on Sundays, and Orthodox Jews were unable for religious reasons to work from Friday nightfall to Saturday nightfall, Orthodox Jews would be at a competitive disadvantage. Yet in 1961, the Court found no constitutional objection to these Sunday closing laws.[14] The Court recognized that laws prohibiting work on Sundays were "undeniably religious in origin," but concluded that the choice of Sunday as a day of rest had, over time, acquired a secular purpose and did not violate the Establishment Clause.[15] Three Justices challenged the logic of these rulings. Justice Stewart said that for the Court to reach the conclusion it did in *Sherbert*, it "must explicitly reject the reasoning" in *Braunfeld v. Brown,* the case involving Orthodox Jews.[16] Justices Harlan and White agreed, concluding that *Sherbert* "necessarily overrules *Braunfeld v. Brown.*"[17]

Given the Court's rejection in *Employment Division v. Smith* (1990) of the constitutional standards established in *Sherbert* (compelling governmental interest),[18] are the unemployment compensation cases still good law? *Smith* treats the unemployment compensation cases as a valid exception because they require "individualized governmental assessment" of religious beliefs, whereas the Oregon law on drug use represented an across-the-board criminal prohibition. That distinction might parse in a law school classroom, but it is extremely strained and unconvincing. The

13. Estate of Thornton v. Caldor, Inc., 472 U.S. 703 (1985).
14. Braunfeld v. Brown, 366 U.S. 599 (1961); Gallagher v. Crown Kosher Market, 366 U.S. 617 (1961).
15. McGowan v. Maryland, 366 U.S. 420, 446, 453 (1961).
16. Sherbert v. Verner, 374 U.S. at 418.
17. Id. at 421.
18. Employment Division v. Smith, 494 U.S. 872 (1990).

heart of *Smith* is that judges shouldn't be making ad hoc rulings to "weigh the social importance of all laws against the centrality of all religious beliefs," and that such disputes are better left to the regular political process, however disadvantageous that might be to religious minorities.[19] How can *Sherbert* and the other unemployment compensation cases still be good law?

A case often cited to demonstrate the Court's solicitude for religious minorities is *Wisconsin v. Yoder* (1972), which held that the religious interests of the Amish outweighed a state's interest in compelling school attendance until age sixteen. The Court found that the Amish provide continuing informal vocational education to their children after the eighth grade, and that high school attendance would endanger the Amish religion and way of life. The Amish deemphasize material success, reject the competitive spirit, and seek to insulate themselves from the modern world, whereas high schools stress "intellectual and scientific accomplishments, self-distinction, competitiveness, worldly success, and social life with other students."[20]

Smith claims that *Yoder* is still good law, but *Yoder* pointed out that Wisconsin's requirement for school attendance to age sixteen "applies uniformly to all citizens of the State and does not, on its face, discriminate against religions or a particular religion."[21] In the same manner, Oregon's drug law applied uniformly to all citizens and did not discriminate against religions or a particular religion. Although *Smith* did not formally overrule *Yoder* and the unemployment compensation cases, they now stand on much weaker ground. Because of *Smith*, there is less reason to expect such liberal decisions in the future.

Smith provided a framework for the Court in 1993 to analyze ordinances issued by a Florida city council to prohibit the Santeria religion from sacrificing animals as a form of devotion. Adherents of that sect kill animals to nurture a personal relationship with spirits. Since the ordinances were aimed specifically at the Santeria religion (even to the point of exempting kosher slaughter), they were not general and neutral. Even if the Florida government had a compelling interest, the ordinances were obviously drafted to suppress a religious exercise.[22]

19. Id. at 890.
20. Wisconsin v. Yoder, 406 U.S. 205, 210–11 (1972).
21. Id. at 220.
22. Church of Lukimi Babalu Aye, Inc. v. Hialeah, 508 U.S. 520 (1993).

What about judicial decisions that do not protect religious minorities? Some cases may have such marginal merit that they would not attract the support of any branch. One example is Louisiana's "Creationism Act," which prohibited the teaching of the theory of evolution in public elementary and secondary schools unless accompanied by instruction in the theory of "creation science." The latter, based on the Book of Genesis, opposes the theory of evolution. The Court rejected the state's assertion that the statute furthered "academic freedom," in part because the legislative record revealed a bias in favor of creationism and religious doctrine.[23]

The Court struck down a compulsory flag salute in 1943, but only after the country denounced the 1940 decision that upheld it. Captain Goldman lost in the Court with his yarmulke case but won in Congress with a legislative amendment. Religious groups interested in securing the rights of conscientious objectors have taken their case to Congress, not the courts. Indians have brought their grievances to the Supreme Court many times, coming up empty on every occasion. What they were unable to achieve through litigation they were often able to achieve though legislation, such as the religious use of peyote and various claims for sacred sites. Narrow judicial interpretations of the social security laws, limiting exemptions for the Amish, were later reversed by Congress to yield broader coverage.

The United States Code is filled with religious exemptions. On hundreds of occasions, Congress has decided to protect religious interests by exempting them from general laws on taxation, social security, military service, peyote use, labor laws, discrimination in housing and employment, census questions, rehabilitative services, medical examinations, and public health measures.[24] The basic protection for religious interests comes from this statutory framework, not from court decisions. Legislative action not only takes the initiative in recognizing and defining religious liberties, but these statutory provisions far outstrip in number and importance the cases that have expanded religious rights.

To draw attention to cases in which courts do not protect the rights of religious minorities is not meant to criticize the judiciary. The American system works quite well when courts limit their reach and decline to

23. Edwards v. Aguillard, 482 U.S. 578 (1987).
24. Previous chapters give specific examples for most of these categories; for the religious exemption on census questions, see 13 U.S.C. § 221(c) (1994); rehabilitation services, 42 U.S.C. § 422(b) (1994); medical examinations, 42 U.S.C. § 1396f (1994).

manufacture new rights. Other political institutions, at both the national and the state level, have greater legitimacy and competence to step in and right a wrong. Rather than expect courts to always deliver a remedy, it is healthier to have that task shared with democratic institutions. Blacks admire the Court for the gains won in *Brown v. Board of Education*, but the statutory victories beginning with the Civil Rights Act of 1964 count for much more. To expect courts to consistently rectify constitutional wrongs, especially in the areas of individual rights and religious liberty, is to expect too much. Liberties are advanced through the public education and support that accompany the legislative process. Aryeh Neier, who spent decades handling cases for the ACLU, offered this advice: "Litigators serving interest groups in advancing causes do not serve their clients effectively if they limit themselves to persuading judges; they must also persuade the public."[25]

Religious groups have learned to consolidate their interests with other denominations to exert the maximum pressure and effectiveness. With ready access to parishioners, religious interests can mobilize more quickly and effectively than nearly any other interest group. As a result, legislatures—supposedly rough institutions designed to satisfy the majority's interests—have shown a keen sensitivity and solicitude in protecting minority rights. For this reason, on matters of religious faith and observance, elected officials more than judges have played an integral role in defining the reaches of religious liberty protections.

An activist member of the judiciary, Chief Justice Earl Warren, recognized that the Court has a limited role in safeguarding individual rights. Commenting on the Court's decisions upholding the deprivation of rights of Japanese Americans during World War II, he gave this candid assessment: "The fact that the Court rules in a case like *Hirabayashi* that a given program is constitutional, does not necessarily answer the question whether, in a broader sense, it actually is."[26] Read those words with care: Just because the Court says that something is constitutional doesn't mean it is. Warren used straight talk to discourage judicial idolatry.

The habit of automatically expecting courts to protect constitutional liberties is ill-advised. Warren believed that the American political system requires the judiciary to play a restricted role: "In our democracy it

25. Aryeh Neier, Only Judgment: The Limits of Litigation in Social Change 242 (1982).

26. Earl Warren, "The Bill of Rights and the Military," 37 N.Y.U. L. Rev. 181, 193 (1962).

is still the Legislature and the elected Executive who have the primary responsibility for fashioning and executing policy consistent with the Constitution."[27] Even here he cautioned against excessive dependence on the
political branches: "The day-to-day job of upholding the Constitution
really lies elsewhere. It rests, realistically, on the shoulders of every citizen."[28] In the search for a reconciliation between constitutional law and
self-government, we must all participate. Who protects minority rights?
In large measure, you do.

27. Id. at 202.
28. Id.

Bibliography

Abrams, Ray H. Preachers Present Arms (New York: Round Table Press, 1933).

———. "The Churches and the Clergy in World War II," 256 The Annals 110 (1948).

Adams, James L. The Growing Church Lobby in Washington (Grand Rapids, Mich.: Eerdmans Publishing Co., 1970).

Ahlstrom, Sydney E. A Religious History of the American People (New Haven, Conn.: Yale University Press, 1972).

Anderson, William L., ed. Cherokee Removal: Before and After (Athens: University of Georgia Press, 1991).

Andrews, William G. Coordinate Magistrates: Constitutional Law by Congress and the President (New York: Van Nostrand Reinhold Co., 1969).

Antieau, Chester James, Arthur T. Downey, and Edward C. Roberts. Freedom from Federal Establishment: Formation and Early History of the First Amendment Religion Clauses (Milwaukee: Bruce Publishing Co., 1964).

Arrington, Leonard J., and David Bitton. The Mormon Experience: A History of the Latter-day Saints (2d ed., Urbana: University of Illinois Press, 1992).

Ball, Milner S. "Constitution, Court, Indian Tribes," 1 American Bar Foundation Research Journal (1987).

Banks, Charles Edward. History of York, Maine (3 vols., Boston: Calkins Press, 1931).

Bartee, Alice Fleetwood. Cases Lost, Causes Won (New York: St. Martin's Press, 1984).

Barton, David. The Myth of Separation (Aledo, Tex.: WallBuilder Press, 1989).

Beaney, William M., and Edward N. Beiser. "Prayer and Politics: The Impact of Engel and Schempp on the Political Process," 13 Journal of Public Law 475 (1964).

Beatty, Kathleen Murphy. "A Group Theory of Religion and Politics: The Clergy as Group Leaders," 42 Western Political Quarterly 130 (1989).

Beaver, R. Pierce. "Church, State, and the Indians: Indian Missions to the New Nation," 4 Journal of Church and State 11 (1962).

————. "The Churches and President Grant's Peace Policy," 4 Journal of Church and State 174 (1962).

————. Introduction to Native American Church History (Tempe, Ariz.: Cook Christian Training School, 1983).

————. "Protestant Churches and the Indians," in William C. Sturtevant, ed., 4 Handbook of North American Indians (Washington, D.C.: Smithsonian Institution, 1988).

Benson, Peter L., and Dorothy L. Williams. Religion on Capitol Hill: Myths and Realities (New York: Oxford University Press, 1986).

Berger, Peter L. "Democracy and the Religious Right," Commentary (January 1997).

Bergman, Jerry. "The Modern Religious Objection to Mandatory Flag Salute in America: A History of Evaluation," 39 Journal of Church and State 215 (1997).

Berkhofer, Robert F., Jr. Salvation and the Savage: An Analysis of Protestant Missions and American Indian Response (Lexington: University of Kentucky Press, 1965).

Berns, Walter. "Freedom of the Press and the Alien and Sedition Laws: A Reappraisal," 1970 Supreme Court Review 109.

Bickel, Alexander M. The Least Dangerous Branch (New York: Bobbs-Merrill Co., 1962).

Black, Hugo, and Elizabeth Black. The Memoirs of Hugo L. Black and Elizabeth Black (New York: Random House, 1986).

Blocker, Jack S., Jr. American Temperance Movements: Cycles of Reform (Boston, Mass.: Twayne Publishers, 1989).

Bodine, John J. "Blue Lake: A Struggle for Indian Rights," 1 American Indian Law Review 23 (1973).

Borden, Morton. Jews, Turks, and Infidels (Chapel Hill: University of North Carolina Press, 1984).

Bordin, Ruth. Woman and Temperance: The Quest for Power and Liberty, 1873–1990 (Philadelphia, Pa.: Temple University Press, 1981).

Bradley, Gerald V. Church-State Relationships in America (Westport: Greenwood Press, 1987).

————. "The No Religious Test Clause and the Constitution of Religious Liberty: A Machine That Has Gone of Itself," 37 Case Western Reserve Law Review 674 (1987).

Braithwaite, William C. The Beginnings of Quakerism (London: Cambridge University Press, 1955).

Brown, Dee. Bury My Heart at Wounded Knee (New York: Holt, Rinehart & Winston, 1971).

Burke, Joseph C. "The Cherokee Cases: A Study in Law, Politics, and Morality," 21 Stanford Law Review 500 (1969).

Burr, Nelson R. A Critical Bibliography of Religion in America (Princeton, N.J.: Princeton University Press, 1961).

Butler, Jon, and Harry S. Stout, eds. Religion in American History: A Reader (New York: Oxford University Press, 1998).

Butler, R. Pierce. "The Churches and President Grant's Peace Policy," 4 Journal of Church and State 174 (1962).

Butts, R. Freeman. The American Tradition in Religion and Education (Boston: Beacon Press, 1950).

Capizzi, Joseph E. "Selective Conscientious Objection in the United States," 38 Journal of Church and State 339 (1996).

Cayton, Mary K. "Social Reform from the Colonial Period Through the Civil War," in Encyclopedia of the American Religious Experience, vol. 3, p. 1430 (Charles H. Lippy and Peter W. Williams, eds., New York: Charles Scribner's Sons, 1988).

Chafee, Zechariah, Jr. Free Speech in the United States (Cambridge: Harvard University Press, 1941).

Choper, Jesse H. Judicial Review and the National Political Process (Chicago: University of Chicago Press, 1980).

Clark, Norman H. Deliver Us from Evil: An Interpretation of American Prohibition (New York: W. W. Norton, 1976).

Cobb, Sanford H. The Rise of Religious Liberty in America (New York: Macmillan Co., 1902).

Cohen, Felix. Handbook of Federal Indian Law (Albuquerque: University of New Mexico Press, 1971).

Cohen, Naomi W. Not Free to Desist: The American Jewish Committee, 1906–1966 (Philadelphia: Jewish Publication Society, 1972).

———. Encounter with Emancipation: The German Jews in the United States, 1830–1914 (Philadelphia: Jewish Publication Society, 1984).

———. Jews in Christian America: The Pursuit of Religious Equality (New York: Oxford University Press, 1992).

Commager, Henry Steele. Majority Rule and Minority Rights (New York: Oxford University Press, 1943).

Complete Writings of Roger Williams, The (7 vols., New York: Russell & Russell, 1963).

Congress Looks at the Conscientious Objector (Washington, D.C.: National Service Board for Religious Objectors, 1943).

Conklin, Francis J. "Conscientious Objector Provisions: A View in the Light of Torcaso v. Watkins," 51 Georgetown Law Journal 252 (1963).

Conway, John S. "The Struggle for Peace Between the Wars," 35 Ecumenical Review 25 (1983).

Cook, Elizabeth Adell, Ted. G. Jelen, and Clyde Wilcox. Between Two Absolutes:

Public Opinion of the Politics of Abortion (Boulder, Colo: Westview Press, 1992).

Corbett, Michael, and Julia Mitchell Corbett. Politics and Religion in the United States (New York: Garland Publishers, 1999).

Cord, Robert L. Separation of Church and States: Historical Fact and Current Fiction (Grand Rapids, Mich.: Baker Book House, 1988).

Cornell, Julien. The Conscientious Objector and the Law (New York: John Day Co., 1943).

———. Conscience and the State: Legal and Administrative Problems of Conscientious Objectors, 1943–1944 (New York: John Day Co., 1944).

Costo, Rupert. "Presidents of the United States in American Indian History," The Indian Historian 4 (1968).

Cousineau, Madeleine, ed. Religion in a Changing World (Westport, Conn.: Praeger, 1998).

Craig, Barbara Hinkson, and David M. O'Brien. Abortion and American Politics (Chatham, N.J.: Chatham House, 1993).

Crawford, Sue E. S., and Laura R. Olson, eds. Christian Clergy in American Politics (Baltimore, Md.: Johns Hopkins University Press, 2001).

Currie, David P. The Constitution in Congress: The Federalist Period, 1789–1801 (Chicago: University of Chicago Press, 1997).

Curry, Thomas J. The First Freedoms: Church and State in America to the Passage of the First Amendment (New York: Oxford University Press, 1986).

Dabney, Virginius. Dry Messiah: The Life of Bishop Cannon (New York: A. A. Knopf, 1949).

Danzig, Richard. "How Questions Begot Answers in Felix Frankfurter's First Flag Salute Opinion," 1977 Supreme Court Review 257.

———. "Justice Frankfurter's Opinions in the Flag Salute Cases: Blending Logic and Psychologic in Constitution Decisionmaking," 36 Stanford Law Review 675 (1984).

Deloria, Vine, Jr., and Clifford M. Lytle. American Indians, American Justice (Austin: University of Texas Press, 1983).

Deloria, Vine, Jr. God Is Red: A Native View of Religion (Golden, Colo: Fulcrum Publishing, 1994).

Destro, Robert A. "The Structure of the Religious Liberty Guarantee," 11 Journal of Law and Religion 355 (1994–1995).

de Verges, George. "Peyote and the Native American Church," 2 American Indian Law Review 71 (1974).

Devins, Neal. Shaping Constitutional Values: Elected Government, the Supreme Court, and the Abortion Debate (Baltimore, Md.: Johns Hopkins University Press, 1996).

———. "How Not to Challenge the Court," 39 William and Mary Law Review 645 (1998).

DeWeerd, Harvey A. President Wilson Fights His War: World War I and the American Intervention (New York: Macmillan, 1968).

Dilliard, Irving. "The Flag-Salute Cases," in John A. Garraty, ed., Quarrels That Have Shaped the Constitution (New York: Harper & Row, 1966).

Dinan, John J. Keeping the People's Liberties: Legislators, Citizens, and Judges as Guardians of Rights (Lawrence: University Press of Kansas, 1998).

Dolbeare, Kenneth M., and Phillip E. Hammond. The School Prayer Decisions: From Court Policy to Local Practice (Chicago: University Press of Chicago, 1971).

Douglas, William O. The Court Years, 1939–75: The Autobiography of William O. Douglas (New York: Vintage Books, 1981).

Doyle, John T. "Dubious Intrusions—Peyote, Drug Laws, and Religious Freedom," 8 American Indian Law Review 79 (1980).

Dreisbach, Daniel L. "The Constitution's Forgotten Religion Clause: Reflections on the Article VI Religious Test Ban," 38 Journal of Church and State 261 (1996).

———. "'Sowing Useful Truths and Principles': The Danbury Baptists, Thomas Jefferson, and the 'Wall of Separation,'" 39 Journal of Church and State 455 (1997).

Driggs, Kenneth David. "The Mormon Church-State Confrontation in Nineteenth-Century America," 30 Journal of Church and State 273 (1988).

———. "After the Manifesto: Modern Polygamy and Fundamentalist Mormons," 32 Journal of Church and State 367 (1990).

Dumond, Dwight Lowell. The Antislavery Origins of the Civil War in the United States (Ann Arbor: University of Michigan Press, 1939).

Dunn, Charles W., ed. Religion in American Politics (Washington, D.C.: CQ Press, 1989).

Ebersole, Luke Eugene. Church Lobbying in the Nation's Capital (New York: Macmillan Co., 1951).

Echo-Hawk, Walter R. "Native American Religious Liberty: Five Hundred Years After Columbus," 17 American Indian Culture and Research Journal 33 (1993).

Eckenrode, H. J. Separation of Church and State in Virginia (Richmond, Va.: Davis Bottom, Superintendent of Public Printing, 1910).

Edel, Wilbur. Defender of the Faith: Religion and Politics from the Pilgrim Fathers to Ronald Reagan (Westport, Conn.: Praeger, 1987).

Edgerton, Henry W. "The Incidence of Judicial Control over Congress," 22 Cornell Law Quarterly 299 (1937).

Elliot, Jonathan, ed. The Debates in the Several State Conventions, on the Adoption of the Federal Constitution (5 vols., Washington, D.C., 1836–1845).

Endy, Melvin B., Jr. "War and Peace," in Encyclopedia of the American Religious

Experience, vol. 3, pp. 1409–28 (Charles H. Lippy and Peter W. Williams, eds., New York: Charles Scribner's Sons, 1988).

Epps, Garrett. "To an Unknown God: The Hidden History of *Employment Division v. Smith*," 30 Arizona State Law Journal 953 (1998).

———. To an Unknown God: Religious Freedom on Trial (New York: St. Martin's Press, 2001).

Epstein, Lee. "Interest Group Litigation During the Rehnquist Court Era," 9 Journal of Law and Politics 639 (1993).

Evans, Bette Novit. Interpreting the Free Exercise of Religion (Chapel Hill, N.C.: University of North Carolina Press, 1997).

Farb, Peter. Man's Rise to Civilization as Shown by the Indian of North America from Primeval Times to the Coming of the Industrial State (New York: Dutton, 1968).

Farrand, Max, ed. The Records of the Federal Convention of 1787 (4 vols., New Haven, Conn.: Yale University Press, 1937).

Fehrenbacher, Don E. The Dred Scott Case: Its Significance in American Law and Politics (New York: Oxford University Press, 1978).

Ferguson, John. War and Peace in the World's Religions (New York: Oxford University Press, 1978).

Findlay, James F. "Religion and Politics in the Sixties: The Churches and the Civil Rights Act of 1964," 77 Journal of American History 66 (1990).

———. Church People in the Struggle: The National Council of Churches and the Black Freedom Movement, 1950–1970 (New York: Oxford University Press, 1993).

Firmage, Edwin Brown, and Richard Collin Mangrum. Zion in the Courts: A Legal History of the Church of Jesus Christ of Latter-day Saints, 1830–1900 (Urbana, Ill.: University of Illinois Press, 1988).

Fisher, Louis. Constitutional Dialogues: Interpretation as Political Process (Princeton, N.J.: Princeton University Press, 1987).

———. American Constitutional Law (4th ed., Durham, N.C.: Carolina Academic Press, 2001).

———. "Nonjudicial Safeguards for Religious Liberty," 70 University of Cincinnati Law Review 31 (2001).

———. "Indian Religious Freedom: To Litigate or Legislate?" 26 American Indian Law Review 1 (2002).

———. "Statutory Exemptions for Religious Freedom," 44 Journal of Church and State 291 (2002).

Fleet, Elizabeth, ed. "Madison's 'Detached Memoranda,'" 3 William and Mary Quarterly 534 (1946).

Flowers, Ronald B. "Tax Exemption and the Clergy: On Vows of Poverty and Parsonage Allowances," in James E. Wood, Jr., ed., Religion and the State (Waco, Tex.: Baylor University Press, 1985).

Foreman, Grant. Indian Removal: The Emigration of the Five Civilized Tribes of Indians (Norman: University of Oklahoma Press, 1932).

Fowler, Robert Booth. Religion and Politics in America (Metuchen, N.J.: Scarecrow Press, 1985).

Fowler, Robert Booth, and Allen D. Hertzke. Religion and Politics in America: Faith, Culture, and Strategic Choices (Boulder, Colo.: Westview Press, 1995).

Freeman, Harrop A. "A Remonstrance for Conscience," 106 University of Pennsylvania Law Review 806 (1958).

Fried, Charles. Order and Law: Arguing the Reagan Revolution—A Firsthand Account (New York: Simon & Schuster, 1991).

Frost, J. William. A Perfect Freedom: Religious Liberty in Pennsylvania (University Park: Pennsylvania State University Press, 1990).

Gardner, George K., and Charles D. Post. "The Constitutional Question Raised by the Flag Salute and Teachers' Oath Acts in Massachusetts," 16 Boston University Law Review 803 (1936).

Gaustad, Edwin S. American Religious History, Publication No. 65 (Washington, D.C.: Service Center for Teachers of History, 1966).

———. Religion, the Constitution, and the Founding Fathers (Rome, Ga.: Shorter College, 1987).

Geb, John. "Native American Culture: The Use of Feathers as a Protected Right," 2 American Indian Law Review 105 (1974).

Gelm, Richard J. Politics and Religious Authority: American Catholics Since the Second Vatican Council (Westport, Conn.: Greenwood Press, 1994).

Ginsburg, Faye D. Contested Lives: The Abortion Debate in an American Community (Berkeley: University of California Press, 1998).

Goldstein, Judith S. The Politics of Ethnic Pressure: The American Jewish Committee Fight Against Immigration Restriction, 1906–1917 (New York: Garland Publishing, 1990).

Goldstein, Leslie Friedman. "The ERA and the U.S. Supreme Court," 1 Law and Policy Studies 145 (1987).

Gordon, Sarah B. "Indian Religious Freedom and Governmental Development of Public Lands," 94 Yale Law Journal 1447 (1985).

Green, John C. "The Christian Right and the 1994 Elections: An Overview," in Mark J. Rozell and Clyde Wilcox, eds., God at the Grass Roots: The Christian Right in the 1994 Elections (Lanham, Md.: Rowman and Littlefield Publishers, 1995).

Green, John C., and James L. Guth. "The Christian Right in the Republican Party: The Case of Pat Robertson's Supporters," 50 Journal of Politics 150 (1988).

———. "Religion, Representatives, and Roll Calls," 16 Legislative Studies Quarterly 571 (1991).

Green, John C., James L. Guth, and Kevin Hill. "Faith and Election: The

Christian Right in Congressional Campaigns, 1978–88," 55 Journal of Politics 80 (1993).

Green, John C., Mark J. Rozell, and Clyde Wilcox, eds. Prayers in the Precincts: The Christian Right in the 1998 Elections (Washington, D.C.: Georgetown University Press, 2000).

Greenawalt, Kent. "All or Nothing at All: The Defeat of Selective Conscientious Objection," 1971 Supreme Court Review 31.

———. "Conscientious Objection and the Liberal State," in James E. Wood, Jr., ed., Religion and the State (Waco, Tex.: Baylor University Press, 1985).

———. "The Participation of Religious Groups in Political Advocacy," 36 Journal of Church and State 143 (1994).

Grimes, Alan P. Democracy and the Amendments to the Constitution (Lexington, Mass: Lexington Books, 1978).

Grinde, Donald. "Cherokee Removal and American Politics," 8 The Indian Historian 33 (1975).

Guliuzza, Frank, III. Over the Wall: Protecting Religious Expression in the Public Square (Albany: State University of New York Press, 2000).

Gunther, Gerald, and Gerhard Casper, eds. Landmark Briefs and Arguments of the Supreme Court of the United States: Constitutional Law (Bethesda, Md.: University Publications of America, 1978–present).

Hall, Timothy L. "Roger Williams and the Foundations of Religious Liberty," 71 Boston University Law Review 455 (1991).

Halverson, Diane. "Humane Slaughter Laws," in Animals and Their Legal Rights (4th ed., Animal Welfare Institute, 1990).

Hamberger, Philip A. "A Constitutional Right of Religious Exemption: An Historical Perspective," 60 George Washington Law Review 915 (1992).

Hamilton, Walton, and George Braden. "The Supreme Court Today," 103 The New Republic 180 (1940).

Hamm, Richard F. Shaping the Eighteenth Amendment: Temperance Reform, Legal Culture, and the Polity (Chapel Hill: University of North Carolina Press, 1995).

Hansen, Klaus J. Mormonism and the American Experience (Chicago: University of Chicago Press, 1981).

Harris, Kathryn. "The American Indian Religious Freedom Act and Its Promise," 5 American Indian Journal 7 (1979).

Hart, James. The American Presidency in Action (New York: Macmillan Co., 1948).

Heller, Francis H. "A Turning Point for Religious Liberty," 29 Virginia Law Review 440 (1943).

Hening, William Waller. The Statutes at Large: Being a Collection of All the Laws of Virginia (13 vols., Richmond, Va.: George Cochran, 1819–1823).

Hertzberg, Hazel Whitman. "Indian Rights Movement, 1887–1973," in William

C. Sturvevant, ed., 4 Handbook of North American Indians (Washington, D.C.: Smithsonian Institution, 1988).

Hertzke, Allen D. Representing God in Washington: The Role of Religious Lobbies in the American Policy (Knoxville: University of Tennessee Press, 1988).

———. "The Role of Religious Lobbies," in Charles W. Dunn, ed., Religion in American Politics (Washington, D.C.: CQ Press, 1989).

———. Echoes of Discontent: Jesse Jackson, Pat Robertson, and the Resurgence of Populism (Washington, D.C.: CQ Press, 1993).

Higginbothan, C. Dean. "Native Americans Versus Archaeologists: The Legal Issues," 10 American Indian Law Review 91 (1982).

Hirsch, H. N. The Enigma of Felix Frankfurter (New York: Basic Books, 1981).

———. A Theory of Liberty: The Constitution and Minorities (New York: Routledge, 1992).

Horsman, Reginald. The Origins of Indian Removal, 1815–1824 (East Lansing: Michigan State University Press, 1970).

Hoskins, Richard J. "The Original Separation of Church and State in America," 2 Journal of Law and Religion 221 (1984).

Howard, J. Woodford, Jr. Mr. Justice Murphy: A Political Biography (Princeton, N.J.: Princeton University Press, 1968).

Howe, Mark DeWolfe. The Garden and the Wilderness: Religion and Government in American Constitutional History (Chicago: University of Chicago Press, 1965).

Humphrey, Edward Frank. Nationalism and Religion in America, 1774–1789 (Boston, Mass.: Chipman Law Publishing Co., 1924).

Hutcheson, Richard G., Jr. God in the White House: How Religion Has Changed the Modern Presidency (New York: Macmillan Publishing Co., 1988).

Hutson, James H. Religion and the Founding of the American Republic (Washington, D.C.: Library of Congress, 1998).

———. "Thomas Jefferson's Letter to the Danbury Baptists: A Controversy Rejoined," 56 William and Mary Quarterly 775 (1999).

Hyman, Harold M. A More Perfect Union: The Impact of the Civil War and Reconstruction of the Constitution (Boston: Houghton Mifflin Co., 1975).

Irons, Diane Gleason. "Religious Discrimination in Employment: Title VII and the Constitution," 29 Journal of Church and State 253 (1987).

Isaacs, Stephen D. Jews and American Politics (Garden City, N.Y.: Doubleday & Co., 1974).

Ivers, Gregg. "Organized Religion and the Supreme Court," 32 Journal of Church and State 775 (1990).

———. "Religious Organizations as Constitutional Litigants," 25 Polity 243 (1992).

———. To Build a Wall: American Jews and the Separation of Church and State (Charlottesville: University Press of Virginia, 1995).

———. "Please God, Save This Honorable Court: The Emergence of the Conservative Religious Bar," in Paul S. Herrnson et al., eds., The Interest Group Connection (Chatham, N.J.: Chatham House, 1998).

James, Edward T., ed. Notable American Women (3 vols., Cambridge: Harvard University Press, 1971).

Jelen, Ted G. "The Clergy and Abortion," 34 Review of Religious Research 132 (1992).

Johnson, Alvin W., and Frank H. Yost. Separation of Church and State in the United States (Westport: Greenwood Press, 1969; originally published by the University of Minnesota Press in 1934).

Johnson, Donald Bruce. National Party Platforms (2 vols., Urbana: University of Illinois Press, 1978).

Johnson, Robert. "Whitehorn v. State: Peyote and Religious Freedom in Oklahoma," 5 American Indian Law Review 229 (1977).

Johnston, John D., Jr., and Charles L. Knapp. "Sex Discrimination by Law: A Study in Judicial Perspective," 46 New York University Law Review 675 (1971).

Jost, Kenneth. "Religion and Politics," 4 CQ Researcher 889 (October 14, 1994).

Kauper, Paul G. Religion and the Constitution (Baton Rouge: Louisiana State University Press, 1964).

Keller, Robert. "Christian Indian Missions and the American Frontier," 5 American Indian Journal 19 (1979).

Keller, Robert H., Jr. "Church Joins State to Civilize Indians, 1776–1869," 5 American Indian Journal 7 (1979).

Kelley, Dean M. "Tax Exemption and the Free Exercise of Religion," in James E. Wood, Jr., Religion and the State (Waco, Tex.: Baylor University Press, 1985).

Kellogg, Walter Guest. The Conscientious Objector (New York: Boni & Liveright, 1919).

Kelly, Lawrence C. "The Indian Reorganization Act: The Dream and the Reality," in John R. Wunder, ed., Constitutionalism and Native Americans, 1903–1968 (New York: Garland Publishers, 1996).

Kerr, K. Austin. Organized for Prohibition: A New History of the Anti-Saloon League (New Haven, Conn.: Yale University Press, 1985).

Keynes, Edward, with Randall K. Miller. The Court vs. Congress: Prayer, Busing, and Abortion (Durham, N.C.: Duke University Press, 1989).

Kleber, Louis C. "Religion Among the American Indians," 28 History Today 81 (1978).

Konvitz, Milton R. Religious Liberty and Conscience: A Constitutional Inquiry (New York: Viking Press, 1968).

Korn, Bertrum Wallace. American Jewry and the Civil War (Philadelphia: Jewish Publication Society of America, 1951).

——. Eventual Years and Experiences (Cincinnati: American Jewish Archives, 1954).

Kraybill, Donald B., ed. The Amish and the State (Baltimore: Johns Hopkins University Press, 1993).

Kurland, Philip B. "The Regents' Prayer Case: 'Full of Sound and Fury, Signifying . . . ,'" 1962 Supreme Court Review 1 (1962).

——. "The School Prayer Cases," in Dallin H. Oaks, ed., The Wall Between Church and State (Chicago: University of Chicago Press, 1963).

——. "The Origins of the Religion Clauses of the Constitution," 27 William and Mary Law Review 839 (1986).

Kurland, Philip B., and Ralph Lerner, eds. The Founders' Constitution (5 vols., Chicago: University of Chicago Press, 1987).

Kutner, Stanley I., ed. The Dred Scott Decision: Law or Politics? (New York: Houghton Mifflin Co., 1967).

LaFantasie, Glenn W. The Correspondence of Roger Williams (3 vols., Hanover, N.H.: Brown University Press/University Press of New England, 1988).

Lash, Joseph P. From the Diaries of Felix Frankfurter (New York: Norton, 1975).

Letwin, William, ed. A Documentary History of American Economic Policy Since 1789 (Garden City, N.Y.: Doubleday & Co., 1961).

Leuchtenburg, William E. The Perils of Prosperity (Chicago: University of Chicago Press, 1958).

Levy, Leonard W. The Establishment Clause: Religion and the First Amendment (Chapel Hill: University of North Carolina Press, rev. ed., 1994).

Linford, Orma, "The Mormons and the Law: The Polygamy Cases" (Parts 1 and 2), 9 Utah Law Review 308, 543 (1964–1965).

Little, David. "Thomas Jefferson's Religious Views and Their Influence on the Supreme Court's Interpretation of the First Amendment," 26 Catholic University Law Review 57 (1976).

Locke, John, The Works of (9 vols., London: C. Baldwin, 1824).

Loevy, Robert D., ed. The Civil Rights Act of 1964: The Passage of the Law That Ended Racial Segregation (Albany: State University of New York Press, 1997).

Long, Carolyn N. Religious Freedom and Indian Rights: The Case of Oregon v. Smith (Lawrence: University Press of Kansas, 2000).

Loveland, Anne C. American Evangelicals and the U.S. Military, 1942–1993 (Baton Rouge: Louisiana State University Press, 1996).

Mahon, John K. "Indian–United States Military Situation, 1775–1848," in William C. Sturtevant, ed., 4 Handbook of North American Indians (Washington, D.C.: Smithsonian Institution, 1988).

Malbin, Michael J. Religion and Politics: The Intentions of the Authors of the First Amendment (Washington, D.C.: American Enterprise Institute, 1978).

Manwaring, David R. Render Unto Caesar: The Flag-Salute Controversy (Chicago: University of Chicago Press, 1962).

Marshall, John. The Life of George Washington (2 vols., Philadelphia: J. Crissy, 1833).

Marshall, Thurgood. "Group Action in the Pursuit of Justice," 44 New York University Law Review 661 (1969).

Mason, Alpheus Thomas. Harlan Fiske Stone: Pillar of the Law (New York: Viking Press, 1956).

Mazur, Eric Michael. The Americanization of Religious Minorities (Baltimore, Md.: Johns Hopkins University Press, 1999).

McCollum, Vashti Cromwell. One Woman's Fight (Boston: Beacon Press, rev. ed., 1961).

McConnell, Michael W. "The Origins and Historical Understanding of Free Exercise of Religion," 103 Harvard Law Review 1410 (1990).

———. "Institutions and Interpretation: A Critique of City of Boerne v. Flores," 111 Harvard Law Review 153 (1997).

McKivigan, John R. The War Against Proslavery Religion: Abolitionism and the Northern Churches, 1830–1865 (Ithaca, N.Y.: Cornell University Press, 1984).

McLaren, John and Harold Coward, eds. Religious Conscience, the State, and the Law (Albany: State University of New York Press, 1999).

McLoughlin, William G. Rhode Island: A History (New York: W. W. Norton, 1986).

McNamara, Patrick H., ed. Religion American Style (New York: Harper & Row, 1974).

Michaelsen, Robert S. "American Indian Religious Freedom Litigation: Promise and Perils," 3 Journal of Law and Religion 47 (1985).

———. "Is the Miner's Canary Silent? Implications of the Supreme Court's Denial of American Indian Free Exercise of Religion Claims," 6 Journal of Law and Religion 97 (1988).

Middlebeeler, Emmet V. "Law and the Conscientious Objector," 20 Oregon Law Review 301 (1941).

Miller, Charles, The Supreme Court and the Uses of History (Cambridge: Harvard University Press, 1966).

Miller, Jeremy M. "A Critique of the Reynolds Decision," 11 Western State University Law Review 165 (1984).

Miller, Perry. Roger Williams: His Contribution to the American Tradition (Indianapolis: Bobbs-Merrill, 1953).

———. Errand Into the Wilderness (Cambridge: Harvard University Press, 1956).

Millis, Walter. The Martial Spirit: A Study of Our War with Spain (Boston: Houghton Mifflin Co., 1931).

Mishler, William, and Reginald S. Sheehan. "The Supreme Court as a Counter-majoritarian Institution? The Impact of Public Opinion on Supreme Court Decisions," 87 American Political Science Review 87 (1993).

Moen, Matthew C. The Christian Right and Congress (Tuscaloosa: University of Alabama Press, 1989).

———. The Transformation of the Christian Right (Tuscaloosa: University of Alabama Press, 1992).

———. "From Revolution to Evolution: The Changing Nature of the Christian Right," in Steve Bruce, Peter Kivisto, and William H. Swatos, Jr., The Rapture of Politics (New Brunswick, N.J.: Transaction Publishers, 1995).

———. "The Evolving Politics of the Christian Right," 29 PS: Political Science and Politics 461 (1996).

———. "The Changing Nature of Christian Right Activism: 1970s–1990s," in Corwin E. Smidt and James M. Penning, eds., Sojourners in the Wilderness: The Christian Right in Comparative Perspective (Lanham, Md.: Rowman & Littlefield Publishers, 1997).

Moore, W. John. "In Whose Court?" National Journal, October 5, 1991.

Morgan, Richard E. The Politics of Religious Conflict: Church and State in America (New York: Pegasus, 1968).

Muir, William K. Prayer in the Public Schools: Law and Attitude Change (Chicago: University of Chicago Press, 1967).

Neff, Jimmy D. "Roger Williams: Pious Puritan and Strict Separationist," 38 Journal of Church and State 529 (1996).

Neier, Aryeh. Only Judgment: The Limits of Litigation in Social Change (Middletown, Conn.: Wesleyan University Press, 1982).

Newland, Chester A. "Press Coverage of the United States Supreme Court," 17 Western Political Quarterly 15 (1964).

Noonan, John T., Jr. The Believer and the Powers That Are (New York: Macmillan Co., 1987).

Norgren, Jill. The Cherokee Cases: The Confrontation of Law and Politics (New York: McGraw-Hill, 1996).

Note. "The Unconstitutionality of State Statutes Authorizing Moments of Silence in the Public Schools," 96 Harvard Law Review 1874 (1983).

Oaks, Dallin H. "The Suppression of the Nauvoo Expositor," 9 Utah Law Review 862 (1965).

Oaks, Dallin H., ed. The Wall Between Church and State (Chicago: University of Chicago Press, 1963).

O'Brien, Sharon. "A Legal Analysis of the American Indian Religious Freedom Act," in Christopher Vecsey, ed., Handbook of American Indian Religious Freedom (New York: Crossroad, 1991).

O'Brien, William V. Nuclear War, Deterrence and Morality (Westminister, Md.: Newman Press, 1967).

O'Connor, Robert E., and Michael B. Berkman. "Religious Determinants of State Abortion Policy," 76 Social Science Quarterly 447 (1995).

Olson, Laura R. Filled with Spirit and Power: Protestant Clergy in Politics (Albany: State University of New York Press, 2000).

———. "Mainline Protestant Washington Offices and the Political Lives of Clergy: Making a Difference or Fostering Indifference?" presented at the annual meeting of the Midwest Political Science Association, Chicago, Illinois. (April 27–30, 2000).

Pacifist Handbook (Philadelphia: Fellowship of Reconciliation, 1939).

Peck, Robert S. "A Wrenching Reversal," 5 Constitution 51 (1993).

Peters, Shawn Francis. Judging Jehovah's Witnesses: Religious Persecution and the Dawn of the Rights Revolution (Lawrence: University Press of Kansas, 2000).

Pfeffer, Leo. "The New York Regents' Prayer Case (Engel v. Vitale)," 4 Journal of Church and State 150 (1962).

———. Church, State, and Freedom (Boston: Beacon Press, rev. ed., 1967).

———. God, Caesar, and the Constitution: The Court as Referee of Church-State Confrontation (Boston: Beacon Press, 1975).

———. "Amici in Church-State Litigation," 44 Law and Contemporary Problems 83 (Spring 1981).

Phillips, Stephen. "Roger Williams and the Two Tables of the Law," 38 Journal of Church and State 547 (1996).

Philp, Kenneth. "John Collier and the Crusade to Protect Indian Religious Freedom, 1920–26," 1 Journal of Ethnic Studies 22 (1973).

———. John Collier's Crusade for Indian Reform, 1920–1954 (Tucson: University of Arizona Press, 1977).

Pierard, Richard V., and Robert D. Linder. Civil Religion and the Presidency (Grand Rapids, Mich.: Academie Books, 1988).

Pilling, Arnold R. "Native American Religious Rights: Constitutional Considerations," 12 The Indian Historian 13 (1979).

Problem of Indian Administration, The (Baltimore: Johns Hopkins University Press, 1928).

Prucha, Francis Paul. American Indian Policy in Crisis: Christian Reformers and the Indian, 1865–1900 (Norman: University of Oklahoma Press, 1976).

———. The Churches and the Indian Schools, 1888–1912 (Lincoln: University of Nebraska Press, 1979).

———. The Great Father: The United States Government and the American Indians (Lincoln: University of Nebraska Press, 1995).

Pusey, Merlo J. Charles Evans Hughes (2 vols., New York: Macmillan Co., 1952).

Rahill, Peter J. The Catholic Indian Missions and Grant's Peace Policy, 1870–1884 (Washington, D.C.: Catholic University of America Press, 1953).

Raines, June Camille Bush. "One Is Missing: Native American Graves Protection and Repatriation Act: An Overview and Analysis," 17 American Indian Law Review 636 (1992).

Ramsey, Paul. War and the Christian Conscience: How Shall Modern War Be Conducted Justly? (Durham, N.C.: Duke University Press, 1961).

Rannow, Robin K. "Religion: The First Amendment and the American Indian Religious Freedom Act of 1978," 10 American Indian Law Review 151 (1982).

Redlich, Norman, and Kenneth R. Feinberg. "Individual Conscience and the Selective Conscientious Objector: The Right Not to Kill," 44 New York University Law Review 875 (1969).

Reich, Donald R. "The Impact of Judicial Decision Making: The School Prayer Cases," in David H. Everson, ed., The Supreme Court as Policy-Maker: Three Studies on the Impact of Judicial Decisions (Public Affairs Research Bureau, Southern Illinois University, 1968).

Reichley, James A. Religion in American Public Life (Washington, D.C.: Brookings Institution, 1985).

Rice, Randolf J. "Native Americans and the Free Exercise Clause," 28 Hastings Law Journal 1509 (1977).

Richardson, James D., ed. A Compilation of the Messages and Papers of the Presidents (20 vols., New York: Bureau of National Literature, 1897–1925).

Rossum, Ralph A. "Congress, the Constitution, and the Appellate Jurisdiction of the Supreme Court: The Letter and the Spirit of the Exceptions Clause," 24 William and Mary Law Review 385 (1983).

Rotnem, Victor W., and F. G. Folsom, Jr. "Recent Restrictions Upon Religious Liberty," 36 American Political Science Review 1053 (1942).

Rozell, Mark J. "Growing Up Politically: The New Politics of the New Christian Right," in Corwin E. Smidt and James M. Penning, eds., Sojourners in the Wilderness: The Christian Right in Comparative Perspective (Lanham, Md.: Rowman & Littlefield Publishers, 1997).

———. "The Christian Right: Evolution, Expansion, Contraction," presented at the Ethics and Public Policy conference, "Evangelicals and American Public Life," Cape Elizabeth, Maine (June 17–19, 2001).

Rozell, Mark J., and Clyde Wilcox, eds. God at the Grass Roots: The Christian Right in the 1994 Elections (Lanham, Md.: Rowman & Littlefield Publishers, 1995).

———. Second Coming: The New Christian Right in Virginia Politics (Baltimore, Md.: Johns Hopkins University Press, 1996).

———, eds. God at the Grass Roots, 1996: The Christian Right in the American Elections (Lanham, Md.: Rowman & Littlefield Publishers, 1997).

———. "Pragmatism and Its Discontents: The Evolution of the Christian Right in the United States," in Madeleine Cousineau, ed., Religion in a Changing World (Westport, Conn.: Praeger, 1998).

Rushmore, Elsie Mitchell. The Indian Policy during Grant's Administration (New York: Marion Press, 1914).

Russell, R. R. "Development of Conscientious Objector Recognition in the United States," 20 George Washington Law Review 409 (1952).

Sarna, Jonathan D., and David G. Dalin. Religion and State in the American Jewish Tradition (Notre Dame, Ind.: University of Notre Dame Press, 1997).

Schlissel, Lillian, ed. Conscience in America: A Documentary History of Conscientious Objection in America, 1757–1967 (New York: E. P. Dutton & Co., 1968).

Schneir, Miriam, ed. Feminism: The Essential Historical Writings (New York: Random House, 1972).

Segers, Mary C., ed. Church Polity and American Politics: Issues in Contemporary American Catholicism (New York: Garland Publishers, 1990).

Seide, David Z. "Daily Moments of Silence in Public Schools: A Constitutional Analysis," 58 New York University Law Review 364 (1983).

Sergent, Gary J. "Separation of Church and State: Education and Religion in Kentucky," 6 North Kentucky Law Review 125 (1979).

Sheffer, Martin S. God Versus Caesar: Belief, Worship, and Proselytizing under the First Amendment (Albany: State University of New York Press, 1999).

Sibley, Mulford Q., and Philip E. Jacob. Conscription of Conscience: The American State and the Conscientious Objector, 1940–1947 (Ithaca, N.Y.: Cornell University Press, 1952).

Slomovitz, Albert Isaac. The Fighting Rabbis: Jewish Military Chaplains and American History (New York: New York University Press, 1999).

Slye, Terry L. "Rendering Unto Caesar: Defining 'Religion' for Purposes of Administering Religion-based Tax Exemptions," 6 Harvard Journal of Law and Public Policy 219 (1983).

Smidt, Corwin E., and James M. Penning, eds. Sojourners in the Wilderness: The Christian Right in Comparative Perspective (Lanham, Md.: Rowman & Littlefield Publishers, 1997).

Smith, Elbert B. The Presidency of James Buchanan (Lawrence: University Press of Kansas, 1975).

Smith, Rodney K. Public Prayer and the Constitution: A Case Study in Constitutional Interpretation (Wilmington, Del.: Scholarly Resources, Inc. 1987).

Smith, William French. Law and Justice in the Reagan Administration: Memoirs of an Attorney General (Stanford, Calif.: Hoover Institution Press, 1991).

Sofaer, Abraham D. War, Foreign Affairs and Constitutional Power: The Origins (Cambridge, Mass.: Ballinger Publishing Co., 1976).

Sorauf, Frank J. The Wall of Separation: The Constitutional Politics of Church and State (Princeton, N.J.: Princeton University Press, 1976).

Stambor, Howard. "Manifest Destiny and American Indian Religious Freedom:

Sequoyah, Badoni, and the Drowned Gods," 10 American Indian Law Review 59 (1982).

Stedman, Murray S., Jr. Religion and Politics in America (New York: Harcourt, Brace & World, 1964).

Stern, Theodore. The Klamath Tribe: A People and Their Reservation (Seattle: University of Washington Press, 1965).

Stevens, Leonard A. Salute! The Case of the Bible vs. the Flag (New York: Coward, McCann & Geoghegan, 1973).

Stewart, Omer C. Peyote Religion: A History (Norman: University of Oklahoma Press, 1987).

———. "Peyote and the Law," in Christopher Vecsey, ed., Handbook of American Indian Religious Freedom (New York: Crossroad, 1991).

Stokes, Anson Phelps. Church and State in the United States (3 vols., New York: Harper & Bros., 1950).

Stokes, Anson Phelps, and Leo Pfeffer. Church and State in the United States (New York: Harper & Row, Publishers, 1964).

Stone, Harlan F. "The Conscientious Objector," 21 Columbia University Quarterly 253 (1919).

Story, Joseph. Commentaries on the Constitution of the United States (Ronald D. Rotunda and John E. Nowak, eds., Durham, N.C.: Carolina Academic Press, 1987).

Strickland, Rennard. "American Indian Law and the Spirit World," 1 American Indian Law Review 33 (1973).

Sturm, Douglas. "Constitutionalism and Conscientiousness: The Dignity of Objection to Military Service," 1 Journal of Law and Religion 265 (1983).

Suagee, Dean B. "American Indian Religious Freedom and Cultural Resources Management: Protecting Mother Earth's Caretakers," 10 American Indian Law Review 1 (1982).

Sullivan, Dwight H. "The Congressional Response to *Goldman* v. *Weinberger,*" 121 Military Law Review 125 (1988).

Swindler, William F., ed. Sources and Documents of United States Constitutions (10 vols., Dobbs Ferry, N.Y.: Oceana Publications, 1973–1979).

———. "Politics as Law: The Cherokee Cases," 3 American Indian Law Review 7 (1975).

Szacz, Margaret Connell, and Carmelita Ryan. "American Indian Education," in William C. Sturtevant, ed., 4 Handbook of North American Indians (Washington, D.C.: Smithsonian Institution, 1988).

Taft, William Howard. "Criticisms of the Federal Judiciary," 29 American Law Review 641 (1895).

Tepker, Harry F., Jr. "Hallucinations of Neutrality in the Oregon Peyote Case," 16 American Indian Law Review 1 (1991).

Thornton, Russell. "The Demography of the Trail of Tears Period: A New Estimate of Cherokee Population Losses," in William L. Anderson, ed., Cherokee Removal: Before and After (Athens: University of Georgia Press, 1991).

Thorpe, Francis Newton Thorpe, ed. The Federal and State Constitutions, Colonial Charters, and Other Organic Laws (7 vols., Washington, D.C.: Government Printing Office, 1909).

Timberlake, James H. Prohibition and the Progressive Movement, 1900–1920 (Cambridge: Harvard University Press, 1963).

Tribe, Laurence H. God Save This Honorable Court (New York: Random House, 1985).

U.S. Selective Service System. Conscientious Objection, Special Monograph No. 11, Vol. I (1950).

Van Alstyne, Arvo. "Tax Exemption of Church Property," 20 Ohio State Law Journal 461 (1959).

Van Kirk, Walter W. Religion Renounces War (New York: Willett, Clark & Co., 1934).

Vecsey, Christopher, ed. Handbook of American Indian Religious Freedom (New York: Crossroad, 1991).

Vile, John R. Encyclopedia of Constitutional Amendments, Proposed Amendments, and Amending Issues (Santa Barbara, Calif.: ABC-CLIO, 1996).

Waite, Edward F. "The Debt of Constitutional Law to Jehovah's Witnesses," 28 Minnesota Law Review 209 (1944).

Wald, Kenneth D. "Ministering to the Nation: The Campaigns of Jesse Jackson and Pat Robertson," in Emmett H. Buell, Jr., and Lee Sigelman, eds., Nominating the President (Knoxville: University of Tennessee Press, 1991).

———. Religion and Politics in the United States (Washington, D.C.: CQ Press, 1997).

Wallace, Anthony F. C. Jefferson and the Indians: The Tragic Fate of the First Americans (Cambridge: Harvard University Press, 1999).

Warren, Charles. The Supreme Court in United States History (2 vols., Boston: Little, Brown & Co., 1937).

Warren, Earl. "The Bill of Rights and the Military," 37 New York University Law Review 181 (1962).

Wax, Murray L., and Rosalie H. Wax. "Religion Among American Indians," 436 The Annals 27 (1978).

Way, Frank, and Barbara J. Burt. "Religious Marginality and the Free Exercise Clause," 77 American Political Science Review 652 (1983).

Weber, Paul J., "Examining the Religious Lobbies," 1 This World 97 (Winter/Spring 1982).

Weber, Paul J., and W. Landis Jones. U.S. Religious Interest Groups: Institutional Profiles (Westport, Conn.: Greenwood Press, 1994).

Weber, Paul J., and T. L. Stanley. "The Power and Performance of Religious Interest Groups," 4 Quarterly Review 28 (1984).

Wharton, Francis. State Trials of the United States During the Administrations of Washington and Adams (Philadelphia, Pa.: Carey & Hart, 1849).

Wiecek, William M. The Sources of Antislavery Constitutionalism in America, 1760–1846 (Ithaca, N.Y.: Cornell University Press, 1977).

Wilcox, Clyde. God's Warriors: The Christian Right in Twentieth-Century America (Baltimore, Md.: Johns Hopkins University Press, 1992).

———. Onward Christian Soldiers? The Religious Right in American Politics (Boulder, Colo: Westview Press, 2000).

Wilkinson, Charles F., and Eric R. Biggs. "The Evolution of the Termination Policy," 5 American Indian Law Review 139 (1977).

Wilson, John K. "Religion Under the State Constitutions, 1776–1800," 32 Journal of Church and State 753 (1990).

Witheridge, David E. "No Freedom of Religion for American Indians," 18 Journal of Church and State 5 (1976).

Witte, John, Jr. "Tax Exemption of Church Property: Historical Anomaly or Valid Constitutional Practice?" 64 Southern California Law Review 363 (1991).

———. Religion and the American Constitutional Experiment (Boulder, Colo.: Westview Press, 2000).

Wood, Gordon S. "Evangelical America and Early Mormonism," in Jon Butler and Harry S. Stout, eds., Religion in American History: A Reader (New York: Oxford University Press, 1998).

Wood, James E., Jr. "Religion Sponsored by the State," 4 Journal of Church and State 141 (1962).

———. Religion and the State: Essays in Honor of Leo Pfeffer (Waco, Tex.: Baylor University Press, 1985).

———. "Equal Access: A New Direction in American Public Education," 27 Journal of Church and State 5 (1985).

———. "Church Lobbying and Public Policy," 28 Journal of Church and State 183 (1986).

Wright, Edward Needles. Conscientious Objectors in the Civil War (Philadelphia: University of Pennsylvania Press, 1931).

Wunder, John R., ed., Constitutionalism and Native Americans, 1903–1968 (New York: Garland Publishers, 1996).

Index of Cases

Subject Index

www.ingramcontent.com/pod-product-compliance
Lightning Source LLC
Chambersburg PA
CBHW050341270326
41926CB00016B/3564